FROM DONNA LEVIN, T
CRITICALLY ACCLAIM
THERE'S MORE THAN ONE WAY HOME,
COMES A ROMANTIC COMEDY SET IN 21ST CENTURY
SAN FRANCISCO

WHERE DIFFERENCES ARE CELEBRATED, AND EVERYONE FITS IN …

EXCEPT WHEN THEY DON'T

HE COULD BE ANOTHER BILL GATES

"Being a good parent is always a challenge. Add a particularly challenging child, acknowledge the daily-ness of the work, add wit, compassion, and imagination, and you have *He Could Be Another Bill Gates*. Levin's story is compelling and her voice authentic. The result is simultaneously hopeful and sobering."
— Karen Joy Fowler, author of *The Jane Austen Book Club*

"Full of **pathos, wit, and tenderness**, Levin's latest novel will appeal to any parent who has felt stuck between a rock and a hard place. Refreshingly, she doesn't shy away from the alternately frustrating and triumphant realities of parenting an autistic child. Fans of Rebecca L. Brown and Mark Haddon will appreciate Levin's **tender and realistic** portrait of a nontraditional yet immediately recognizable family."
— Stephanie Turza, *Booklist*

"A delightful, witty tale of contemporary San Francisco life, featuring a single mom, her autistic teenage son, and a precocious five-year-old daughter. Donna Levin's comic sensibility lifts a story of tough lives into the realm of enchantment."
— Joan Steinau Lester, author of *Black, White, Other*

"A complex and insightful rendering of contemporary love and family … Jack's teenage point of view is striking for the glimpse it provides into Asperger's."
— *Kirkus Reviews*

HE COULD BE ANOTHER BILL GATES

A NOVEL

Donna Levin

This is a work of fiction. Names, characters and incidents are either the product of the author's imagination or are used fictitiously.

ISBN 978-0-9997569-3-5

Front cover illustration by Kelly Airo

Book design by Daniel Middleton

Chickadee Prince Logo by Garrett Gilchrist

Visit us at www.ChickadeePrince. com

First Printing

DONNA LEVIN

HE COULD BE ANOTHER BILL GATES

A Novel

Donna Levin is the author of three acclaimed previous novels, *There's More Than One Way Home, Extraordinary Means* and *California Street*, all of which are available from Chickadee Prince Books. She has also written two books on the craft of writing: *Get That Novel Started* and *Get That Novel Written.*

Her work is included in the Howard Gotlieb Archival Research Center at Boston University and in the California State Library's collection of California novels.

She lives in San Francisco.

Visit her at *www.DonnaLevin.com.*

HE COULD BE ANOTHER BILL GATES

A Novel

Chickadee Prince Books
New York

For Nancy Nicholas:
Editor
Mentor
Longtime Friend

Ah, *Vanitus Vanitatum*! Which of us is happy in this world? Which of us has his desire?—or having it, is satisfied?

> William Makepeace Thackery
> *Vanity Fair*

There are many admixtures of feeling we call love.

> George Eliot
> *Middlemarch*

CHAPTER 1

It was the first day of school, and Jack had a new locker. He only had to hear the combination once to memorize it, but he still had trouble opening the door.

Finally it gave.

It was empty. It was supposed to be empty, because it was the first day, but the emptiness was the same as the emptiness in his chest. Another year of school. He liked middle school, but last year he started here at George Takei High and he was a freshman and didn't know anyone. There were three older boys who wanted to be his friends and they would invite him to the convenience store to buy potato chips so they could go to the park and eat them together, but once Jack got the potato chips they all got separated.

Now that his locker was in the new place he was all turned around and didn't know how to get to his first class.

"You want some help?"

He looked up. It was a girl he'd never seen before. Her voice was like Bambi's mother.

"You okay?"

What happened? He was thinking how he had to be in class.... Now the hallways were getting empty and one of the bells had rung, and he was sitting in the center of papers that formed an asteroid belt with him as the star.

Then he remembered: Some time ago — usually he knew exactly how long ago something happened, but the girl confused him — his binder had slipped from his hand and broken open, sending every sheet flying up and then floating to the ground. He'd shrieked in delight; he was inside a snow globe.

"Here." The girl bent down on one knee, pulled his binder toward herself and snapped it closed to keep the few remaining pages safe. "Let's get you together."

She collected the yellow dividers, and then began to gather the loose filler paper. "H'm." She squinted. "Is this from last year?"

"I guess so."

"Oh-kay." Her hair was the color of the pumpkin ice cream that would be back in Safeway on October 12th. But faces were mostly useless to him. He would sometimes notice something like missing front teeth. But it took a long time before he could recognize a person by their face.

"This is all homework," she said, holding some papers up. "So it *has* to be from last year, right?" She sounded like he'd played a joke on her and it was a funny joke.

"Uh ... yeah."

His mother had given him a new backpack for sophomore year but he had put a lot of stuff from his old backpack in. She had thrown the old backpack away but he'd found it in the trash before the garbage truck came and now it was in his closet.

The girl put the homework in a pile and smoothed the edges. "Well, I guess that's one way to do it."

He heard each word and he knew what each word meant, he just didn't know exactly what they meant together. Jack's own language was complex and nuanced, but it was an unspoken language in the same way that some languages were unwritten. He'd had to learn English the way some of the other kids learned French or Korean in those immersion programs. At sixteen, he spoke and understood fairly well — but it was still his second language, and so much of what he thought didn't translate into it.

In English, the name for his problem was Asperger's Syndrome. People like therapists and his mom and even his dad told him he shouldn't feel bad about it, but he didn't see how they could know that it was like being on the track field when everyone was passing you for the second time. They called that "being lapped."

"What if we separated the old stuff into one part? So you could put your new stuff from today in a new part? And we wrote down the name of the class on the dividers? On the white tabs, you know?"

"Yeah, good idea."

"I tell you what." The girl rose from her squat. "We're both going to be late if we don't hurry. What if I helped you organize your binder after school?"

"Yeah, good idea." *Why do I say such stupid things? No wonder everyone thinks I'm stupid. What could I say now to make her know how much I think inside?*

"I'll meet you back here, then." She wriggled into her own backpack. "See? This is my locker." She tapped the metal door that was at her shoulder level. "I'm Ashleigh, by the way."

DAMN CUPCAKES. Damn bake sales. Why didn't they just have the kids sell blood?

Not their *own* blood. I wasn't a monster. Just a bit overwhelmed at the moment.

I was running in four-inch heels, because 1) I always wore four heels and 2) the rear end of my mini-van was sticking dangerously over the edge of a driveway curb cut. I had to hope that I could drop off the cupcakes and return before the enraged homeowner got DPT to tow my car to the bourn from which no cars returned for less than $500.

Who the *fuck* has a bake sale the first day of school?

I hadn't baked the cupcakes. I had a job, two kids and no husband. Also I hated doing anything that involved the stove, or a mixing bowl — or silverware, for that matter. I did not have money to throw at problems, yet here I was, bringing a $40 box of cupcakes that would retail for $28, all to keep up the illusion that Jack's mother (me) was a cheerful participant in the ongoing community life at George Takei High.

Ooomph.

Suddenly my hands and knees were on the pavement. I felt the sting of violated skin. One heel had caught on a bulge in the sidewalk.

In the next half-second I saw that the bakery box had flown from my hands and landed face down. A black stain was already forming on the side. I could almost hear the frosting squish.

"Need some help, Ma'am?"

"No, I'm fine." I was inspecting the damage (one scraped palm, one skinned knee, torn pantyhose), and I didn't need someone helping me to my feet so that he could ask for the address of my nursing home.

"Are you sure?"

"Yes, I'm — "

And then I looked up, and saw that it was a policeman.

I was afraid of policemen. Policewomen, too. It didn't help that I occasionally failed to notice a NO LEFT TURN sign. The mere sight of a black-and-white cruiser had me white knuckling the steering wheel at ten and two o'clock.

This policeman was large, and looked larger still since he towered over me. I tried to arrange my legs under myself so that I could stand again.

He held out his hand.

I feared taking it. I feared not taking it.

I took it.

He pulled me up with such strength that my heels momentarily left the sidewalk.

"Are you sure you're all right?" he asked. "I don't know how you girls get around in those shoes."

Women, I corrected him silently, but as I was only weeks away from turning 40, the appellation "girl" had lost its condescension and become a compliment.

"Yes, yes." I could feel blood pooling on my skinned knee. "It's my cupcakes I'm worried about."

"Cupcakes. Is that what they are?" He squatted to pick up the box. "But we like doughnuts, my people, you know."

The box was still upside down, but the officer was smiling and I wasn't about to turn that grin outside in by giving him any grief. What to do? Return to the bakery? I was already late for work.

"Let me take you to the school nurse," he said.

"There is no school nurse."

"Oh." He looked around sheepishly. "We're new here."

"'Who's 'we'?" I asked, before blurting, "You and your evil twin Skippy?"

Even fear couldn't shut my big mouth.

"Me and my son," he said, with an ever-so-slight hesitation before the word "son."

"Really."

"He's a transfer student this year. We don't really know anyone at the school."

"You'll find people friendly." I didn't; not particularly. But then, I was a prickly person who didn't make friends easily.

"I'm a single dad," he went on. "I was just meeting with my son's counselor trying to fix his schedule."

"Yeah, there's always some problem with that."

He took a step closer. I took one back. "What teens do you have here?" he asked.

"A son. Too." My eye was on his badge. *Oro en paz, fierro en guerra.* Something about peace and war. And the weapons on his belt! Handcuffs, a nightstick — and a service revolver. Jesus take the wheel and get me outta here.

"Two sons?" he asked.

"No, I mean one son, like you — like you have one son." His shirt was tight across his broad chest. He had yellow eyebrows that matched curly blonde hair. "And a daughter, but she's only five — " When nervous I tended to babble.

He took another step closer, and I thought I smelled shaving lotion.

"Your cupcakes?" He held them close to my bosom. "Can I carry them to the office for you?"

"No! I mean...." I snatched the greasy box. "I mean, I'm fine, thank you. Thank you."

I stepped sideways to get around him and I was mightily relieved when he let me pass.

I took the steps down into the courtyard. My knee twinged, but I was mostly concerned with my cupcake-challenged state.

The courtyard still had a number of students in it, some heading to class with a speed that told me they were late; others sitting on the benches that rimmed the sides; still others gathered around the flagpole at the center. Many displayed George Takei jackets, with the blood-red porcupine against a white background.

As soon as I reached the main building I made a 360 degree turn to make sure that the cop was out of sight. Then I yanked the string off the box and peeked inside. Every single cupcake — all chocolate with pink frosting — was upside down.

I closed the lid and dumped the box in the nearest garbage can.

Then I pushed my shoulders back and marched into the school office.

"Is Rose in?" I asked the school secretary, Olive.

Rose Gonzales was the full-inclusion specialist, in charge of the students with special needs, and she emerged without further summoning. She was stout, with coarse skin, a large nose and ultra-thick hair cut in practical comb-and-go layers. "Anna." She rubbed her hands together. "You brought something for our bake sale?"

"I had three dozen cupcakes," I said. "All stolen from my car."

"How awful."

I let out a resigned sigh. "That's the city for you." I got out my wallet. "I'll just have to make a contribution instead."

I couldn't even remember to what fund I was donating: musical instruments or a part-time art teacher or a new computer.

"Oh, you don't need to do that," Rose said, while reaching for my two proffered twenty dollar bills.

Simultaneously, I crunched the money between my fingers and withdrew my hand.

"We spoke about moving Jack's locker," I reminded her. "Where is it?"

I'd looked for Jack on my way in, but except for a few stragglers the hallways were empty.

The previous year, when Jack's locker had been on the second floor of the building, he had fallen prey to three spawns of Satan who had lured him to the local convenience store, where they had him buy a giant bag of Ruffles, promising that the four of them would share. Once Jack made the purchase the largest boy would grab the bag and the three would run off.

As often as I explained the ruse, he went off with the same boys every time they asked.

So I had requested (firmly) that Rose put his locker in front of the office. Last year's tormenters were history, thanks to a few phone calls from Jack's dad, my ex-husband Alex, but tormenters had a way of reproducing.

"I'll show you." Rose stepped out of the office and pointed to the end of the bank of lockers. "Right there."

"Not exactly full view," I observed.

"This way he won't feel self-conscious," she said.

I was about to argue, but was abruptly distracted. I had assumed that Jack was safely in class by now, but there he was, at his newly-assigned locker, wriggling to keep his backpack from falling off one shoulder. He was doing his usual juggling act with additional books, which somehow always outnumbered, outweighed and outclassed him. When he tried to hoist the backpack up by raising one shoulder, he dropped the pile of books that was in his arms.

It was then that I saw the girl who was with him. A lissome redhead who bent over to gather the books that had fallen. Her hair was a copper waterfall pouring over her shoulder as she leaned forward.

She was in thrift shop clothes. A plaid shirt — they were trendy that year — and bell bottom jeans frayed at the hem. But, like Dorothea Brooke, this young woman "had the kind of beauty thrown into relief by poor dress."

They didn't see me, but walked off down the hall together. Jack moved with his usual lumbering gait, made more awkward by the weight of his backpack. The girl glided next to him, so smoothly that she might have had wheels on her feet.

How many times can your heart break before the pieces are too small to break any more?

"We'll keep an eye on him," Rose said. "Won't we, Olive?"

WHEN ALEX and I made a baby I didn't actually think we'd send it to high school. I was in denial about many aspects of the parenting experience.

And when I was pregnant, I knew that something might go wrong, and I knew that the going wrong could happen to me, but I thought that by worrying about what could go wrong I could stave it off, so I worried, and worried hard, about a long list of going wrongs, like a missing finger, or a cleft palate, or a late-term miscarriage.

I forgot to worry about autism.

Jack clumsily flipped the pages of the binder that Ashleigh had begun assembling for him after school.

"See now, if you have one section in your binder for each subject, then you know where the pages go."

He heard himself giggle. Here with Ashleigh, it was like listening to a recording of his own voice on the answering machine and it made him cringe.

The school was quiet. Everyone had either left or gone into one of their clubs or out to practice sports. The linoleum floor was sticky, but Ashleigh didn't seem to mind: She sat on one butt cheek with one leg tucked under her and the other stretched out. Jack was plunked down, somehow taking up more room than he should. "Tell you what," she said, "why don't we look through your new books first?" She piled the new books into a tower, laughing while she did. "How'd you get so much stuff in your books in one day?"

There were a lot of papers sticking out from between the pages. "They gave me the books that way," he said.

"You're funny," she said, and he didn't know if she meant it in the nice way or the mean way but he thought it was the nice way. Sometimes even when he could understand the words he couldn't hear the difference between teasing and insulting.

Ashleigh sucked in her lower lip as she sized up the books. Just her lip made him feel the stiffness between his legs. And then she ran her hand over the sticking-out pages and her hand was the most beautiful thing he'd ever seen. He wanted to hold it. He pictured himself walking down the street, just holding hands.

Like the other guys with their girlfriends.

They had talked when she first got here, so he knew that she was the same age as he was, even though she was a grade ahead. She was taller than he was, too, but lots of guys had girlfriends who were taller — or did back when he was in middle school. Not so much anymore, but still, there was nothing to keep them apart.

Except he knew that there was, and it was a crushing weight to replace the emptiness in his chest.

Ashleigh was still staring at the tower of books. She sighed deeply. "We'll do this book by book."

Ashleigh spent the next 28 minutes going through his textbooks, flipping through the pages and examining each paper.

When she looked into his backpack, she found his collection of bus transfers. Receipts from purchases of candy bars and the potato chips crumbs from last year. Little crumpled, colored pieces of aluminum foil from Hershey's Kisses. Pennies and nickels. It had all been in his old backpack, the one that was in his closet now, but he had moved it to the new backpack.

Jack was afraid of throwing anything away. He knew he wasn't going to need all of these things, but he might need one of them, and he didn't know which one, or when.

"Let's make a pile of paper to recycle. And I have some extra spiral notebooks. We're going to label them. See? The notebooks have holes like the filler paper so they can go in your binder, too."

He wasn't listening. He was practicing a question in his head.

"Earth to Jack?" she prompted.

"Where...."

"H'm?"

"Where — where do you live?"

There! It came out!

"On Corcoran."

He wanted to ask if he could walk her home. And he knew where that street was! It was a long street. It stopped at a couple of small parks and then started up again at the other side. It wasn't very far out of his way, either.

But all his words were gone, flown away like the pigeons from the wires that hang across those same streets. He made fists and squeezed hard.

"Are you all right?" Ashleigh asked.

"Yes." Yes. He never forgot *that* word. *C'mon, Jack!* "Where on Corcoran Street?" That was a safe question. She couldn't say no to a where question.

"Near Sloat. Are you going that way?"

"Yes." It was only three blocks out of the way.

And just like that, their plans were made.

As I'd told the cop while I was bleeding out on the sidewalk, I had a five-year-old daughter, too: Marissa.

So for the second time that day I was running in heels, and for the second time hoping to move my van before the rightfully enraged residents of a nearby apartment building could have it towed away. I'd gone straight to work from Jack's school, but I kept an extra pair of pantyhose in the cargo hold.

The scene in front of me was the chaos of school letting out: children milling on the sidewalk; the older boys punching each other; the older girls huddled in gossipy clusters; the younger ones waving greetings to their approaching nannies or mothers, and a couple of little girls in tears.

I couldn't single Marissa out right away, as she was one of the smaller children, but I did spot a tall woman in a sari of vivid shades of turquoise and cantaloupe, and a moment later, when three boys ran out to a waiting SUV, there was a gap through which I saw that she had her hands on Marissa's shoulders.

"H-hi," I panted as I stopped short in front of them.

"You must be Marissa's mother. I was wondering where she got those eyes."

Marissa's Margaret Keane eyes were an unusual and striking teal when the sun hit them; in dim light they were simply dark. When she looked up at me silently, though, as she was doing now, I was less concerned with their color than with what was going on behind them.

"And you're Miss Persons." The first-grade teacher.

"It's *Mrs*. Persons, but please call me Lakshmi." She spoke perfect English with a posh British accent.

"Lakshmi," I repeated.

Switching from the role of "Jack's mom" to "Marissa's mom" was a vertiginous experience: the emotional equivalent of one of those holy-shit Six Flags rides that loop you around until you're pretty sure that your head is going to fall off.

Marissa would be six in February, which would have made her one of the older children in a kindergarten class. This was unacceptable to Alex since Marissa was clearly of above-average intelligence: She could read most of Dr. Seuss, except for the made-up words, and do double-digit addition and subtraction in her head.

So Alex "made a few calls," and she had started first grade that day — not only first grade, but first grade at an elite private school targeting gifted children: Sunrise Academy.

I had been against Marissa skipping kindergarten, but I'd lost that argument, and so here I was with Lakshmi in front of this Robber Baron mansion-turned-private school.

"How did it go?" I asked timidly. Looking around at how large the other children seemed, I was seized by fear that I'd been right all along and that first grade was too big a leap even for the devil-with-the-blue-green-eyes.

"It was fine. She's delightful."

"I'm so glad." But there was a reason that Lakshmi was standing with Marissa, and it wasn't to tell me that Marissa was a delightful child with big eyes.

"I had a lovely talk with your husband early this morning."

Ex-husband, I almost — but did not — inform her.

"He's delightful, too. I'm impressed with a man so involved with his daughter's education."

"He certainly is that," I said.

"And I look forward to working with you."

"I, um … I beg your pardon?"

Lakshmi continued, "Sunrise is a parent partnership school, and it's parents like you who make the difference."

"If you have any bake sales coming up, you can count on me."

Lakshmi laughed. "He said you had a sense of humor. Believe me, we could use a little more of that around here." She glanced around and put a finger to her lips. "No more telling tales out of school. But we really could use your input on several committees."

"Several committees," I echoed. The sidewalk was emptying very quickly now, as the school children disappeared into waiting Mercedes, Beamers and what I thought was a Tesla.

"I most appreciate your being a room parent. Those slots are dreadfully hard to fill."

"I'm sure they are," I murmured. What fresh hell was this? I was horrifically unqualified for the job description of room parent: fundraising, corralling volunteers, sending cheery notes home, and most of all, taking mornings off from my own job to be in the classroom to help these supposedly gifted children learn to read.

"You'll want to attend the first parent meeting," Lakshmi said.

"Right." Marissa was too big for me to carry for more than a few steps, but swooping her up, Power Puff Girls backpack and all, would be a diplomatic exit strategy.

"Don't pick me up," Marissa commanded, but calmly, as we were still in the presence of the new teacher.

"You have many things to do," Lakshmi said, "but I must give you this."

"I won't pick you up! … I'm sorry, Mrs. … Lakshmi, what — ?"

She was handing me a depressingly thick packet. "Emergency forms, class roster, the usual."

And you need this all tomorrow, I bet.

"I'm afraid we need it tomorrow," she said.

Jack didn't know what to say to Ashleigh. He was counting on her to do the talking.

"Can I — I can — "

"Yes?"

"I can carry your books."

"You don't have to do that."

"But I *can*."

Her hair wiggled when she shook her head. "You're a little guy."

That isn't good.

She stepped off the sidewalk in front of the school, but then stopped. "Are you okay crossing the street?"

His chest stiffened. *I've been crossing the street since I was nine!*

"Yes."

"Well, then, be careful."

He remembered to look both ways.

"Good job," Ashleigh said. "That backpack looks so heavy. Did you really have to bring all your books home?"

"Yes."

When she first said "Corcoran," he pictured it in his head, but after they walked for a while he didn't know where they were. He let her get a step ahead of him so that he could follow but not look like he was following. So many houses looked the same. They all had the same doors and they were almost all the same color. He knew his house because of the Princess Tiana doll that Marissa put in the front window.

"I had Mrs. Rawlins last year," Ashleigh said. It took a moment but then Jack realized that she was talking about one of his teachers. *What class? Right, English.* That was his worst subject.

"She's tough. Don't let her get to you."

"I won't."

They had gotten to a street where the houses were bigger, and not quite as much alike. He kept looking for things he'd remember, and he found a van that said "One Mean Carpet Clean Machine" on it, and a door with a Christmas wreath on it (which shouldn't have been there because it was August).

"*Way* too much homework."

The little curly parts at the bottom of her hair bounced as she walked. She walked fast. He could walk fast but the backpack was slowing him down. Ashleigh didn't have a backpack; her books were in some other kind of carrier that hung from her shoulder. It was black and there were words written in white: WORLD PEACE OR THE WORLD IN PIECES.

They turned one more corner.

"That's where I live." Ashleigh pointed ahead. He couldn't tell which house she meant. "Are you okay, now? Can you find your way home?"

"Of course I can — I can find my way home!"

Ashleigh put her hand on his shoulder. "You are very sweet," she said, and he felt a little flutter at her words and tiny bit of stiffness at her touch.

Scientists should investigate the specific ratio of ex-husbands to ulcerative colitis, delusional parasitosis, and other often psychosomatic diseases.

There he stood, outside my little three-bedroom house, big as life: Alex.

I didn't mean "big" solely as metaphor. He was five-foot-ten and … let's say "portly." He carried it well: conferring on himself all the dignity he thought he deserved. And damn it, did deserve in many ways.

I pulled my Town and Country into the driveway and came around to let Marissa out of the booster seat.

"I had to let Jack in," Alex said lightly. "He was waiting outside when I got here."

"Daddy!" Marissa sprung from the booster seat and slammed into him.

"Didn't he have his key?"

"Oooph! You're a big girl now. Go easy on your old Dad!" To me: "Apparently not."

"He's never forgotten it before." I tried not to sound defensive.

"May I make a suggestion? You might keep a spare under the doormat."

"Daddy, I started first grade today!"

"You didn't think I forgot, did you? We're going to talk all about it."

I made a couple of calculated grunting sounds as I lifted one of the three bags of groceries from the cargo hold.

Alex came over. "I'll take those." With some effort he managed the other two and led the way into the house through the open door.

Jack was in front of the television, laughing his loud, maniacal laugh. He didn't look up as we passed. Alex went ahead into the kitchen, sending Marissa to her room to "see if HannahSophia wants to come with us." HannahSophia was Marissa's daughter, best friend and confidante, though to the uninitiated she was a stuffed pink leopard.

While I started unpacking groceries, Alex dug around in one of the other bags until he found a box of ice cream bars.

"Your hair is getting very long," he said.

"Yes, I like it this way." My hair was black and cascaded well past my shoulders.

"So you see I was right about Marissa starting first grade." Alex spoke through his first (very large) bite of ice cream bar. "Do you buy a lot of Lean Cuisines?" he asked, peering over the top of the bag.

"They're just back up."

"H'm. I'm just curious — have you thought about eliminating lecithin from Jack's diet?"

"I'm still thinking." This was the latest in a very long series of dietary and other suggestions-read-demands that came from Alex: often the latest theory espoused by some Internut.

"There are some very convincing studies." He jammed the stick in his mouth and then pulled it out slowly, having snatched the last glob of ice cream. "So you see, I was right," he repeated, "about Marissa starting first grade."

"Today was only the first day." His complacency brought out my perverseness.

"I talked to her teacher this morning."

"I know you did. I understand you volunteered my services in a number of areas."

"You don't mind, do you?" He tilted his head inquisitively. "I thought you'd want to get involved."

After all these years of knowing Alex, I still couldn't decide if he was able to believe anything he wanted to believe, or if he was simply that masterful a liar.

And perhaps Alex wasn't inflating Marissa's gifts; perhaps I was blind to them. We were worse off than new parents: We were second-time parents whose only reference was our Asperger's son.

Every divorced couple is divorced in their own particular way. Alex and I had a deep, complicated, and dangerous history: Marissa had divided us, and then brought us together again.

And to me, Alex was a napping lion. Poke him with a stick and he would wake up in a very bad mood. The kind of mood that makes men take their wives to court for custody.

I shut the cabinet door on a row of cans of Progresso.

Marissa twirled into the kitchen. "When are we leaving, Daddy?"

"Right now, Wissy," Alex said. To me: "I'll have her back before eight, so be sure she gets to bed by 8:30. She needs ten hours to maximize her learning power. And the principal asked me to remind you not to block any neighbors' driveways."

I merely grumbled to myself, Marge Simpson-style.

Marissa bounded out again, twirling and jumping past Jack who was still in front of the television, and still emitting the unholy sounds that we called laughter for lack of a more accurate term for a sound that could ferment grapes.

But when his father and sister reached the front door he followed them. "Have fun! Have fun!" he parroted. "Have fun! Have fun!"

"G'bye Jack," Marissa said solemnly.

Jack loitered in the open doorway. "Maybe — maybe next time I'll get to come."

Daddy had a big white car called a Cadillac. But if Marissa was so big and smart why did she have to sit in the back, in this dumb baby seat?

"I'm going to take you to my office," Daddy said, as he pulled the car into the street.

"But what about dinner?" Marissa didn't care about dinner; she just knew that she had to eat something "healthy" before Daddy got her the giant ice cream sundae at Mel's. She'd force down a hamburger, which wasn't even that healthy.

"You don't want to see the plaque your old dad got?"

Daddy had a lot of plaques: They were like awards.

"This is from a victim's rights group," Daddy said.

Daddy was very important. Marissa wondered how other children felt about their fathers who weren't important, the ones who had time to pick them up from school.

"So," Daddy said in his big Daddy voice, "you like Sunrise Academy, don't you?"

"Y-yes." Her classroom had tight little desks. At pre-school they could go wherever they wanted. "The teacher is strict," she admitted.

"How so?"

"We have to sit still all the time." The thought made her wiggle in the booster seat, straining against the belt that held her in. "And we have to write real neat."

"Real*ly* neat*ly*. You'd be bored in kindergarten. Not that there's anything wrong with going to kindergarten."

"You said kindergarten was for babies."

"It's just that you don't need to go."

"You promised I didn't have to stay in first grade if I didn't like it."

"Of course not. May I tell you a story?"

"Okay." She tugged at the shoulder harness, trying to loosen it.

"Don't do that, babe. It's not safe. Well, a friend of mine has a daughter. When she was your age she was just like you. She skipped kindergarten, too."

"Uh-huh."

"She worked very hard and she got very good grades."

"Uh-huh."

"Then, when she was in fourth grade, her teacher decided to put her in sixth grade. Later she skipped another grade and she got to start college when she was sixteen. She was out of law school at 21, so she got to start her political career very early."

They were driving down the long street that had the park on the side. Soon they'd get to where there were men on corners holding signs. Their signs usually said HUNGRY or FOOD.

"Did you hear my story?"

"Yes."

"Can you tell it back to me?"

She could, especially since he told her the same story last week. But she had a hard feeling in her stomach now that made her not want to.

"Heh-heh-heh." That was Daddy's laughing sound. "You're tired."

"I'm not tired."

"Would you like to hear more about my friend's daughter, then?"

"Is this about me becoming a Phi Beta Krappa?"

Daddy didn't say anything for a while. At first Marissa didn't pay attention, because she was trying to see the freeway overpass that would mean that they were almost there. It was nighttime, but there would still be lawyers in Daddy's office and they'd all talk about how big she was getting and how they remembered her from when she was a baby, which she used to like but now it was just annoying.

Then she realized that Daddy's quiet was the mad kind of quiet. "Did your mother call it that?" he finally asked.

"Call what what?"

"It's Phi Beta *Kappa*. And it's something to be very proud of." Daddy coughed a little. "If you get your Phi Bet key, I'll give you mine and we can make them into earrings."

"I can wear earrings?" That was exciting news!

"You can wear those earrings every day, Wiss. How much is four times six?"

"Twenty-four. *When* do I get to be a Phi Beta — "

"You'll be surprised how fast the time goes."

That wasn't an answer, but she could tell when she wasn't going to get one. She had already pictured the earrings: big and sparkly, hanging from her ears, but now they were just hanging in a dark empty space in her mind, floating farther and farther away....

Then she saw the big red billboard: BAIL BONDSMAN. That meant that they were really really close.

And finally Daddy slipped his Cadillac into the parking spot with the words RESERVED FOR THE DISTRICT ATTORNEY.

He turned off the engine. "You know, Wiss ... if you wanted to, you could come live with me."

"Live in your house?"

"Mmm h'm. It'd be easier to study there."

Marissa squirmed, more impatient than ever to get out from under the seat belt. She used to like Daddy's house. It was like Magic Land, because there were so many doors that led so many places, and two staircases! She and Jack spent the night there sometimes.

But Jack didn't spend the night anymore and Marissa was scared to be there without him when it was dark. Mommy once said that her grandma's ghost was on the third floor "to make sure her little boy behaved himself." The "little boy" was Daddy. Then Mommy said she was joking, but Marissa couldn't get it out of her mind.

Daddy clicked the seat belt open and Marissa almost leapt in the air. "What about Mommy?"

"Heh-heh-heh. You don't need to worry about your mother."

CHAPTER 2

My younger sister Darya and I had had a difficult relationship over the years. But she was my only family, and I was all of hers, and so I tried to make it work.

What better friend than a sister? Who else knows why you're as crazy as you are?

Have you noticed, though, that the most neurotic people have the least patience for your neurosis?

"So you've been hurt!" she told me on the phone. "We've all been hurt! Get over it!"

This from a woman whose last boyfriend had nearly slapped her with a restraining order. She was lucky to have an ex-brother-in-law who knew every judge in town.

"I am over it," I said gamely.

"Then why aren't you dating? Get an online profile! That's how —"

"You. Met. Sean. I know."

But Darya was off and running. *Put it out to the universe. I said exactly what I was looking for. A man who would love me for myself....*

Why hadn't Val loved me for myself?

And want to grow with me....

Val — that was his name. What a stupid name. An effeminate name.

You're 40....

God, how I'd loved him!

I hate to tell you, it doesn't get easier after this.

Why hadn't he loved me enough to stay? Had he loved me at all? Had he ever loved me?

"Anna, are you listening to me?"

"Yes, yes, of course."

"So will you go out with him?"

"Who?"

"Who have I been talking about? Jesus, you're a space cadet. Damien's friend! You know what you need," she finished with a giggle.

"Don't say it." What I *needed* was help with the laundry. And some company at night: company that I didn't have to clean up after.

"You need to get laid."

I sighed. "I asked you not to say it."

Damien's friend was Sean, Darya told me; he was a stockbroker, and a Capricorn. He and Damien had been friends — best friends! — since high school. Or was it college? And he was dying to meet me!

Her closing argument was a rhetorical question, "What have you got to lose?"

"The last shred of my self-respect?"

But I agreed to dinner with Sean at The Destination, which he insisted was the hottest new restaurant in town, quoting a review from a website I'd never heard of, but which he described as "'Yelp' for *true* gourmets."

The Destination was South of Market, aka SoMa, where I usually got trapped behind the eponymous Market, and then circled around one-way streets until I was halfway to the airport. The restaurant sign was small enough that I passed it three times, but when I did arrive, I identified Sean right away, as he was only man sitting by himself.

He was studying the menu through reading glasses. Alerted by the noise of my arrival (the click of my heels and my panting from having run the last block) he looked up, looked puzzled, then removed the glasses.

"That's a relief."

"I beg your pardon?"

"You're beautiful," he said, putting his menu down.

No one had complimented me on my looks for a very long time.

I took a deep breath, then sucked in my abdomen, the better to squeeze into my seat (as well as to deserve the compliment), for the tables were crammed close together.

"You know, someone wants to set you up...." Damien shrugged. "Darya isn't the most reliable source in town."

"Wouldn't take a stock tip from her?" I wanted to keep the tone light.

"I don't think so," he said, but pleasantly.

Now we were in on a joke. And Sean wasn't bad-looking himself: Post-40 men fall into one of two categories: Good Hair or "but I *like* balding men!" and Sean was in the former. He was well-dressed, too, a quality about which I was unabashedly judgmental: tweed sport coat and a royal blue button-down shirt of good make.

So it was with a feeling of optimism that I made fun of the haute cuisine menu. "Whoever thought arugula and radicchio belonged in a salad? In my day they were weeds."

Then when Lawrence-our-server dropped off the breadbasket I turned the breadsticks into chopsticks and mimed eating invisible food.

And Sean laughed.

Lawrence-our-server returned, and Sean pressed me to order the salmon. I agreed; I wasn't crazy about salmon, but it was one of the less expensive entrees, and if Sean insisted on picking up the check I didn't want to be beholden.

"Holy shit." Sean had his finger on the wine list. "We've got to get a bottle of this Pinot Noir. This is the optimal wine for salmon."

"I don't drink wine," I said. "It upsets my stomach. Which is funny because — "

I was about to say that I could down quarts of espresso without adverse effects but Sean interrupted. "Be a good sport and try it."

He meant well. I told myself I'd take a few sips.

"You'll like it," he promised, and he seemed hopeful that I would.

We fell into a conversational trough, which I intended to pull us out of by asking him about work — realizing only too late that this was a bad time to ask a stockbroker about his job. The stock market had all but bottomed out earlier that year; we were in the middle of what would soon be called The Great Recession.

But it was not a bad time to ask Sean: His career was on an upward trajectory. As for the Dow's recent troubles: "I sold Apple at a thousand a share. Pretty happy clients when that tanked." He went on to list other victories, and rhapsodized about his prospects for promotion.

Then he asked me what I did.

"I have a Ph.D. in psychology." I was proud of those three letters. "But I don't want to be an actual therapist. I do research for a group of psychoanalysts and psychologists." It often involved interviewing people in their homes, which for me was a good excuse to dress up, although my colleagues usually wore jeans.

"Can you make a living doing that?"

"Not a very good one."

Food arrived. I was amazed at how small the portions were, but when I said, "I finally found the salmon — it was hiding under the parsley!" he remarked, "Pretty expensive parsley."

I'd gone too far. Sean had chosen the restaurant and the entrée, so I was criticizing *him*. "This is really very good," I said, and let that lead to a number of other banal, ingratiating observations about the décor (it was so dimly-lit that it was almost a literal blind date) and, God help me, even the weather. Nervous=babbling.

"Aren't you going to drink that?" He was refilling his wine glass; his narrowed eyes indicated my own glass, untouched.

I raised it, forcing a smile. "*L'chaim.*"

He grunted. "My ex-wife was Jewish."

"Really?" I put the wine to my lips, but recoiled at the taste.

"And she's crazy. She's always claiming the kids need something new that doesn't make sense. Since when does a six-year-old boy need the latest iPad? I think she's spending the child support money on herself."

He was drunk. It had happened while I was making the smallest of small talk.

Lawrence returned to ask if everything was all right. I said, "yes," but now I just wanted to get out of there — no, no dessert, and no, not even coffee. I had enough cash to offer to pay half the check.

"I told her I was coming for the rest of my clothes, and do you know what she did? She donated my three best suits to the Salvation Army. Two-thousand dollar suits. I tried to get them back and they wouldn't give them to me! The goddamn Salvation Army!"

"It's funny," I said, "but every divorced man I've ever met has a crazy ex-wife. How can that be? Statistically?"

"She had me buy $200 tickets to Disney on Ice and when I came to pick up the kids they weren't even there!"

"Maybe the two of you should consider family therapy. For the kids' sake."

"No way. I tell you, she's crazy."

Sean was scraping up the last dabs of the dill-and-horseradish sauce that had not-very-generously topped the tiny salmon filet, when I noticed a man talking to a couple at the table behind him. He wasn't a waiter: He was in a wrinkled gray suit that was too big for him and he carried what looked like a large white poster board. The wife had her mouth half open. When the man with the poster board turned toward the husband, I saw that his suit was double-breasted. That made it a good fifteen years old.

"Shall we order another bottle?" Sean asked. Rhetorically.

Suddenly the man was at the side of our table and I got my first look at his face. Half of it was covered in a port-wine stain. In the candlelight it was a dark purple.

He looked only at me and whipped the poster board around his waist. It wasn't just a board, though: It was a portfolio. He opened it and displayed a watercolor.

It was a simple watercolor, and though far beyond any skills I possessed (which were limited to spilling paint on myself), it was fairly crude. I recognized it, though, as Ocean Beach, the user-unfriendly shore a few short miles away, with Seal Rock and its rough sand. Several strata of pink and gold indicated that it was sunset.

"I'm selling these," the man said. He hesitated and added, "I'm helping my son through school."

"I came here to eat a good meal," Sean barked. "I don't appreciate being interrupted."

My ears heated up. The man slowly began to pull the portfolio away.

"I'll buy one," I said. "How much?"

His lower lip trembled. "A hundred dollars."

"How did you get in?" Sean demanded.

"I — I only have sixty on me." I reached into my purse. "A good time for PayPal, huh?" My ears burned hotter.

Sean took a gulp of wine from my glass. "What are you doing?"

"Buying a painting." I handed my three twenties to the artist and carefully slipped the watercolor under my arm, hoping, I confess, that it was dry enough not to stain my white satin blouse. "And leaving you with the bill."

Ashleigh's mother, Kimberly, was standing between her and the front door. Just leaving for school had become like getting through airport security.

"You're not going out in *that,* are you?"

Ashleigh was wearing jeans and her t-shirt from the Gay-Straight Alliance. "What's wrong with it, Mother?" she asked coolly.

"If I have to tell you then there's no point."

Ashleigh launched her Mother exercise: Take a deep breath, and silently recite the affirmation, *I must accept my mother's limitations. I must accept my mother's limitations.* "I don't have time to change." She said this matter-of-factly.

"Well, I need you home for dinner, anyway."

"I might be late." Ashleigh raised her chin. "Won't you be showing a six-million-dollar house to a Silicon Valley billionaire anyway?"

"You should be so lucky! Selling homes is what pays *our* mortgage. Puts clothes on your — "

"Puts clothes on *your* back and that diamond the size of my head on your finger." No! No! *I must accept my mother's limitations, I must accept....*

Ashleigh had hoped that things would be better between herself and Kimberly this year. They'd hardly seen each other over the summer: Ashleigh volunteered at the Goodwill Store a lot of hours, and for a few weeks she was a counselor at a drama camp for inner city grade school kids. That even paid a little money.

But since school started, she and her mother had been going at it every day: Ashleigh needed to study more; if she insisted on doing volunteer work it should be for the symphony guild; and no more second-hand clothes, because even if Ashleigh didn't care, it reflected badly on both of them.

"I suppose you have the *One World Club,*" Kimberly sneered. "And Freddie will be there."

"What do you hate most about Freddie, Mother?" Ashleigh asked. "That he's black or that he's gay?" Freddie was Ashleigh's best friend, but at first Kimberly thought Freddie was her boyfriend.

"For God's sake! You know I'm not prejudiced against anyone!"

"Not if they have the right credit score, you aren't."

"Can we have one adult conversation!" Kimberly pressed her fingernails into her forehead. "Why do you do this to me?"

And just that fast, Kimberly whipped out the weapon that could have ended the Cold War thirty years early: guilt.

Kimberly had Ashleigh when she was only 17. Her family wanted her to have an abortion, was going to *force* her to have an abortion, but Kimberly ran away from her home in East Palestine, Indiana, and came out west, all to save Ashleigh's life.

"I'm sorry, Mother," Ashleigh murmured.

Kimberly stretched out her hand, like she wanted to make up. "Freddie sounds like a perfectly nice boy. But if you want to get into Stanford — "

"*You* want me to go to Stanford. I never said — "

" — you need to be meeting better people than the sort ... the sort you meet at your high school."

"Like Freddie?"

Kimberly shrugged. "Like Freddie."

That was it. "Maybe you'll be glad to know that there's a new guy in my life, Mother."

"Don't tell me. This one has an arrest record."

"Not hardly. He comes from a really important — a *prominent* family. And he's been walking me home from school, too."

These two bits of information seemed to catch Kimberly off-guard. Then suspicion kicked back in. "What's his name?"

"Jack."

"Jack Whitfield! I didn't know he went to Takei!"

Ashleigh didn't know a Jack Whitfield but her mother knew all the rich people in the city. Jack Whitfield must be the son of one of those early Silicon Valley billionaires, the ones who were old already.

"No. Jack Kagen."

"I don't know any Kagen family."

"His father is the District Attorney."

Kimberly frowned. *Mother knows so damn little about anything that doesn't affect her.* If Ashleigh could get her into a mental ward, and they asked her who the president was, she probably wouldn't know, so they'd end up keeping her there. Something to keep in mind for the future.

"You're not just saying that are you?" Kimberly asked.

"I never lie to you, Mother. Look it up on the Internet. His father is Alex Kagen, and really rich."

"Really? Why didn't you tell me about him before?"

"I knew you wouldn't approve."

"And why not, pray tell?"

"He's autistic."

The word in her own ears was dangerous, a warning, the screech of the late bell (which she was going to hear pretty soon if she didn't get past her goddam mother).

Kimberly noisily tapped the toe of one Christian Leboutin shoe. "What does that mean?"

Did her mother really not know what "autistic" meant? Although Ashleigh didn't either at first, not really. She had asked around about Jack, and even though none of her friends knew him, Sue said that it sounded like he had Asperger's Syndrome.

Ashleigh looked it up. Now she knew about the autism spectrum and that Asperger's was the high-functioning end. She also found out that there were something like two dozen kids on the spectrum at Takei. Part of her rebelled against this. Asperger's sounded like yet another label: dyslexia, ADHD. Stoner. Nerd.

So she tried not to think *autism* or *Asperger's* when she was with Jack. She'd let him walk home with her that first day because it felt like a good deed, and her motto was "no good deed too small." It still felt like a good deed, but he was an incredible listener.

"It means he's a human being, like you or me."

"I can't take any more of this." Kimberly moved away from the door. "I don't care how many mentally-challenged kids you're babysitting, you can be home by 6:30. If I don't do something with the tilapia tonight, it'll go bad."

Marissa gathered a handful of my skirt and squeezed. "I don't want a shot," she pleaded.

We were at the pediatrician's office. I'd taken her out of school an hour early, praying that Alex wouldn't find out and have a grand mal seizure.

My blind date had been three days before, but I hadn't been able to shake off the memory. The image of the man with the port wine stain haunted me.

I confess, however, that most of my thoughts were more self-centered.

When my marriage was breaking up, I'd had an affair with a man named Val. If his name were effeminate, it was the only effeminate quality he possessed: He was a hiker and a biker, an athlete, and a lover *par excellence.*

"I'm sorry, honey, but it's to protect you from getting sick."

I hadn't been entirely lying to Darya. I was mostly over Val, at least Val-qua-Val. What I couldn't get past was that *I had been as stupid as I had been.*

I had overlooked the fact that the job he held was temporary. That the apartment he lived in wasn't his. That the way he spoke of past adventures made it clear that he longed for more. He slept with his passport under his pillow. (Metaphorically.)

And just as Val's past had predicted his future (that he was not going to stay with one woman), so did my past predict mine: I was going to choose the wrong man. The man I chose would be a man whose past, if I considered it honestly, would reveal that he was unavailable for the long haul.

But I would not consider his past honestly.

So it was just as well that Damien had been a jerk. If I'd liked him I would only have been setting myself up for another heartbreak.

There were good men in the world. Jonas Salk. Martin Luther King, Jr. Atticus Finch.

"Can we go home now?" Marissa pleaded.

I put down the *People* magazine I'd grabbed from the top of a pile, even though *People* always depressed me, with its stories of rich 'n' gorgeous celebs who had found true love but who deserved it because they'd overcome shyness or bulimia or food allergies on their way to the top.

After what felt like an archeological dig in my tote bag, I brought out *On the Banks of Plum Creek.* We'd started it a few nights before, after I'd made the unilateral decision to skip the dreary *Farmer Boy.*

Laura and Mary were living in a "dugout": a house underground. I knew the story well, and I knew how badly it would end, with the plague of grasshoppers that devoured their crop and, in the following book, the blindness that would descend on Mary. But meanwhile, Marissa giggled whenever I mentioned Laura's dog, because his name was Jack.

"Marissa?"

It was the nurse.

Up until now The Shot had been an abstract threat, something I would never really make her do if she didn't want to. Once the shape of the nurse blocked the light from the doorway, she knew that it wasn't April Fool's after all.

"Don't make me, Mommy!" she cried, and this time she grabbed not only a fistful of my skirt but a large chunk of my thigh and squeezed until I cried out, too.

CHAPTER 3

Jack could memorize anything. People always asked him how he did it. There was a way that he did it but he didn't have the words in English to explain.

Ashleigh didn't ask him how he memorized her schedule after she only told him once, on that first day, but he did, and that was how they got in the habit of walking home together, because he always knew just when she was going home.

That first day he could tell that she was just being nice, but Jack could be patient. And persistent. So in the beginning he always asked her, even though his heart was pounding so hard he wondered if he could have a heart attack. But teenagers never had heart attacks on TV. They only died from drugs and drunk drivers.

Then one day Ashleigh flipped her locker door closed, with this little sigh she had, and said, "So, are you ready?" and he knew that it had become an understanding that they walk home Mondays and Wednesdays *and* Thursdays.

Ashleigh described him as a real gentleman for walking her home. She didn't know that he waited an extra two hours so that he'd be ready at the same time that she was.

And every girl wanted a gentleman for a boyfriend. He'd heard that on at least four Disney Channel shows, like *The Suite Life of Zack and Cody* and *Drake and Josh*.

After that first walk Ashleigh asked him about himself. What were his parents like? What was his house like? Did he ever go on vacation? Just Disneyland? *She* wanted to see the world. What exactly bothered him about traveling? Strange bathrooms? Really?

There was surprise, but no condemnation, in her voice.

His short, vague answers prompted longer, and more specific questions, but the wonderful thing he discovered was that he didn't have to talk, didn't have to struggle so hard with how to translate what he was thinking. Because the more he stayed quiet, the more she talked for both of them.

Today they had just gotten away from the school when she fingered the strap of her book-carrier and said, "Are you in a hurry? I mean, would you mind if we took a walk to the beach?"

"Okay." Jack would walk to the moon with her. (It would be so fun if they *could* walk to the moon.) The beach was kind of far away, but after a few blocks Jack could see the section of the sky at the bottom that was darker than the rest.

When they got to where the sidewalk ended there was the highway to cross and it was very windy, and they waited a long time for the light but finally they got across and went down some steps and there they were.

Jack didn't like the beach much, because, when he was little, a wave almost swept him away. Ever since then, the water made him a bit nervous. His mother and even Marissa insisted that standing in the little waves was safe, but everyone said that it wasn't safe to swim. He hoped that Ashleigh wouldn't want to go in the water.

When he stepped on the sand his feet sank down, but this sand here was grainy and full of rocks so his feet didn't go down very far. He was intent on not letting sand into his shoes.

It was hard to follow Ashleigh, who walked ahead. Fortunately they stopped before they got very far. Ashleigh sat down on the sand, and let her book-carrier go down next to her. Jack didn't want to let his backpack touch the sand, so he kept it on and plunked next to her.

Ashleigh was quiet for a while, but then she sighed, louder than usual. "I dunno, Jack. My mom — "

She stopped. The wind was making her hair flap. He'd never thought about the color of anyone's hair before, but he saw that each strand was its own distinct shade of gold, orange or dark red. In the sunlight it glowed like fire, but beneath the unkind fluorescent lights of the school hallway it turned almost green.

"I know that every teenage girl is supposed to have problems with her mom, it's such a cliché, but with me and my mom it's worse than it is for my friends, so they don't understand."

She stared out to the ocean while she talked. The ocean was loud, a steady whooshing sound. There were other people on the beach but not very many. The wind on his face stung.

"We're so different is the problem. She wants to be in the Nob Hill Gazette every week. Like, as real estate agent to the stars." She pulled her book-carrier on her lap. THE WORLD IN PIECES, he read again. "Parents, huh?"

"SpongeBob doesn't have this problem," Jack mused, and Ashleigh laughed. Her laugh was like the spray of the shower, the little tickles on his chest.

"You are *so* funny, Jack."

He flushed with pleasure. He had no idea why what he said was funny, but he knew a compliment when he heard one.

"She doesn't give me any privacy at all. I tried putting a lock on my door, I got my friend Freddie to help, and she had a handyman take it off! He took out the whatever — the mechanical part — so now the door won't even close all the way, you know, it won't click shut." She mimed slamming a door. "So now I keep my journal in my locker."

He felt like he was supposed to say something about that, but he wasn't sure, so he followed his rule and kept quiet.

Ashleigh took off her sneakers and then spent a lot of time fiddling with the legs of her jeans. "You can't really roll up bell bottoms," she said, which he didn't understand. "I mean, the micro-managing! She wants, like, a resume from everyone I hang out with. And she only wants me to hang out with — "

She stopped so suddenly, just when his heart was speeding up, because he was someone she hung out with and maybe she was going to say something about hanging out with him, but the next thing she said was, "Can you believe she doesn't want me to go to the dance on Friday?"

Jack felt like she wanted an answer. "Yes," he said. There was a 50-50 chance he'd be right.

Ashleigh made one short laughing sound. "Yeah, me too. You get her now. Everyone goes to dances! A lot of us girls don't even dance one-on-one. We get on the dance floor as a group, or we just hang out."

Jack loved to go to the dances, the ones open to sophomores, and last year he volunteered to work in the coat check at the junior prom. There were some problems with the coats getting mixed up. So many of them looked alike. Anyway, he didn't think they'd let him do it again this year.

"Can you believe that I'm not supposed to wear makeup? At my age?"

Jack was pretty sure that these were more of those questions that he didn't need to answer. There were some questions you weren't even *supposed* to answer. Why did everyone call *these* people "normal"? What they said rarely made sense. And the things they did really didn't make sense! They spent hours on homework when they were going to forget the whole class by the following year; the girls went on scary-to-think-about diets, and then never thought they were thin enough anyway; the moms washed everyone's clothes that just got dirty the next time someone wore them.

For the next seven minutes they were quiet. Jack liked it when they were quiet. He liked being near her, and even sitting on the sand wasn't bothering him so much anymore.

"Can I tell you something, Jack?"

"Yes."

"It's a secret. I haven't told anyone yet."

"Okay."

"Promise you won't tell anyone?"

"Yes."

She was looking at him and he was looking back at her, right in her eye.

Finally: "I want to join the Peace Corps."

"What — what's the Peace Corps?"

"You don't know.... Never mind. I'm sorry." She looked away, digging her toes deeply into the sand. Even her toes were cute. "Well, I have to do more research, because there are a lot of programs, but..."

She talked too fast for him. He heard the word "Africa" and "water" a lot of times. Something about a girl walking....

"Three miles *each* way just to get water for her — for her — " She choked up. She might have been crying.

"And then one day she dropped the — the — " She waved her hands over her head. "The container she used for the water and — "

Tears dripped down her cheeks. Jack felt terrible but he didn't know what to do. Would it be okay if —

"*She hanged herself.*"

Ashleigh put her face down against her knees. Her shoulders trembled.

Jack edged closer to her, pushing up a ridge of sand, and dropped one arm across her back.

Ashleigh sniffled and pulled herself up. "I'm okay now. Do you have a Kleenex?"

"Yes!"

He opened his backpack. There *was* Kleenex in there. Where was it? He shoved his hand between the books and fluttering papers.

Ashleigh took a deep breath. "I can stand it because I know I'm going to make a difference." She started talking fast again. She wanted to take a Gap year, which must have meant that she would spend a year shopping at The Gap.

He found some Kleenex, but it was all in shreds. "It's like snow," he said, "but it's August."

She laughed, even though her cheeks were still wet. "*So* funny. You've made me feel better." Suddenly — so suddenly it scared him — Ashleigh grabbed his hand. "I can really talk to you, Jack," she said. Her face changed, and though he couldn't read any meaning into the change, still, this was probably the first time he'd seen a face so clearly.

I wondered.

Student body president or swirly victim, would anyone go back to high school?

Once a year it was the privilege of us parents to do so, on Back to School Night — or "B.S." night, as I privately called it.

We were supposed to go from class to class, following our own sons' and/or daughters' schedules, thus to listen to their teachers describe the upcoming year's curriculum, grade requirements, needs for extra school supplies, yada, yada, yada.

Parents like me, with students in the full-inclusion program, also attended a separate session, the better to learn about the accommodations that would be made for our kids: untimed tests; an extra aide in the classroom; audio books for the aural learners.

That special presentation for the special was taking place even as I stood in the school cafeteria, gulping coffee that tasted like brown crayon juice. I was a veteran of full-inclusion programs and did not feel the need to expose myself to the worries of the incoming parents, who would only arouse my own not-so-dormant anxieties.

The cafeteria itself had been transformed into a festive bazaar, with the various clubs and sports teams selling food and *tchotchkes* to raise money: t-shirts, bumper stickers, brownies, cupcakes, Korean BBQ, chow mein. The walls were plastered with banners ("Go Porcupines!") and anti-drug posters ("Stay Alive – Don't Drink and Drive!" "Wasted? So Is Your Life!"), while crepe paper in the school colors of red and white looped from the ceiling.

I nibbled at a chocolate chip cookie, purchased from the Ballroom Dance Club. I wanted to go home badly, but Jack's 7th period class was algebra and the teacher was new to the school. It would be in my and Jack's interest for me to appear and to make nice. Maybe mention the tutor that Alex would hire. Maybe hint at a reduced homework load.

"You're looking very nice tonight."

It was a disembodied voice I didn't recognize, and when I turned around, I saw a man I didn't recognize, either. But I smiled, making sure that all my upper teeth showed. Flirting was fun. Flirting was safe.

The man was tall, blonde, and big-boned. A mustard-and-brown hound's-tooth sport coat that told me he might have dressed in the dark. To be fair, I wasn't exactly surrounded by Project Runway: There were a lot of unintentionally-faded jeans on both men and women and even *men in flip flops,* which I considered less a fashion statement than a declaration of war.

"Of course, you always look nice," he added.

I simultaneously preened and panicked, as the "always" implied that we had met before. I'd met hundreds of people when I was married to Alex and on the speeding handshake-and-air-kiss merry-go-round that was local politics. *Nice to meet/see you again/why yes, I'd love to see a picture of your new twins/kitchen remodel-in-progress/rescue dog.* I'd learned to remember the number, gender and names of their children, but I still had trouble with faces.

What the hell. I'd faked recognizing people more often than I'd faked orgasms, though I didn't get away with it nearly as often. "Thank you."

"You know I didn't realize it was you at first."

Awkward suddenly became creepy.

"You don't remember me at all, do you?"

Oh, shit, I thought. *Just get it over with.* "No."

"How soon they forget." He smiled and the creepiness dissipated. It was a half-smile: just one corner of his mouth turned up. He looked friendly and timid and even a tiny bit *nebbish*. The sport coat contributed to this last quality. His teeth were big and straight and of a natural shade, instead of that blindingly white look that I and much of the rest of the Bay Area was chasing. "Well, it has been five years."

"Five...."

Suddenly I wished for two tectonic plates to shift so that the earth could swallow me whole. It was not only the policeman from in front of the school, it was a policeman from another life: Jason Armstrong.

Five years earlier two of Jack's classmates accused him of causing the death of another boy. In retrospect, my fear that Jack would get sent away, to a brutal camp for wayward youth, if not worse, seemed a classic case of what Alex would have described as "Anna being hysterical and overreacting." But if anyone had been hysterical it had been the other parents, who then spread the hysteria beyond Jack's school and to the public. Orson Wells couldn't have done any better with a second *War of the Worlds* broadcast.

It was over now, thank God, thanks in significant part to the policeman in front of me.

"I'm so embarrassed," I said.

"I know I look different."

"No! You don't. I've always had trouble with facial recognition. Really, ever since — "

I babbled a little longer. He did look somewhat different, though: He had crow's feet that I didn't remember. His nose was crooked, and I didn't remember that, either.

"I meant — " I finally interrupted myself. I wanted to say that I meant to get in touch, to write him a thank you note, or at least to send an e-mail. "I never thanked you enough."

He raised his shoulders in an exaggerated shrug. "Maybe you'll have another opportunity."

"I hope so," I said as the spirit of the eternal flirt re-entered my body. Then, newly-embarrassed, I tried the radical tactic of asking him about himself. "So ... five years. What's new?"

"Well." He shuffled his feet. "Trevor ... you know ... Trevor."

He stopped. And I remembered: this policeman who had helped me, back in the day when policemen were my friends because I was married to the District Attorney, had a son Jack's age, who was also on the spectrum.

I didn't remember any other details about Trevor; again, at the time of our original meeting, I'd had a lot on my mind. And when he'd said at our earlier, cupcake-centric reunion, that his son was a transfer student, he hadn't mentioned the Asperger's.

"But he's a student here now," I said, to prove that I wasn't a complete amnesiac. The next logical questions would have been where Trevor had transferred from and why he had transferred, but Aspies transferring schools was common and usually for reasons uncomfortable to discuss.

"And ... um, I'm a single dad now."

"Right. Right, right." Here it came. The story of his divorce and his crazy ex-wife. I swished the remaining coffee around the bottom of my cardboard cup. Could I be forgiven for hoping that he was a widower?

But a moment passed and he didn't mention whether a tragic, surgically-aimed fragment of a meteor had killed his wife or if they'd divorced amicably after she had a vision of the Virgin Mary telling her to become a Carmelite nun. Instead he peeked over the edge of my cup. "Can I buy you another cup of coffee?"

"Sure." I pointed to the table where I'd purchased the one I held. A poster hanging over the side proclaimed it "The One World Club."

"Decaf?"

"Puh-lease. Decaf coffee is like lean pastrami."

"Not sure I get that, but okay."

I watched him make a wide circle around a couple with a double stroller and do a quick side-step to avoid a trio of teenage girls carrying pom-poms.

But the coffee urn wasn't far away and when he stopped there I got a good look at his left hand. No ring.

Why did I bother to look? He'd just said he was a single dad.

He folded what appeared to be a five-dollar bill into the empty pickle jar and I interpreted from his traffic-cop raised palm that he was telling the redhead behind the table to keep the change. She'd looked familiar when I bought my own "coffee."

"It must be fate bringing us together," he said as he handed me my cup. "My last fortune cookie predicted I would meet a lovely stranger."

"But I'm not a stranger," I reminded him.

A man with disturbingly muscular shoulders stretching the short sleeves of his T-shirt appeared behind Jason, and thumped him on the back in the hail-fellow-well-met spirit of a sports bar. "Yo, Jace," he said. "Can you come by the bungalow tomorrow?"

The man's hearty thump caused a wave of dark liquid to slosh over the side of Jason's cup. "Tomorrow?"

"Yeah, tomorrow. Before practice. Hey, where'd you guys get the coffee?"

I pointed to the urn.

"See ya tomorrow then."

As he walked away, the crowd of parents parted for him. "Who was that masked man?" I asked.

"The track coach. David Takanawa." Jason gulped. "I'm a-sceered, Ma," he said, looking after the coach, who had moved on, and was chatting with the same redhead at the urn, though without putting any money in her jar.

"Why should you be scared?" I lowered my eyes to the empty cup and regarded him through heavily mascaraed lashes. "You look like you could take him twice over."

"I probably could, especially since I'll be sure to be packing heat."

"Hardy-har-har." I cocked my head. "Is — um, your son trying out for the team?"

"Nope." He toasted me with the paper cup. The use of Styrofoam was now a class A felony in California. "Trevor is *on* the team now. Try outs were last week."

"Mazel tov." An athletic Aspie was a rarity. I was ashamed of a moment of envy.

"It'll be a bigger whatever-you-said if he stays on the track team. He has some, er, let's say 'issues.' "

"Who doesn't?" I was dying to hear more. "When you say issues, do you mean...." I cut myself off instead of asking, *Counting the people in the bleachers?*

"Things... kind of have to go his way."

"Most of us like things to go our way." It was a commonplace among the parents of kids on the spectrum to politely assert that their kids' oddities weren't really oddities.

"He's one of the top runners in the city." Jason's voice thickened. "He's a miler."

"What's his best time?" I asked, though I had no idea what a good or bad time would be.

"Six-fourteen-nineteen."

"That's fantastic." I knew it was fantastic because Jason had implied as much.

"So, he's on the track team here already, but... We left Harvey Milk High because of some problems, and I thiiink..." He wiggled his eyebrows, Groucho Marx-style. "They may be about to, shall we say, resurface."

"Ah."

"He throws fits. I hate to describe it that way, but...."

"My son used to have that problem."

I immediately wanted to take it back. Yes, there was a bond among us special need parents, but there could be a perverse competitiveness as well. "Mine isn't as bad as yours," *or* "Mine is worse than yours." It makes ordinary parents sound pathetically self-absorbed: "*My* kid is going to Princeton." "*My* kid is going to Yale." Your kid is going to college. Shut the fuck up.

"I'm worried." He was more serious now. "The track team means a lot to Trevor — and to me."

"You'll have to call me to tell me how it goes."

"Yeah — well, you know, I'd better get to that full-inclusion talk."

I was surprised to feel how this last cup of coffee was traveling backwards, burning my esophagus on its return trip. Did he think I was asking him to call me? I looked at my watch. "That started twenty minutes ago."

"I know." He grinned again. "But I saw you and I just had to say hi." He reached into the inside pocket of his sport coat and pulled out a cell phone. "I guess if I'm going to call you to tell you how it goes, I'll need your number."

I caught myself humming as I put the key in my front door. A single guy with a friend for Jack. Jason's single state was a plus not because I saw him as relationship material, but because I'd found that it was much easier to be friends with singles, male or female, than with couples.

The porch light was on and through the drawn curtains I saw that the lights were on in the living room as well. I had been sure that I would be home no later than eight, which was why I'd left not only Jack alone but Marissa in his care. They both knew not to answer the phone (though Marissa did defy me on occasion) and I'd fed them before I left.

Jack knew to switch the deadbolt behind me, too, but when I turned the key and found it *un*bolted, I froze. *He just forgot,* I told myself. Please God, he just forgot....

A hairline crack of time later I stood inside, looking at Alex and a strange woman while they looked back at me.

Someone died. There was no other reason for Alex to drop by unannounced this late. And that woman with him ... she was the grief counselor or the Highway Patrol officer out of uniform who was there to break the news.

"What did you think you were doing?" Alex asked.

"I — I went to Back to School Night." Adhering to the principle that the best defense is a good offense, I added haughtily, "I thought I might have seen you there."

"You left your children at home alone." Alex was using the same strategy against me. "Do you think that's safe?"

"As a matter of fact, I am later than I expected," I said, as I slipped off my coat. "I had a chance to speak privately with Jack's new algebra teacher. I won't be able to help him once they get past the basic equations." Was the strange woman a social worker here to officially declare me an unfit mother? "I told her you'd be hiring a tutor."

No, she couldn't be a social worker: She was too relaxed, sitting sideways with her feet on the couch, flipping through a magazine. This make-herself-at-home position told me that she and Alex were well-acquainted. That didn't give her the right to put her shoes on my couch, though. Just because soiled diapers and half-eaten burritos had been there did not mean — oh my God, was she wearing *penny loafers?* And a red pullover sweater with snowflakes on it?

"Where *are* our children?" I asked. I referred to them as "our" for the benefit of the silent woman, who had yet to make eye contact with me. She was in her late 30s, possibly younger, with brown hair of a shade that could fairly be called colorless, and pale, pasty skin with the finish of a marshmallow. A plain woman. But perhaps I was not the most objective observer.

"The children are in their rooms. I wanted to talk to you alone."

"I have made it clear that I do not want you to drop by unannounced. Your key is for emergencies."

"This could easily have been an emergency," he countered. "With Jack and Marissa — "

This was literally where I came in, so I addressed Alex's companion cheerfully, "Hi! We haven't met. I'm Anna. Anna Kagen — but you knew that second half, right?"

"This is Linda," Alex said. "Linda Bartlett."

At last the selective mute in the Christmas-in-September sweater spoke. "'Linda' is on my birth certificate. My professional name is Violetta." She smiled over the top of the magazine: *The Garden of the Future.* Then she raised her bottom from the couch so as to pull a card from her back pocket. I didn't move, but she held it straight out in front of her and finally I stepped forward to take it. Lavender flowers obscured all but the words THE GARDEN and VIOLETTA BARTLETT.

All at once I knew who Linda/Violetta must be.

Alex's fiancée.

I should only be surprised that he hadn't remarried years ago. Divorce had been good for his sex life. I'd heard that he always brought a date to the many events he attended. He had no trouble finding those dates: Women circled him as if he were a Target about to open on Black Friday. Except for that little bit of excess weight he was a handsome man — and that was the least of it. He was rich and influential, when a Y chromosome and a pulse was more than enough for most women over thirty in a city like San Francisco.

Or maybe she was Alex's wife already! We hadn't seen him during the weekend just past. He could have gone to Nevada and married. He would avoid so much discomfort by presenting this situation to me and the kids as *fait accompli.* No tears, no awkward introductions — because he'd leave it to *me* to break the news.

I didn't love him anymore. What did I care if he had a new wife? What did I care if he had more children with this younger-than-me-wife? What did I care if he had another son?

"*Enchanté*," I said weakly.

Linda wasn't his usual type, who were svelte, well-educated brunettes who showed off their legs in skirts just above the knee. Linda wasn't even wearing makeup. *And* she had a receding chin.

I'd remained standing all this time. Now I sat down heavily.

Alex leaned forward. "Now you and Linda are going to be seeing a lot of each other, and I know you can have a little trouble with new people, Anna, so I just couldn't wait to bring her over."

"Why are we going to be seeing a lot of each other?" I asked warily.

"Linda is an education consultant."

Linda smiled with her lips only and went back to her magazine.

"An education consultant?"

"She's going to help us with Marissa."

"What help — "

"It's called The Garden. The Chinese military started experimenting with it two decades ago — why do you think they're turning out the world's top scientists now? It's almost unknown in the United States. Here's what they've discovered."

He continued in an intense whisper, "The human brain — especially in childhood — learns the same way our metabolism burns calories. There's a learning metabolism, too, and you can speed it up with high intensity intervals alternating with short breaks." He looked at Linda — perhaps for approval? "We'll use the first cycle to reinforce what Wissy's learning in school and the second to launch subjects Sunrise Academy can't address, like Mandarin, or even Cantonese, although we're starting awfully late for that."

"The best time to plant a tree was twenty years ago." Linda touched her finger to her tongue and turned a page.

"But the second-best time is now!" Alex concluded, more animated than I'd seen him since the night he'd been elected to his third term. "You'll want to hear more, Anna."

"Not really," I said.

He took that as a yes and launched into a lengthy spiel. Every cult has its own vocabulary and I picked up words like "greenhouse," "plowing," and "topsoil." In the background I heard Jack yelping at the television in his room. Distracted, tired, I fell into a kind of stupor. My mind wandered back to Jason, and our plans to get the boys together.

"Linda's The Master Landscaper," was the first full sentence I caught in a while. "She can set up right here." Alex indicated my modest living room. "We'll be adding at least two computers — possibly a third, so it'll be a little cramped. *Your* job — " he pointed at me — "is to make this 'fertile ground.' "

"Are you going to actually truck dirt in here?"

"No. Will you listen? 'Garden' is a *paradigm.*"

"We've trademarked the term," Linda said. "Also the slogan, 'Where flowers bloom so does hope.' "

"Your other job — " Alex slapped the back of Linda's magazine — "will be to keep Jack quiet during the afternoons. Linda — "

"Violetta," Linda corrected him, "is more appropriate in this context."

"Violetta and her gardening team will be here at least four hours a day."

On cue we all heard another yelp from the direction of Jack's bedroom. Alex grimaced.

"Why don't we make sure he has detention every day?" I asked.

"Don't be dramatic. This can be an opportunity for him, too. You're right." He paused to let me savor these unfamiliar words. "I haven't been spending enough time with him. So I'm going to find a good afternoon program for him, too."

"You're — "

"Yes, I'm paying for everything, if that's what's worrying you."

"I was going to say that you're scaring me," I said. *Don't let this become a blow-out.* "Let's just not rush into this."

"You're holding Marissa back."

"No. You're pushing her way too hard." I shook my head. "You've already got her a grade ahead in a high-pressure school. You've got to see how it can backfire. She'll end up a runaway hooked on heroin and supporting her pimp with a day job at Walgreen's."

"Please. Do not. Talk that way."

I turned to Linda. "Are you familiar with the musical *Little Shop of Horrors*? About the plant that eats people?"

"There are no plants that eat people," Linda said. "Where did you get that idea?"

"Technically it drinks blood," I corrected myself. "Alex, Marissa has got to have some kind of normal childhood. If — I mean, I'm sure she's destined for great things, but why such a rush? Why does she have to graduate college at fourteen instead of twenty? I don't want her to miss out on her prom or having a high school boyfriend. The normal things that — "

"Seventy-seven percent of children who enter The Garden before age six enter Ivy League schools," Linda interrupted. Her face had an otherworldly glow, so now it was like a very *shiny* marshmallow. For some minutes I had been wishing that she were Alex's fiancée after all.

"You know, Zuckerberg's parents had him enrolled in an early version of The Garden. That is a well-kept secret, isn't it?"

I looked from one to the other. I'd never imagined Alex could fall for such a scam. Because it was obviously a scam, as surely as Scientology, as surely as those "better than Botox" ads.

In the early days with Jack, Alex had undergone a torturous period of denial during which he was sure that Jack would snap out of his odd behaviors once we got him into pre-school. That passed, though, and after that, Alex had been the pragmatic one. When I heard about places like the ranch in Wyoming where the owner/director claimed a 90% complete recovery rate, it was Alex who had brought me back to Earth.

But at the moment, he was beyond reason, and I wasn't going to waste any more time.

"Okay, that's all folks," I announced, getting to my feet. "This Kid Farm or Wheat Crop — *not happening.*"

Alex gave Linda an indulgent this-is-what-I-warned-you-about look.

Linda quoted, "'Raise your voice, not your words. It is rain that grows flowers, not thunder.' "

"Let me ask you this," he said to me. "Would you be willing to try it for two months? Just to see what kind of results we get."

"I just told you — *not happening.*" I liked the way it felt to tell him what I thought. Let him cut off all spousal support. Let him go to the press, to Child Protective Services. Let him frame me for bank robbery.

"Would you be willing to try it for three weeks?"

I cracked.

"For the love of God!" I stomped my heel hard enough to make a divot in the carpet. "Get out of Marissa's life! Get out of my life!"

The thrill of standing up to Alex faded rapidly in the silence that followed. But I'd finally made myself clear, because Alex brought his eyebrows together much as Marissa did and lowered his head like a bull about to charge.

I pointed to the door. "Why don't you two go out and plant a tree somewhere? Did you have a coat, Lindale, or should I call you 'Vi' in 'this context'?"

"This is going to happen," Alex said.

I strode to the front door and held it open, letting in a draft of cold air. "Over my dead body. Drive safely now."

CHAPTER 4

The weekend came and with it, my once and perhaps future policeman friend Jason arrived.

He'd shaken the hound's-tooth in favor of a celadon polo shirt, which was flatteringly tight across his broad chest.

"And you must be Trevor!" I squealed at Jason's companion, like a nervous pre-school teacher, which sounded all the more odd because Trevor was just a tiny bit shorter than his father, probably six-two, though of a much lankier build, as one would expect in a runner.

"I got a new rainbow fish," Trevor said. His unwashed hair was in a ponytail that hung down his back, and when he spoke I noticed a pronounced under bite. I recognized both from my years as an Aspie mom: I knew kids who wouldn't let anyone cut their hair, and it was by the grace of God that Jack hadn't needed braces.

"This is Jack." I reached for Trevor and Jack at the same time, then I pulled back. Perhaps Trevor didn't like to be touched? I ended up flapping my hands in much the same way that Jack did.

Both boys stared at each other.

"Trevor's on the track team!" I said.

"I run *cross-country*," Trevor corrected me. "Track is in the spring. The *spring*."

"Running is — running is fun," Jack said.

"I run the mile. I run the fastest mile in the city."

An unnerving silence fell, punctured by a soft huh-huh-huh coming from Jack.

"Why are you doing that?" Trevor asked Jack. He had a nasal voice that made it sound more like a taunt than a question.

"Your dad has told me a lot about you!" I chirped, when Jack didn't respond. "You boys have a lot in common."

"I'm not a *boy*."

"No, of course not — "

"I'm not a *boy*."

"I'm sorry! You *young men* have a lot in common."

"Like what?" Trevor challenged me. "Do you have fish?"

Jason squirmed. "Trev...."

"Like...." I saw that Jason was wearing a Giants cap. "Like baseball!" I said. Jack wasn't what you would think of as a fan, really, but

Alex had taken him to many games when Jack was younger, and he had memorized the players' names and their jersey numbers.

It was a good guess, though, because Trevor smiled, making the under bite more prominent. "Who's your favorite player?" he asked Jack.

"Barry Bonds."

"He doesn't play anymore." Trevor's smile disappeared. "Besides, he was caught using drugs. *Drugs.*"

Jason slapped his son on the back. "Hey, kids, why don't you let us old coots talk about the good old days, when candy bars cost a nickel?"

"Did candy bars ever cost a nickel?" Jack asked. "I could afford a million of them!"

"Me, too," Trevor agreed. "I'd get a million."

"Jack, why don't you show Trevor your room?"

"Ok!"

Jack waddled off with Trevor slouching just behind.

Jack was used to people being taller than he was, but Trevor was *really* tall.

"Do you guys have an aquarium? I have a really big aquarium," Trevor said. "A really big aquarium. I have more fish than anybody."

Jack didn't like bragging.

But if Trevor was going to be bragging, then Jack would, too. "I have every season of *The Simpsons* ever on DVD."

"No, you don't."

"Yes, I do!" If he didn't, it was only because not every single season was available, and also because his dad hadn't bought Seasons 16 and 17 yet like he promised.

"Show me Season 15." Trevor sounded like a foghorn. "Season *15.*"

Jack's DVDs were scattered all around the room, little UFOs crashed to earth. But Jack could spot each one in order. "Here!"

"Is that Season 15?"

"Yeah."

The first episode on Disk One was the Treehouse of Horror episode. Jack could recite all the dialogue from memory. He had plenty to brag about, too.

"That went well," Jason decided, at the slam of Jack's door.

"Yes," I agreed tentatively. I wasn't ready, after five minutes, to declare them BFFs.

"I think I'd better stay here," Jason said casually, looking up at the ceiling. "I mean, at the house. You know, in case there's a problem."

"They should be good for an hour." I cleared my throat. "I hope."

"Oh, at least," Jason said. He was shifting his weight from foot to foot, with his hands in his back pockets.

"You can always call for back up." Were police jokes kosher? "I suppose, uh … I suppose I should offer you something to drink."

"Yeah, uh … I could go for a beer." He quickly added, "I never have more than one. I mean, I don't *have* to have a beer."

"That's good." I was still standing, too, bizarrely shy about inviting him to sit. "I don't have any beer."

"You're more of a white wine gal."

"Don't have any alcohol in the house."

"Mineral water? You must be that much of a yuppie."

"Huh. For that, Officer, you get a juice box."

I had a selection of Odwalla juices and I grabbed one at random. Staying away from soda, diet or otherwise, was a nod to the healthy-food-only home I could never quite manage. Meanwhile, the coffee in my French press was still fresh enough that I filled a mug for myself.

In my living room I had a shabby sofa and two lumpy armchairs, neither of which matched the sofa nor each other. When I returned with what turned out to be Mango Tango, Jason was seated in one of those armchairs and I took the opposite one.

Awkward.

Then I remembered the bulked-up man who had passed us in the cafeteria on Back to School Night. "What did the coach — what was his name? — want to see you about?"

When Jason didn't answer right away I was nervous for him. He straightened up in the armchair.

"Coach Takanawa. He had a special meeting of the team without Trevor — "

"No!" I gasped, thinking the worst.

" — to talk to them all about Trevor's special needs." The corner of Jason's mouth went up again; it mirrored the bend in his nose. But his voice caught when he went on, "It's been a 180. Trevor was on the team at his last school, and that coach — well, that's in the past." He looked into the distance above my head. "Coach T rallied them all around Trev and they … well, they accept him."

I nodded, afraid that I might (quite uncharacteristically) choke up a little myself.

"He did the whole spiel about how we're different."

Jason pronounced "spiel" as it was spelled, rather than adding the "h" to make it *shpiel*.

"And of course he had the whole 'team' mentality to work with." Jason dismissed this gruffly, as if to say, *it's a guy thing*.

"Why aren't there more people like that?" I asked.

"Trevor worships him," Jason said. "Anyway — " he adopted an air of forced modesty — "that was a week ago and things are going good. It's good for the whole team. Everyone's showing up on time for practice and no one tries to duck out early."

My envy from Back to School Night returned; this time it lasted more than a moment. Jack had skills that could briefly impress a stranger but after all these years we had yet to find a way to put any of these skills to practical use. If only he'd been born in China before they invented the abacus.

Jason had dropped the pretense of modesty. "One of Trevor's big rules is that he win, but they don't have to 'let' him win because he wins all the time anyway."

Before this bragging could annoy me, he continued, "Back at Harvey Milk — his old school ... they weren't going to let him run this year. The coach wanted him off the team."

"Because...."

"He was having blow-outs on the field."

"Blow outs...."

"'Tantrum' is such a baby word."

"True that."

He was silent for a bit, fiddling with the cap on a shoelace. The opposing cap was missing and the shoelaces, once white, were now mostly gray. "We've paid our dues," he said finally.

"I bet," I said, adding quickly, "haven't we all."

"Trevor's been through some tough times." More cap-fiddling, then, "His mom and I split up when Trev was just eight."

"That *is* hard. Not that there's an easy time."

"No," Jason sighed. "And when we split we decided that it was better if we didn't do the joint custody route."

"That route has fallen into disfavor." I nodded wisely.

"Denise wanted to travel and I said 'vaya con Dios.' For the first couple of years it was okay but I know he misses her now."

"Do you mean, you haven't seen her since then?"

Jason shook his head. "I told you I was a single dad."

"I know, but — " *But being a single dad isn't the same as never seeing your son's mother.*

Onscreen, Krusty the Clown was having his Bar Mitzvah. Jack didn't have his Bar Mitzvah until he was 15, but then he got this TV for his room because he did a really good job.

Trevor announced, "I want refreshments. Why don't you serve refreshments?"

"We have to finish this episode first."

"No, we don't. We don't."

Jack knew that he had to be flexible if he wanted to have friends. Trevor wasn't making it easy. Why couldn't *Trevor* be flexible?

Ice cream will make things better.

Jack's mom and Trevor's dad were still in the living room. That was good, because his mom would give him a hard time about eating ice cream, when there's nothing wrong about eating ice cream.

Trevor opened the refrigerator. "You have lots of food. Lots of food."

Jack took out the Neapolitan ice cream, which was the best because it was three kinds, but it only counted for eating one. Why didn't they make Neapolitan ice cream with a different three kinds, like mint chip and cookie dough and rocky road? He should write a letter, but he didn't know the address.

He and Trevor both wanted some of each of the three flavors that there were, and it was hard to get it just right so they used up the whole carton.

They were just scraping up the last of it when Marissa came in. "You're gonna be in trouble," she said.

"I'm not in trouble."

"He's not in trouble," Trevor echoed, like he thought it was funny. "He's not in trouble."

"I'm not in trouble," Jack repeated.

"You are so in trouble!" Marissa pointed to the stove. "There's ice cream on the burners! You could make a fire!"

Can ice cream burn?

"He's not in trouble. *Not* in trouble."

Jack saw the ice cream dripping down the side of the stove, all the way to the floor.

"I'm telling." Marissa whirled around.

Telling was the same as "tattling," which was a mean thing to do. Jack didn't know if Trevor's dad was mean or nice and he didn't want Trevor to get in trouble.

Maybe if they went to Jack's room no one would see the ice cream.

But when they got back there, Trevor said, "I'm bored. *Bored.* Do you have an X-box?"

"I have a Game Boy."

"Game Boys aren't as good. They aren't — "

"Game Boys are good."

"They aren't."

But Trevor agreed to play Game Boy *Attack of the Killer Tomatoes* and *Bart Simpson's Escape from Camp Deadly*. He won every time. Jack didn't care about winning, if it meant that he and Trevor could have fun.

After four games the ice cream had melted. "It's soup now!" Jack said, and then he saw a long brown hair stuck to the side of Trevor's bowl. "It's hair soup!" He laughed so hard his body shook.

"Don't do that," Trevor said, putting his hands over his ears. "It hurts."

"*Okay.*" Jack had an idea. "Let's have ice cream soup."

He took the melted ice cream, tipped the bowl to his mouth and poured.

Trevor grabbed his own bowl and did the same.

Under the sound of their glugging and slurping Jack could hear that they were *both* laughing.

"You know," Jack said, "If our mom and dad got married we'd be like Drake and Josh. It's perfect!"

Drake and Josh on the TV show were stepbrothers. They stopped making new shows two years ago but it was in re-runs and Jack had seen every episode three times. They had it that Drake lived with his mother and his little sister, Megan, when Josh and his dad moved in.

Jack lived with *his* mom and had a little sister and her name even began with "M"!

Trevor thought for a second. Then he said, "They have an aquarium!"

"Yes!" Jack pumped his fists.

"Don't do that," Trevor said. "Let's play until my dad calls me."

JASON'S CONDENSED divorce story turned the atmosphere somber, but not for long.

When we moved on to sharing stories of life with Asperger's it was to see the humor in our common situation.

Me: "There was this time he tried to shoplift a huge bag of fun-sized candy bars by hiding it under his jacket. He looked like he was pregnant — "

Jason: "When he got caught cheating on his math test — "

Me: "I had to drive to *Concord* to pick him up from a field trip—"

Jason: "For a long time he counted cars on the way to school — "

Me: "And you know what I *really* hate?"

I leaned forward. I'd found my way up to the sofa and somehow, at some point, Jason had found his way next to me.

"What do you really hate?" he whispered close to my ear.

"When the teacher or whoever says, 'Can you talk to him about it?' You know — " I pitched my voice high to mimic a stereotypical school marm — " 'Can you talk to him about not making inappropriate remarks?' " I slapped my forehead. "And I want to say, 'Wow! Talk to him! What a breakthrough idea!' "

Jason laughed. I loved to make people laugh.

Marissa's arrival made us both shut up immediately.

"Mommy, Jack and his friend are making too much noise. HannahSophia needs her nap."

Jason started to get up. "I guess that's my cue."

"They made a really big mess in the kitchen."

"No, don't — " *Don't go.*

Jason stretched. "He's lasted much longer than I thought he would. Trevor, I mean."

"Oh. I mean, that's good. Right?" *Shut up, Anna.*

"Trev!" Jason called.

"You got to see this mess, Mommy."

"I will, hon."

Jason looked down at me. "Um ... we should do this again sometime, don't you think?"

"Sure."

"Maybe even...." He ran his thumb up and down the wood of the front door, and I wanted to stop him, for fear he'd get a splinter. "Maybe even ... what about Stinson Beach on Sunday?"

I only shrugged agreement, but in my mind I was repeating, like Molly Bloom: *Yes, yes, yes.*

MARISSA BRACED herself against the doorframe of the kitchen and leaned in as far as she could without losing her grip.

Mommy was opening the salad bag that she bought at the store. She saw Marissa and smiled. "See? I'm making you 'a real dinner' like you asked."

"Thaaank you, Mooommeee." Marissa leaned a little farther forward, testing the strength of her arms, but then —

"Marissa, hon, don't do that, you'll hurt yourself."

"Mommy, that's the 'throw up bowl'!"

When Marissa was little, they had a "throw up bowl" for when she or Jack was sick and they couldn't make it to the toilet in time. Mommy still gave it to them, although *Marissa* always made it now.

"You know it isn't," Mommy said. She shook the last of the lettuce out, then reached down to one of the cupboards below the sink to bring up an orange plastic bowl. The sight made Marissa feel queasy. "See, baby?" Mommy tipped the bowl upside down. "If this bowl could talk." She slipped it back in the cupboard. "Let us speak of it no more."

Mommy was in a good mood and Marissa knew that it had to do with the people who just visited. Marissa didn't like Trevor. He was big and his voice was scary.

And she had a feeling that he'd be back.

First grade could have been really hard. In the beginning the girls teased her and called her "Baby," because she was the youngest. But she knew that if she cried, she would be "Baby" forever.

So she stopped herself from crying. It hurt her eyes and her neck but she heard herself shout back, "You're the babies! You went to kindergarten! Kindergarten is for babies!"

First grade got a lot easier after that.

In pre-school you couldn't choose who you played with, because the teachers paired you off even though they were always saying "do your own thing," which was supposed to mean "do what you want," but didn't.

In first grade the kids went to their moms and told them who *they* wanted to have a play date with, then the moms called up other moms they didn't even know. Kids went over to other kids' houses and they got to play in rooms by themselves.

Marissa had already been to Mommy a jillion times, asking her to do those calls, and so she'd had at least one play date, usually two, every weekend since school started. She already divided the class into two parts: the ones she wanted to be friends with and the ones who weren't worth the bother. She knew by the end of the first week who belonged to which group. Some girls had the right lunch boxes and some girls didn't. Some girls had the right clips in their hair and some girls didn't.

A few days ago Mommy called Emma's mommy, and Emma came over after school.

Emma and Marissa went to play in Marissa's room. Marissa told Emma that she could be her friend, but that Katie wasn't going to be her friend, so Emma couldn't be friends with Katie anymore either. "But Katie is already my friend," Emma said.

"You can't have us both," Marissa said. "You can hold HannahSophia if you want. She likes you. But she doesn't like Katie."

When Mommy came to say that Emma's mother was there, Marissa walked Emma to the front door, because Mommy had taught her that that was good manners.

HannahSophia wanted to say good-bye, too, but Marissa was done sharing her, so she carried the leopard, graciously passing on the news to Emma that "HannahSophia says you can come over again."

The two mommies were talking. Mommy had on her Fake Voice, but Emma's mommy didn't seem to notice.

"Say thank you to Marissa," Emma's Mommy instructed.

That was when Emma turned around — Emma who had been so excited to come over, Emma, who played by all of Marissa's rules, just like Jack always did — Emma turned around and asked, "Why is your brother so weird?"

There was a little gasp from the Mommies. Marissa never had a chance to think of what her answer would be because she was still trying to figure out what Emma meant when Emma's Mommy was running out to her car, holding Emma's hand, and calling out more thank you's to Marissa's Mommy.

Marissa went to her room and put HannahSophia down for a nap. She lay down on the bed next to her and thought hard. When Emma first came over Jack came in her room and asked if he could play with them. Mommy called him away. Was *that* weird?

Marissa was afraid to ask Mommy. It felt like she would be stepping into the throw up bowl.

Marissa had always thought that Jack was such a good big brother, because he was a lot like the big brothers on TV: he was home and he talked to her, not like the *real* big brothers. He couldn't do what the TV brothers could: have a rock band in the garage or a job in a store, but that's TV, and no one could do what kids *or* grown-ups could do on TV, like keep their houses clean all the time.

It was true that Jack didn't play with her the way he used to. But since last summer she hadn't wanted to play with him so much, either. And now that she had her first-grade friends they didn't play at all. But while yesterday she had decided that Jack wasn't weird, today there was another big brother, well, he was nobody's big brother but he could have been, and he was scary. His voice was so loud it hurt her ears, but Jack's voice was always loud....

He was annoying, too. He kept saying the same things over and over again, even when she said that she heard him the first time. He asked her a jillion times if she had any fish.

She stayed in her own room, playing with HannahSophia, thinking that it wasn't fair that Jack had a playdate when she didn't, *and* that Mommy was too busy for her. But it wasn't until she saw Trevor taking every item out of the refrigerator, one by one, opening the lids of the containers and putting his nose all the way up to the insides, that the word tolled in her mind. *Weird.*

Marissa kept holding on to the doorframe while she pushed herself in and out. In the kitchen. Out of the kitchen. In, out. She had to ask, she had to ask. "Mommy, is Jack weird?"

Mommy froze. Then she started tossing the salad again. "Well ... he can be different sometimes."

"What do you mean?"

"We're all different." Mommy shrugged. "Right?"

Grown-ups could be really mean about not answering questions. "I *know* that."

Mommy walked away and looked in the refrigerator. "Are hamburgers okay?"

This was another mean thing that grown-ups did: change the subject.

"Did Hannah mean the way he talks about Crime Conquerors so much?"

"What's that, dear? Have you seen the mustard?"

Marissa got really annoyed then. But it gave her time to keep thinking how Jack sometimes made her impatient, when he kept starting the same sentence over and over. And then she thought about how he made those noises that sounded like car alarms. She always told herself that it was something boys did but not girls, like pee standing up.

Mommy said that's why he got pee on the floor sometimes. When Marissa saw that she called Mommy to clean it up *right away.*

Mommy looked at the ceiling. Her head tilted farther and farther back until her neck was very long and Marissa was afraid that she would fall.

"You know," Mommy said, still looking at the ceiling, "maybe we should sit down now and have a real talk about this."

But Marissa could tell that Mommy *didn't* want to talk about it. And even though Marissa was suddenly afraid to "talk about it," that made her not just annoyed, but really, really mad at Mommy.

Mommy bent over the sink again. When she spoke she sounded real relieved. "Whenever you are ready to talk about it," she chirped in her Fake Voice, "you let me know. Right now, why don't you help me with this salad?"

"No!" Marissa stomped her foot. "HannahSophia needs me!"

And she marched off to her room.

CHAPTER 5

I was running late for work when the phone rang, but I grabbed it. In the old days a phone call during school hours often meant a trip to pick up an out-of-control Jack, and although that hadn't happened for some time, I had been trained never to let a call go to voice mail.

"Is this Anna?"

A sweet voice; an ingratiating voice.

"Speaking."

"I'm Kimberly Allen."

I didn't recognize the name, but she sounded too nice to be a telemarketer. So I was apologetic: "I'm sorry — I don't know — "

"Funny — I always think people know me! Just because my face is on buses. I'm embarrassed now." She laughed a tinkly, wind-chime laugh. "I'm Ashleigh Allen's mother."

She pronounced the name "Ashleigh Allen" as if that would answer every possible question, all the way up to what music I wanted played at my funeral.

"I'm afraid I don't know an Ashleigh Allen either. Are you sure you have the right Anna?"

"Is your son Jack?"

With the name "Jack" her sweetness went from sugar to aspartame.

"That's me," I said with defiant pride. "Jack's mom."

Kimberly Allen laughed again. The sound was still light and airy but self-conscious, too. "Your son and my daughter have been walking home together." *Doesn't that beat all?* Her tone implied. *Katy bar the door!*

"Oh? Um, well, that's nice." Nice? It would be fantastic if Jack had another new friend. And a female friend! Trevor's and Jason's visit had given me hope that Jack's social life was about to expand. The girl must be a full-inclusion student, too. I pictured her *zaftig*, with blue eyes, slightly crossed.

"What kind of work do you do? May I call you Anna? I should have asked before. You need to call me Kimberly."

Her change of subject put me on guard. "I have a Ph.D. in psychology, so I guess you could call me *Dr. Kagen*."

"I'm a realtor myself." Again the laugh, by now a nervous tic. "It's been a very challenging year. I'm doing all right, but do you know anyone in the market? A first-time buyer or someone who wants to upgrade? Perhaps you'd like to take a look at what's out there. With so many houses under water, there are bargains to be had, that's for certain."

"What can I do for you, uh…." Having made it an issue, I didn't know what to call her.

"I think these walks home are harmless enough," Kimberly said. "I just don't want to create any unrealistic expectations on your son's part."

I had been wandering up and down the hallway with the cordless phone, looking at my watch repeatedly, which was my own nervous tic. Now I abruptly stood still. "Perhaps you could be more specific."

"Aren't there afterschool programs for kids like him?"

That was specific enough. I controlled myself long enough to ask rhetorically, "So your daughter isn't a full-inclusion student."

"I hardly think so! She's headed for Stanford. She's at the top of her class and she's a graduate of the American Conservatory Theater's Young — "

"Before you say that she was short-listed for the Nobel Prize in physics, why don't you tell me exactly what you want?"

"I don't want anyone to be hurt, that's what I want. And you know Ashleigh's still young and she takes these wounded birds under her wing — that's a funny way to put it, isn't it? 'Under her wing?' "

"Hilarious, yes." I started moving again, but I was no longer "wandering:" I was stomping.

"So perhaps you could talk to your son. He's autistic, isn't he?"

"Mildly. You do know it's not contagious, right?" I spoke through clenched teeth so that I wouldn't scream. Somehow I thought that I — that *Jack* and I — were past these humiliations. "Let me ask you something — what are you afraid of?"

"Don't worry, I'm not afraid of anything sexual, given the circumstances. I'm afraid he might expect … an invitation."

"What, to the White House?"

"Somewhere. Ashleigh has some particular events coming up, and if — "

"*Mrs.* Allen," I interrupted. "I think it's your job to talk to your daughter."

"But you'll be able to speak to Jack in a way he understands."

"And your daughter only speaks Urdu? Don't you have termite damage to shred, Kimmie?"

"Mrs. Kagen, there's no need — "

"Oh, I think there's a very great need," I snapped, and then, having returned to the base for the purpose, I slammed the handset down.

After that I paced the hallway again, arms crossed and chest heaving. Bitch! Sanctimonious bitch! Her and her headed-for-Stanford daughter. Why do people with high-achieving children think they can take the credit for those achievements? What I wouldn't give for her to know what it was like when....

As my pacing slowed and my lungs wouldn't fill with quite as much air, I had to fight to keep my anger on her. What did she mean by "not afraid of anything sexual, given the circumstances"? How dare she call him a "wounded bird"!

It was no use.

She *was* an insensitive bitch. But some of my best friends were insensitive bitches.

No, what Kimberly had done was far worse even than openly calling Jack the "R" word. Like the hurricane that indifferently destroys what stands in front of it, she had blown down the mental house that I had carefully constructed.

The early years with Jack had been pretty damn tough. We'd reached our lowest point five years before, when it seemed that half the city had cast Jack as the star of *Killers on the Spectrum.* Coming soon to a theater near you.

For once his autism had been a good thing: Jack had been insulated from most of the frenzy, which had taken the form of press coverage and even a demonstration in front of the house I had shared with Alex.

I had a feeling that Kimberly Allen only read the Real Estate and Business sections of the paper (and I wasn't sure about the Business section) and thus belonged to the half of the city who didn't know about our family troubles.

Jack's private school expelled him. Parents were funny about murder suspects as students. But when he started fifth grade, it was at a welcoming public school, and when the excitement died down we had entered a relatively peaceful time. Teachers loved him and accepted the work he did without complaint. The other kids liked him, and with the rare and usually easy-to-handle exception, never teased or bullied him.

I quickly learned to ignore off-campus social life. "Playdates" morphed into "hanging out." Parents no longer felt compelled to invite the whole class to birthday parties.

Jack was Jack, school was school, I had a job and a baby and then a preschooler, and the hamper was always full.

Most of the time I didn't think about his future. After all, it was still possible that before high school was over he'd take the developmental leaps that would allow him to enter the mainstream. He'd always have his quirks, but who doesn't?

I met with his teachers. I made the doctors' appointments. I unloaded the dishwasher, and once in a while I ran the vacuum, even while knowing that there were black demons under that very carpet.

Ashleigh joined the One World Club when she was a sophomore. She had read about it on the bulletin board where all the students posted information about their clubs, and it was exactly what she was looking for. Their mission statement was "To bring the diverse cultures of the world together in harmony."

Then she joined and discovered that they only called themselves the One World Club because they needed a name like that for administrative approval. *Their* idea of "bringing diverse cultures together" was to celebrate the holidays of other countries — granted, some of the lesser-known ones, like *Nossa Senhora Aparecida*, which was Brazilian — by partying. Sometimes they'd get inspired and decorate, but that was mostly just so Gloria Leemis, the then-President, would have a chance to boss everyone around.

A couple times one of the seniors even brought beer, on a Friday afternoon when the party was going to run late and the chance of getting caught was so low.

Ashleigh didn't have much of a voice then. The underclassmen got bitched around by all the seniors, not just Gloria, but even by the juniors. Ashleigh was biding her time until she was a junior herself, and Gloria and her posse would move on to whatever online degree school would have them.

The morning that Kimberly gave Ashleigh a hard time about the One World Club, it hadn't even started up yet, but Ashleigh was looking forward to it. That afternoon, though, after the last bell, when she went to Room 134 where Mr. Lyu, the club sponsor, taught Spanish, it was only to find a teacher she didn't know gathering up her things. When Ashleigh asked New Teacher about Mr. Lyu, New Teacher snapped, "I don't think that's any of your business," which mostly hurt Ashleigh's feelings but also worried her enough that she tracked down another club member from sophomore year, Sarah Manus, at lunch the next day.

"You mean you didn't *hear?*" Sarah acted as if it were the attack on the World Trade Center.

When Ashleigh admitted that she had not *"heard,"* Sarah told her that Gloria went back east to a college that wasn't even accredited and that Mr. Lyu took early retirement.

"And this is big news *because…?*"

Well, Sarah whispered, over the summer there were rumors that the glorious Gloria and Mr. Lyu had a hook-up. "So the club's charter's been suspended," Sarah concluded, scooping up the last of her macaroni and cheese, "until you get a new faculty sponsor."

"Why me? Isn't it *our* club?"

"I can't believe you didn't hear any of this."

"I don't like to listen to gossip," Ashleigh said, while reluctantly admitting to herself that she didn't like being out of the loop.

"How do you stay so thin?" Sarah asked her mournfully.

Girls asked her this often. She always said, "I think about the hundreds of millions of people who go hungry every day."

Sarah looked down at her plate, on which there remained only an orange swirl of pretend cheese.

Ashleigh didn't have time to go into Lecture Mode about how so much corn in the U.S. and how many vegetables in Europe were being turned into fuel instead of food. She was back to picturing that bitchy teacher in Mr. Lyu's room. Then she had one of those epiphanies they talk about in AP Lit. *In order to do good you must have the power to do good. You have to play the game.*

Ashleigh didn't have to think long about whom to ask to replace Mr. Lyu: Mr. Takanawa, the Advanced Placement U.S. History — APUSH — teacher. He was young for a teacher, and passionate about his subject: He was already talking about the Native American genocide as if it happened to one of his own relatives.

He was also hella intimidating, so she kept putting off talking to him.

But today was going to be the day.

"Can I help you, Miss Allen?"

Mr. Takanawa smiled at Ashleigh as he slipped papers into his leather briefcase.

"Mr. Taka — " *What am I ever going to accomplish if I can't just come out with it?*

"Taka*nawa*," he finished for her.

Her mouth froze half-open. OMG, did he think she didn't know his name? That she was a total racist? "I — I know." Pause. Then she forced it out in a rush. "Mr. Takanawa, we need someone to sponsor our club. It's the One World Club and it already has a charter, but the faculty sponsor from last year … uh, retired…."

He smiled as his zipped his briefcase. But instead of tucking it under his arm, as she expected, he placed it under his desk, leaning it against the fake wood so that it stood upright. "I'd be honored."

"Gee, that is *such* a relief!"

Mr. Takanawa grinned slyly at her. "You sound like Beaver Cleaver."

"Beaver — " she started, then stopped. "Beaver" was slang for female genitalia.

"A TV show before your time," Mr. Takanawa explained. "Before my time, actually. Beaver said 'gee,' a lot."

He'd had this same expression since they started talking, like she was being really funny and didn't know it. She hated nothing more than not being taken seriously, like her dreams about the Peace Corps and starting a worldwide movement after that — yeah, sure, she had to wait a few years before she could get all that started, but a lot of young people, young women, too, had made a big difference. Anne Frank and Joan of Arc. They were both murdered before they were twenty years old, but still had time to change the world.

"It won't be an inconvenience?" she pressed.

"Not at all." He was smiling again, but just when she thought that he was *really* patronizing her, he added, "I am looking forward to seeing what you can accomplish," and she couldn't doubt his sincerity.

She'd thought that getting the sponsor would be the tough part, but now it felt like the next step would be the hard one: getting members.

The room was even emptier than it was when she first walked in. Then students from Mr. Takanawa's last class were still hanging around. But now, for the club, there were only a few of the people she'd specifically asked, and a few club members from last year.

Jack still hadn't arrived. Would he be able to find the room? Maybe she could find some Good Samaritan type who would go out in the hall to keep an eye out for him. She had to stay; she had to talk to Freddie.

He was right where she expected: in the corner in the back, whispering with his new b.f., Edward.

Ashleigh met Freddie at the Gay-Straight Alliance when they both joined as freshmen. The Gay-Straight Alliance had a totally awesome motto that Ashleigh wished she could take credit for: "Being gay isn't a choice. Being homophobic is." No one seemed to know who came up with that, so when Ashleigh told people about it, she didn't go out of her way to explain that it wasn't her idea. Ideas were just out there, right?

But the GSA wasn't just an organization that worked to stop homophobia, it was a safe place for kids in the closet to get comfortable enough to come out. In the spring of the year most of the meetings revolved around the girl or guy who cried tears of joy and relief while everyone applauded.

So last spring Freddie finally came out, after trying to get people to believe that Ashleigh was his g.f., and then the very next week it was Edward's turn and the two fell into each other's arms like Romeo and Juliet at that dance. For a couple of weeks they were Freddie-and-Eddie but thank God, that didn't last.

Freddie had constructed a fort of desks around himself and Edward. Ashleigh was happy for them, but she was sorry he didn't have the same kind of time for her that he used to. *They* used to walk home together, in fact, although he refused to come into her house for fear of running into her mother: "The Leona Helmsley of San Francisco." Ashleigh had to google Leona Helmsley, and when she read about her she was a little sorry that someone saw her mother the same way she did.

"Hi, girl," Freddie said. His arm was around Edward's shoulder. Edward was Korean-American so they were the perfect San Francisco couple.

"Yo, Trashbag."

Edward turned "Ashleigh" into "Trashleigh" and then into "Trashbag" in a week.

"We're kinda short of peeps, aren't we?" Freddie asked quickly.

"Yes." She looked behind her. Still no Jack. The girls she called The Unholy Trinity, Parker, Blake, and Sue, had arrived. When she turned back she saw that he and Edward were rubbing cheeks. "Cool it with the PDAs, okay? This is the plan." She leaned over the nearest desk, and lowered her voice. "One of you is going to run for president of the club and make it a force for good."

"Not me, child." Freddie shook his head. "I'm not executive branch material."

Ashleigh instinctively glanced at Edward. He hadn't even been listening; he'd been too busy twirling the rings on Freddie's hand. She was glad that *she* wasn't in love. It made it impossible to accomplish anything else.

"All right," Ashleigh sighed. She didn't want to be the face of the one in charge but she had to be honest with herself, and with her idea about Freddie running, she really *was* trying to install a puppet government, like the CIA with Iran or Chile. "Would you support me if *I* ran?"

"What? Girl, no way. I'll be voting for John McCain or Karl Marx."

"I'll take that as a show of your support." An evil thought occurred to her. With a small turn-out today, this was the day to have the election! There was nothing in the club charter demanding that a certain number of members be present for a vote.

"When are we getting outta here?" Edward asked. "I've got a lot of — " he fluttered eyelids at Freddie — "*homework* to do."

Ashleigh looked over her shoulder for Jack again. Still not here! She told him to come to room 222 right after the last bell. She found herself thinking, *how hard can that be?* — but quickly replaced that with the affirmation she designed specifically for him: *Compassion for others will bring compassion for me. Compassion for others....*

But she had to get her own future settled. "You're not going anywhere until after you vote for me for president."

"Who will be your First Hubby?" Edward asked. "Maybe someone we haven't met yet?"

Ashleigh had brief second thoughts. If she told people what to do then they wouldn't be doing it of their own free will and the mission wouldn't be taking hold of *them*.

But Plato said that the best ruler was the man who didn't want the job. He didn't think far enough ahead to include women in his vision, but she could overlook that. She had to.

Jack could hear noises from the classroom, even though the classroom door was closed. He couldn't make out any words. The noises were a dark color with sometimes a little light color thrown in.

The rest of the hallway was quiet because it was after school. All the noise he could hear was coming from the other side of this one door.

Whatever other noise was going on in the school — the maintenance people cleaning up the cafeteria, the kids in the courtyard waiting for rides, or stalling before they headed off for the bus — had become inaudible.

She wanted me to come, he reminded himself. *She said so. She said room 222, and that that was an easy number to remember.* As if he couldn't remember any number she gave him!

Don't be scared.

But he was scared. He could feel the weight of his backpack, pulling him down, the pain beginning in between his shoulder blades and traveling down to his lower back. It could pull him right through the floor. Then what would happen? He'd sink down through the ceiling of the first floor and then through the floor of the first floor down to the ceiling of the basement, if there was a basement, he didn't know, and he didn't know what was below that … just earth? Earth … dirt and worms and bones.

He could feel his back sliding a little lower.

She wanted me to come.

But did she really? How often had people said to him, "Sure, come along," and then when he got there they were gone already? Or maybe they told him the wrong place. Or maybe they told him the right place but he got it wrong.

English is funny. There were way too many words to understand and sometimes the differences between them were so small that he would get in trouble. Like "taking" something could also mean "stealing" it.

And then there were words like "friend." The friends that were older than high school age were his friends but they were a different kind of friend than the friends the other guys had.

Jack felt his backpack slip down another notch. He had to take it off. *If I'm going to take it off I might as well take it off inside the room. If I take it off here I'll never pick it up again.*

So he walked in.

Ashleigh jumped at the *uh-huh-uh-uh-uh* sound that made her, and everyone else, look toward the door.

Jack had arrived.

His fists were clenched and pumping up and down. He stood blocking the path of several people trying to get in and several others trying to get out. "Get a clue, Dude," someone said, and Ashleigh's cheeks burned for him.

"Jack!" she called, "come over here!"

That snapped him out of his arm-pumping. He clumsily made his way among the desks and when he got to them, he said, "So, what are we going to talk about?"

Freddie and Edward both blinked. Ashleigh had told them about Jack, but this was the first time they'd met. She could trust Freddie to be decent, but she was afraid of what snarky comments might be coming from Edward. Another guilty thought: Jack might not understand them anyway.

"What do you *want* to talk about, Dude?" Edward mocked him.

Ashleigh stood up so fast that her chair slid out three feet behind her. "Come on, Jack. I'm going to show you around." She took Jack by the arm and led him over to the opposite corner of the room where Grace and Sarah were digging for something at the bottom of Grace's tote bag. Grace was doing most of the digging while Sarah kept watch.

iPod speakers, Ashleigh guessed. *Damn.* This was just what she *didn't* want to have happen this afternoon. No music, no shoving the desks aside to dance, not even future party planning. But then, perhaps Mr. Takanawa would stay to keep an eye on them.

"Hey, guys," Ashleigh greeted Grace and Sarah. "This is Jack. I told you about him?"

Jack's elbows were going up and down. "I just got the new ConquerZomb!" he announced. "You can come see it if you want."

Both girls stopped mid-search, their arms jammed into the backpack up to their elbows. Sarah made a choking sound that meant she was trying not to laugh.

"*Serious* congratulations, Dude," Grace said.

Ashleigh's cheeks heated up again. How did you find compassion for people like Grace and Sarah?

"Guys, I'm running for president of the club this year?"

Grace shrugged while Sarah did not give any indication that she'd heard.

"Will you vote for me?"

Grace snorted. "Why do we need a president anyway? Let's be socialists."

Jack stared at Grace and Sarah, like he wanted to say something but didn't know how. Sarah sidled around Grace's back to block Mr. Takanawa's view as Grace slipped the iPod speakers out. "Is there a problem, Dude?" she challenged Jack, who kept staring in that way he had, that *could* be kind of creepy.

"There's no problem," Ashleigh said.

She quickly dragged Jack away, to the threesome that there was no avoiding: Parker, Blake and Sue. The Unholy Trinity. Parker was the unacknowledged leader. You could tell just when you looked at the three of them: Parker in her dad's pinstriped suit jacket, and the full lacy skirt, arms folded under her push-up bra, and holding forth with instructions.

"Ashleigh." Parker addressed her with all the warmth of one of those blizzards you saw on TV that hit the east coast.

This was the first time that Ashleigh had spoken to Parker this year. Parker liked a guy last year, a junior named Nicholas. Nicholas had a thing for Ashleigh. Ashleigh *did not* encourage him. But when Nicholas asked her out right in front of Parker, it was war. Even though Ashleigh said no — and right then, too, with Parker still standing there!

"Hey," Ashleigh greeted her.

Parker didn't turn toward her. One eyebrow, at least the eyebrow that Ashleigh could see, went up. *Oh, for fuck's....* Parker banged the side of her head with the heel of her hand and said to her groupies, "Do you hear a buzzing in the room?"

"Parker. Is this really how you want it to be?"

"That buzzing," Parker sneered, "it's started again."

Blake's and Sue's eyes shifted simultaneously from the one to the other.

"I'm running for president of the club today," Ashleigh said with dignity. "I hope you'll vote for me."

"Everyone should run for president!" Jack declared.

The very last of Ashleigh's self-satisfaction crumbled. She'd wanted to help Jack make friends and so far all she'd done was to expose him to ridicule: more with each encounter.

"Miss Allen."

It was Mr. Takanawa. "Ooh, you startled me," she said, putting her hand over her heart.

But it was Jack who got the attention. When Ashleigh jumped, he gave out a short, sharp yelp, loud and sudden enough to cause everyone else in the room to laugh (nervously or derisively) and for a couple of them to shout, "Shut up!"

Ashleigh glared at the offenders before she asked Mr. Takanawa, "You're leaving?"

"No." He looked up from the book he'd been reading and smiled. "You asked me to be the club sponsor."

"Yeah, I know, but — " *But the other teachers never stayed.*

"I'm not here because there's nothing better on television," Mr. Takanawa said. "I'm here to participate." He closed the book. She saw the title: *The Limits to Capital.* She took a deep, deep breath. She had to get up the nerve to tell him that she was going to run for president of the club.

"HI, JACK!"

Ashleigh didn't recognize the super tall boy who strode in then, but obviously Jack did.

"HI, TREVOR!"

Ashleigh closed her eyes.

Jack and the new boy named Trevor quickly got involved in a shouting match that seemed to be their idea of a conversation. The others, mostly girls, yelled at them to shut up.

Then Mr. Takanawa's voice rang out. "Time for everyone to calm down and sit down." That smile again. "Not necessarily in that order."

Ashleigh grabbed a seat. Then she looked around and saw that everyone was not only sitting, but quiet! Except for....

"Gentlemen?" Mr. Takanawa addressed Jack and Trevor. When they didn't respond, he called more loudly, "Mr. Armstrong!" — and Trevor turned sharply. So Mr. Takanawa must know him already from somewhere else.

"Please sit."

They complied.

"Miss Allen has said that she would like to run for president of this year's One World Club," Mr. Takanawa continued.

"Not fair!" Grace called out. "She's the only one running! So it's like — it's just like a dictatorship!"

"Not at all," Mr. Takanawa countered. "We are going to run this according to parliamentary procedure."

"What's this got to do with Parliament?" a girl whined.

"If you're thinking of the English Parliament, Miss Ferlinghetti, we don't have time for a discussion of that now," Mr. Takanawa said. "I'll explain the process. The floor is open to nominations. You can't nominate yourself; someone must nominate you and someone must second the nomination."

Freddie jumped in right away. "I nominate Ashleigh Allen!"

Edward seconded it. They put their arms around one another, and Freddie gave her the thumbs up from behind Edwards's shoulder. *Good friends,* Ashleigh thought, regretting the mild irritation she'd felt toward them earlier.

"Perhaps you'll be running unopposed," Mr. Takanawa said. His words were so formal, yet with — with an *arch* tone. To the class he said, "If there are no other nominations then the vote will be considered unanimous."

Then someone shouted, "I nominate the new dude!"

It was Parker. An unkind label came to Ashleigh's mind — and almost to her lips.

"What new dude?" someone asked.

"I don't know." Parker pointed to Trevor. "Him."

Trevor snapped to attention.

"This is Trevor Armstrong," Mr. Takanawa said and he was just as cold to Parker as Parker was to Ashleigh. "He's on the track team, and holds the school district record for the mile."

"I second it!" Blake shouted.

Trevor clearly didn't understand what was going on. Neither did Jack, but Ashleigh could see he was getting excited from the way his fists were pumping.

Mr. Takanawa did some authoritative shushing and then explained both to Jack and to Trevor that the latter would be running against Ashleigh in a contest for president of the club.

And just as it seemed that the guys were catching on, there was the sound of a cell phone text, as embarrassing as a fart.

It was Mr. Takanawa's. He looked at his screen. "I have to deal with this," he said, pocketing the phone and slipping out of the classroom. He moved so gracefully, that it made her think of the girls she knew who stuck with ballet. It also made her think of the rumors that he was gay.

"Let's wait for Mr. Takanawa to come back?" Ashleigh said, but not loudly enough, or not in charge enough, or something, because everyone ignored her. The second Mr. Takanawa was gone Parker called out, "Trevor, make a speech!" then everyone chorused, "Speech! Speech!" Even Jack was shouting it.

Trevor stumbled to the front of the room. So this boy was a champion runner — in what universe was that possible? Had things gotten so bad in the world that even gravity had turned against them?

"I don't know anything about this club. Jack told me to come. To *come*."

Trevor's laugh was one of those all-in-the-nose sounds that people make when they aren't sure if something is funny or not.

"But I could make it a really good club, so you should vote for me."

Everyone laughed, and the laughter encouraged him. "Vote for me!" he repeated.

"But how are you going to make it a good club?" someone challenged.

"Uh … Uh…. We'll order pizza!"

Somehow the way Trevor said it made it sound stupid, when actually it was a good idea. Sure, someone would have to walk up to Irving Street to pick up the pizza, but....

Semi-intelligible whispers and snorts went around the room.

"And will you pay for this pizza?"

"Can you promise us all A's?"

"Any other genius ideas, Einstein?"

Trevor announced, "We'll travel back in time to live with dinosaurs!"

Ashleigh closed her eyes again. She was willing herself not to recognize the voices so she didn't have to hate the person.

"And no more homework!"

"And we get Fridays off every week!"

That was unmistakably Jack. And he was laughing the hardest at Trevor's answers.

"Just vote for me!" was Trevor's frequent answer. "Vote for *me*." But his expression had become confused.

Jack was probably trying to rescue Trevor when he declared, "A president can do anything!"

Then Mr. Takanawa burst in. "What is going on in here?"

He hardly raised his voice. The question was almost ironic.

Ashleigh insisted, "I want the club to be so much more than what it was last year. Last year — " She stopped. Did Mr. Takanawa know what happened — what *allegedly* happened with Gloria? Oh, fuck that, what happened.

"Now, now. What's past is past," Mr. Takanawa said.

Mr. Takanawa had his calendar laid out on the screen of a totally flat computer that only had a monitor. He said it was an iPad.

He tapped a little white square and typed in the next club meeting, a week from now. "You're president of the club now, Miss Allen."

"Thanks to you."

When Mr. Takanawa had re-entered, the room fell as silent as the world will be after the last nuclear bomb explodes. Parker broke that silence when she smirked, "We voted Trevor club president."

"Did you now?" Mr. Takanawa had asked, sort of surprised and puzzled, but very calm. "I don't see how that's going to work. Trevor has practice with me every afternoon."

"I do have practice," Trevor had said with a big smile that showed only lower teeth. "*Practice*."

Mr. Takanawa had emphasized how much the team relied on him. Jack chimed in to reinforce Mr. Takanawa's argument, and said something about how proud Trevor's father was of his running.

Within three minutes Trevor had resigned his office and Mr. Takanawa proclaimed Ashleigh president, quoting something to do with government that Ashleigh couldn't remember anymore.

"And what will your first executive order be?" Mr. Takanawa asked now.

"I do have a lot of ideas," Ashleigh said. "A charity walk, and a bake sale — "

"I know you'll do a fine job." Mr. Takanawa slipped the iPad into his briefcase. "Madam President."

CHAPTER 6

I visited the grocery store four times a week just to keep us in bananas (Jack, Marissa) and Hostess cupcakes (me — for very bad days). That's where I was with Jack the afternoon when he spoke the seven words I had prayed never to hear come out of his mouth:

"I want to get a driver's license!"

I yanked at a cart from the line at the entrance. It was stuck to the one in front of it.

"I can do it!"

"No, that's — " *Let him do it, Anna, he needs* — "Okay, you try."

Jack tugged uselessly on the metal bar.

"Try pulling from the mid-"

"No! I can — "

Enter Grumpy Old Lady stage right, first clearing her throat with a wet rattle, then demanding, "Can I get a cart, please?" in the tone that she would have used to say, "I thought they used people like you to test experimental medication."

"Ma'am, if you'll just be patient." I pulled with both hands at the gritty bar, gently elbowing Jack to the side. The cart came loose with the grating of metal on metal. "Here you go, Ma'am." I stepped back to swing it in her direction, but now the wrong end was facing her. I started to make a counter-clockwise turn, but one of the rear wheels jammed, and the cart almost tipped over by the time I had it right.

Our neighborhood supermarket, Cal-Smart, had little of the "super" about it, but I liked that. Jack and I were on first-name chat-about-the-weather terms with a few of the checkers. Sometimes when I was having a pity party I reminded myself that there had been a time when taking Jack to the grocery store had been like a scene from *The Exorcist*. There were three or four stores around town that to this day I was still too embarrassed to walk into. More than once people stepped over Jack while he was having a good old-fashioned kick-your-heels-into-the-floor tantrum. *Ma'am, I'm sorry, but we're going to have to ask you to leave/to pay for that/to rend your garments and cry mea culpa....*

But now we had a new neighborhood, and a new neighborhood store, where various maroon-smocked employees nodded at us from the height of their ladders as they stocked their merchandise while we negotiated the aisles.

"So … so…."

"'So' what, dear?"

"So, can I get a driver's license?"

A driver's license. When Jack was as old as twelve, I was still determined that he would learn to drive. Without that definitively American skill, he'd be confined to living in a very few high-density areas. True, San Francisco was one, and perhaps he could invent himself as a hero of the environment, a soldier who left no carbon footprints.

"You're thinking too far ahead," was one of Dr. Fairchild's, Jack's erstwhile therapist, favorite aphorisms. Easy for *her* to say. She had since retired, while still in her late 40s.

"So, can I?"

I pretended to study my list.

"Jack, I could really use some help. We need pasta. Why don't you take the cart and get some of the kind that you like."

I loved pasta. All you had to do was to boil it and open a can of sauce and it was almost what Marissa called a "real dinner like on TV."

Jack trundled away with the shopping cart, his butt swaying a little, and I pulled a plastic bag down from the spool at the produce section.

Even when Jack was ten and got expelled from the private school Alex had insisted on sending him to, I was sure — no, I was *positive*, that he was going to take giant developmental steps forward in his teens, get his license, join the soccer team, and earn straight A's — thereby wreaking my revenge on the heartless administration that had humiliated me — I meant *us* — in such a way.

But six years had passed and in each of those years I had peeled another layer off my roll of hopes, just as I peeled off successive plastic bags to hold oranges, and then apples.

Things could still change. Many things. My sanity rested on that belief.

But for now, it was clear that Jack would be a menace on the road. As of that afternoon, he couldn't even help me look for cyclists or pedestrians when I was backing out of the driveway. He would alert me with a yelp, all right, but not until someone was already directly behind my car. Praise the Lord, so far I had stopped in time. So far.

I picked up a bag of baby carrots. I figured that if I had fruit and yogurt and finger-sized veggies in the front of the refrigerator the kids were less likely to go digging in the back to find where I had hidden my box of See's candy (under a row of cottage cheese cartons, where they were never going to be touched).

I was just about to get a second cart for myself when Jack came rolling back with his. He'd half-filled it with boxes of pasta.

"So, can I get a license?" he asked.

"Jack, we don't need this much pasta."

"Yes, we do!"

I counted quickly, and estimated that he had at least a half dozen boxes each of rotelli, spaghetti, bowtie, seashell, linguine, and a couple of shapes I'd never seen before.

"Here's six boxes of linguine. Take four of them back."

"But we need them!"

"Jack, if there is ever, and I mean *ever*, a night when you want linguine and we don't have it, then I promise you, I swear to you, that I will go immediately to the store to buy it."

"But the store might be closed."

"There's a 24 hour Safeway out by the ocean."

"That store closed!"

"It did not. It just isn't open 24 hours anymore."

"So you lied!"

"I fibbed a little. Okay, let's keep three boxes of linguine." God, I wished I could drink. The only thing keeping me going was the thought of stopping at Starbucks when we were finished here.

"I want a driver's license."

"You know, a lot of kids are choosing not to get their driver's licenses now." I unloaded my produce into his cart and took it from him. "C'mon, we're going to put some of this back." Stocking up on an item was a fairly benign grocery store prank. Once when we'd gone shopping he'd filled the cart when I wasn't looking with two-liter soda bottles and jumbo bags of chips. He told me that it was for a party he was having that weekend. He didn't have a Facebook page back then, but said that he was telling all his friends. What could I say — that no one would come? I let him have the soda and chips, and no one came.

"Trevor's going to drive!"

"No, he's not."

"It's true! Ask Trevor!"

I knew from Jason that Trevor had failed the written test for the learner's permit four times. If he ever did pass that test, though, he might well drive, like many Aspies on the mild end of the spectrum. Trevor simply had the reflexes that my own son lacked.

"Well, what if I talk to Trevor's dad about it?" Ah ha — brilliant move, even though I was only postponing the inevitable: Eventually I'd have to explain not only the physical dangers but the liability issues. Our legal system was such that even when he was thirty, anyone he hurt (or their families, if he killed someone) could sue Alex for every penny he had. They'd say that Alex should have known that Jack couldn't drive.

After I convinced Jack to replace a few more of the various pastas, we turned down the cereal aisle. The colors were like something out of an acid trip — or so I was reliably informed. I wanted to buy Mini-Wheats and Cheerios, but this was yet another battle with both him and his sister. Even I could taste the chemical dye in Fruit Loops.

Jack bent over, his weight almost lifting the front end of the cart.

"Honey, don't."

"If I got a driver's license, I could get a car."

I was momentarily distracted by the Special K. Could I get either of the kids to try it? Maybe the strawberry flavor?

"All the guys with cars have girlfriends."

I pictured myself pulling an invisible knife from my chest. "Not necessarily," I said. I had dreaded this day far more than I'd dreaded hearing about the license. A girlfriend. He'd never talked about girls before. What had I thought — that he would never be interested in girls, or if he wasn't, that he wouldn't be interested in boys? Was bestiality the only way for him to nab a consenting partner? No, God, no, I was selling him short. Way short. There was someone for everyone, although I might be the exception that proved the rule. It was just ... I remembered the first day of school, the graceful girl who was bending over to help him pick up his books and binders from the floor.

"Hey, Boychik, I tell you what — *you* get the cereal while I go around and get us some soup. Let's see if you can stick to just three boxes, okay?"

"Trevor has a girlfriend."

"I don't think he does, Boychik."

"He said so."

Remind me to get a polygraph machine for the house.

"Don't forget, *three boxes.*"

I walked down the canned foods aisle wondering if it could be possible someday. It couldn't be harder for Jack to learn to drive than it had been for me. I was famously uncoordinated, with the reflexes of a corpse, but after five driving instructors, including one who felt me up, and three visits to the DMV, the State of California had, in its infinite generosity, issued me a license.

The capacity of humans to delude themselves in the service of their desires is unlimited. Who knows that better than a psychoanalyst?

I was gathering soups in one arm, looking for the ones labeled "low sodium," when I heard the crash.

You know how when you first hear the police siren behind you, even see the flashing lights in the mirror, you think, *oh, no, it's not for me, I'm such a good citizen!* So you pull over to make it easier for the police car to pass —

But the lights are still in your mirror.

Part of me was still imagining that the crash was just some poor schlemiel dropping a case of wine bottles, or cans from another shelf....

Then I heard the ungodly shriek. Like rabbits being tortured in a cosmetics lab.

Jack.

I raced around the end of the aisle.

He lay on the floor, surrounded by brightly-colored boxes. A lone orange rolled toward me.

"*Jack!*"

He sat up.

The cart was on its side, but it had not fallen on him. I covered my face with my hands and waited for the shaking to stop.

When I lowered my hands, two employees were running towards us. I recognized Timothy and Pat.

"I'm sorry." My voice quivered.

A crowd had already gathered around us. "Do you think he's okay?" "That poor boy." "I didn't see what happened — what happened?" "She should sue."

Jack grinned up at his audience. "That made a *ka-pow!*" He liked the sound he made, so the second one was louder. "*Ka-pow!*"

"*Jack, get up,*" I hissed.

"Are you sure you're not hurt?" Timothy asked. He was a middle-aged man with a large handlebar moustache.

"I'm not hurt!" Jack declared, rising and puffing out his chest. "The Sword of the Mighty Quarko protects me!"

Pat, the other clerk, a diminutive African-American man, was picking up cereal boxes and I quickly joined in. There were at least a dozen brands, everything from Choco-Loaded Fake Flakes to Marshmallow & Lard French Toast Bricks.

Jack was chasing the orange, but each time he got close enough to pick it up, he accidently kicked it farther away.

A couple of spectators had wandered off but more had joined up. "What happened? I didn't see what happened." "The cart fell on that boy." "Have they called the police?"

"No, really, it's all right." I tried shooing them away with one flattened palm. What would Jason say? "Nothing to see here, folks."

No one seemed to hear me. Jack kicked the orange again; now it was a game.

I waited until we got out into the parking lot. "How did the cart fall over?"

Jack was carrying one of the grocery bags. It was heavy for him and he leaned backwards as we walked.

"Maybe ghosts knocked it down!" Grinning. He was not at all embarrassed and I couldn't decide whether this was a good thing or a bad thing.

"Jack, really, please. Tell me how the cart fell over."

I didn't expect an explanation. Einstein said that insanity was doing the same thing repeatedly, expecting different results, but it's also a good definition of masochism.

Jack imitated the sound of an engine gaining speed. "I was r-r-r-racing it!" He hefted the grocery bag a little higher. "I wanted to prove to you — "

"Yes?"

"I wanted to prove to you — that I can drive."

I took Jason up on his offer the following Sunday, and the five of us drove to Stinson Beach.

Even with Jason ostensibly in charge, I was anticipating car sickness (Marissa), sulking (Trevor), agitation (Jack), and arguments (everyone). Instead, when Jason took the wheel to maneuver us down the winding roads of Marin to the isolated town, a calm settled over all five of us, sure as the fog that blanketed the shore.

He set us all up on the beach, pledging that the fog would lift by noon and, being September, it did. But although it became sunny, it never got hot, so when the kids were finished with the beach, we wrapped all three in towels. When they were dry enough to change, we went up into the woods above the shore where Jason threw coals into one of the brick barbecues and cooked a package of hot dogs, along with two steaks: one for himself, one for me.

Whether it was because Jack was enlivened by the presence of a boy his own age or simply because Jupiter was aligned with Mars, he acted as an emissary between Trevor and Marissa to find mutually acceptable games. Trevor did not respond to Marissa's domineering ways as Jack did, but a simple command from his father kept him in line.

On the winding drive home we sang "99 Bottles of Beer." If you want good audience participation for that song, you gotta get yourself a five-year-old and two Aspie teens.

Jason had thought I was joking when I described my absolute lack of skill in the kitchen. Then I let him watch me fry an egg, and he believed me. So when we made plans for him and Trevor to come over for dinner the following Friday, Jason offered to bring food.

I expected take-out along the lines of Chinese or pizza, but he brought ingredients for a salad that didn't even come in a bag, and a chicken to roast. *To roast at my house.* (I was touched even though I didn't really see the point, when the Cal-Smart had chickens already roasted.) He kept calling from the kitchen asking me for utensils I'd never heard of, but in the end, when we sat down, Marissa declared, "This is dinner like on TV!"

She gazed at her food in awe before picking up her fork; the boys devoured theirs noisily.

I hadn't realized how lonely our meals were when it was just the three of us. I would slap something together for the kids and we would sit in the darkening room, me picking at whatever nutrient-challenged garbage I'd put in front of myself, wanting to save my appetite for a bowl of ice cream that I would eat in bed while watching *The Daily Show,* starring the man who had never yet let me down: Jon Stewart.

That night, after dinner, Jason and Trevor played video games for a couple of hours. I didn't enforce any bedtime on weekends (I barely enforced it on weekdays), but by 10:00 Jason said he should take Trevor home. "It takes him a long time to wind down at night."

"Jack and Marissa, too."

They left.

There was no *Daily Show* to watch on Sunday nights.

Bowling was Jason's suggestion for the following weekend.

There was an alley in the Presidio, a former Army base that by the year 2025, I feared, would either be another Six Flags or three square miles of luxury condos. But that was a good 15 years away, and for now it was still a pleasant wood of giant eucalyptus, cypress and pines, crisscrossed with running and biking trails, though the sound of automobiles was never very far away.

The noises of the little bowling alley (originally built for the recreation of servicemen) bothered both Marissa and the boys: the *whirr* of racing balls and the clatter of pins, often followed by even louder whoops and catcalls.

But Marissa cheered immeasurably when Jason introduced her to bumpers, the thin rails that magically arise on either side of the lane and protect the bowler from a gutter ball. Bumpers turn bowling into a game of pool, but Marissa chose to ignore that: She only knew that she was winning against Jack. She looked up at the computer screen after every turn, including Jason's and mine.

Trevor had strength, but not much of an aim. Jason had it all: He would hold the ball up to his chest, fingers placed deeply into the holes, and study the arrows as if he were at target practice. Then he'd move, slowly at first, then faster, pulling the ball far, far back and releasing it just at the moment he hit the lane. The ball rushed forward, gathering speed, and usually hitting dead center, causing the pins to collapse in surrender.

As the game went on, Trevor began to improve. He never paused to aim the way his dad did. But when he threw, he threw hard, so if the ball stayed out of the gutter it would knock down anything its path.

This was a turning point for Marissa. Up until now she had confined her boasting to whispering to me, cupping her hand over her mouth, and dabbling tiny dots of spit along the edge of my ear. But when she first saw that Trevor's score had exceeded her own, she exclaimed aloud, "It's not fair! He's so much taller!"

The next time Trevor's turn came around she cried, "See, he can lift a really big ball!"

When Jason took Trevor and Jack to get fries, forcing me to reproach myself for not packing carrot sticks or at least trail mix in Ziploc bags, I spoke firmly to Marissa, telling her that I would tolerate no more such outbursts.

She pouted.

I explained, "Honey, you can't win at everything every time."

"But I always win over Jack." She squinted up at the computer screen.

I knew that. When she was three I'd caught her lying about her hand during a game of Go Fish, and another time (or two) flipping dice to a more propitious number when Jack wasn't paying attention.

But now there were no more three-year-old tricks involved. She just won: at cards, at Monopoly Junior, at Sorry. How skillful she would have been at bowling without the bumpers was another question — for now.

I hesitated. The constant dilemma: point out Jack's limitations, which she took as natural since she'd never known anything else?

Someday, someday. But not yet.

"You can't always be the winner."

She was looking up at me with big, big eyes, while her brows formed the mighty V of disapproval.

"Why not?" she asked.

The menfolk returned, Jason holding two orders of fries. At ten paces I could see the fluorescent ceiling lights reflecting off the grease.

"I've got to go back," Jason said. "I forgot to take soda orders. No Coke, Pepsi," he finished with a slight accent.

"Wasn't that nice?" I asked Marissa. "Jason waited to hear what you wanted before he ordered for the boys."

Marissa was still frowning. "Don't get us sodas," she commanded. "Trevor makes too much noise when he drinks."

Ashleigh thought that Freddie was acting like a baby.

"Oh, Lord, let's not and say we did," he groaned. "You know I hate camping."

"But you've never *been* camping."

"I hate the *idea* of camping. I hate the *word* camping."

"I should never have used that word anyway! This isn't real camping. It's a — a field trip."

Freddie rolled his eyes, and then fell backward on his bed.

When Ashleigh remembered the day she was "elected," and how she said she wanted to organize a charity walk and a bake sale, she was humiliated that she threw out such lame-o, overdone ideas. She was too intimidated by Mr. Takanawa to think straight. And how was that going to work out for her when she got to meet, like, state leaders?

But the second she left the classroom, the real ideas started flooding her brain. *Overflowing.* Organize volunteers to clean up Ocean Beach; start a tutoring program for at-risk kids in elementary school; raise money to send to the Red Cross.

When she got to her locker, Jack was staring at the combination lock while he spun it around. But then he saw her, and his smile was so spontaneous and bright.... Only young children smiled like that, before they got corrupted.

And she knew.

Why did she want to join the Peace Corps? To help the people of a nation! It didn't matter if it was Somalia or El Salvador. But she couldn't join the Peace Corps yet, right?

But they were all around her. The Nation of Autism.

"It was like a *vision*," she told Freddie. "All these guys who have trouble making friends.... They need to get into nature. Away from all this concrete and pollution." She had to get Freddie to feel it, too. "You know how there's this big autism epidemic? And nobody knows why? It's technology. We've all gotten so alienated from our roots.... Oh, that's not the right word."

"I would definitely agree that 'Roots' isn't the right word."

Jesus, Freddie was sensitive.

"C'mon. You know what I'm trying to say. Nature will be healing. This is our chance to help them — "

"What you mean 'our' chance, Kemosabe? No means no. Did you cut class when we talked about sexual harassment?"

She fell back on the bed next to him. On the ceiling was a poster of LeBron James. There were so many posters of athletes, especially basketball players, on Freddie's walls that you could hardly see the walls. He put them there so that he could look at beefcake while fighting off his parents' growing suspicions about his sexuality, in spite of the time he spent with Ashleigh. They would prefer she was black, too, but they were mostly just happy she was a she. They didn't know that Parker called her "a hashtaghag."

She and Freddie *were* an unusual couple. If you just watched TV, you'd think that white kids and black kids are best friends all the time, like those doctors on *Scrubs,* or that show she liked when she was little, with Raven-Symoné as a psychic. But in real life ... not. There was still a black kid table at the school and even though there was more integration in the clubs, and plenty of black kids in sports, you hardly ever saw the black kids and the white kids really pairing off.

She and Freddie were kind of like girlfriends, but better. Ashleigh had never done real well with girl-girlfriends. It seemed that a guy always got in the way.

"I need you," she said finally.

That was her secret weapon. They always promised that they would be there for each other.

He didn't answer and she smiled to herself, knowing that he was about to relent.

She was wrong.

He sat up and almost shouted, "What part of 'I don't have time' remains unclear? This is *junior year*. This is the year that counts. Some of us don't have a four-point-oh average."

"I don't have a four-oh! Besides, your grades are good."

"Good enough to live at home and go to City College, right?"

"Freddie, *chill*." She made the time out sign by forming a lopsided T with her hands. "You and I both know that you are very, very bright. You just have to relax." She leaned on her elbow. "Tell you wha-at. I bet we could get some independent study credit for this project. And then how's *that* going to look on our college apps?"

"Most universities don't look at that shit." He pouted a little, pursing his lips.

"But a lot of them do," she soothed him. "You have to focus on the positive. I wish you'd at least try doing affirmations."

For the hundredth time that afternoon, he rolled his eyes.

"I bet Mr. Takanawa will help with that extra credit, too." She was deliberately ignoring his complaint about colleges. He was right about some, wrong about others. But that wasn't the point. Didn't anyone do *anything* without expecting a reward? "Since he's the club sponsor? That'll be worth something. And a college recommendation next year?"

"You haven't even asked Mr. Takanawa to sign on."

"But I will." *Eventually.* She was scared about that part, she had to admit.

"Well ... I'll think about it," he said grudgingly.

Suddenly Ashleigh was assailed by all-too-familiar feelings of self-doubt. She picked at the threads that were the beginning of another hole in her jeans. Unlike the girls who bought expensive jeans in the chain stores at the mall, she didn't pay for her jeans to be worn out: She bought these jeans second hand and now she'd had them for years. They were as short as Capris on her because of how much she'd grown since then. "Maybe it's not such a good idea."

"Don't guilt-trip me. Of course it's a good idea. Just because *I* —"

All Ashleigh needed to hear was *of course it's a good idea*.

"This isn't going to be the wilderness," she said. "I'm thinking of that place in Marin County with indoor plumbing and phones — "

"Will Verizon have coverage there?"

" — there's a place we can stay where we can take nature hikes and just roll around in the grass — "

"I've never seen you roll around in the grass!" Freddie *hah'd*.

"I meant — uh, metaphorically."

"FGI. That stands for For. Get. It."

But he laughed when he said it, and now she could tell him what she really felt, at the bottom of it all: "I owe this to Jack."

"Explain that to me?" he asked sardonically.

"Well, I've learned something from him."

"Like how to dance without a partner?"

"That it doesn't matter if people laugh at you. Remember that day, when Mr. Takanawa helped me get elected?"

"As if I could forget."

"*I* won't forget. When I was trying to introduce Jack to our so-called friends, everyone laughed at him. Then when he was talking to Trevor, everyone laughed at him harder. But he doesn't care what people think."

Freddie put his hands behind his head. "All right, then. But you owe me *bigtime.*"

CHAPTER 7

Daddy was teaching Marissa how to play chess. He promised her it would be fun and so far mostly it had been. She liked how so many of the pieces were different from each other, not like checkers where the only difference was red and black.

"The Queen always goes on her color," Daddy said, switching her King and Queen.

"Oh." She didn't like being corrected but with Daddy she was as used to it as she'd ever be.

They were at Daddy's house, in the room that Daddy called the "east parlor," which she'd never heard a room called anywhere else. It had really high ceilings in a triangle, like a church.

At the first lesson he had taught her how to set the pieces up. The pawns were easy because they all went in the front row, and then there were the hard pieces, but except for the King and Queen, the two sides were the same, only in reverse: bishop, knight, rook. Easy-peasy-lemon-squeezy.

The next time he taught her how the pieces move, and that was more interesting than checkers, too, where every piece moved the same. And Daddy was so proud!

"How are things at home?" Daddy asked. He was twirling his own queen by the throat.

He always asked this when they were alone together.

She had mixed feelings about "things at home." She loved the fun adventures that they all went on now. But she missed how she and Mommy used to have outings, just the two of them. Mommy would take her shopping alone, because Jack still wandered off at the mall (Mommy said it was because men hate to shop) and then he wouldn't answer his cell phone.

Sometimes her and Mommy would go to the movies just the two of them because Jack still yelled out in the middle, and once they had to leave, and it was before the end of *Meet the Robinsons*, and Marissa had a tantrum in the car, even though Mommy said she'd bring her back the next day. Marissa was ashamed of acting like such a baby, but she was only three, so it didn't really count.

She couldn't say now that she wanted to spend more time with Mommy, though, because then Daddy might have thought she liked Mommy better than him and be jealous.

But it felt safe to start with, "Jack has a new friend."

"Really? That's good." Daddy was looking at the board and rubbing his chin. It made a scratchy sound. "Do you like his new friend? I assume it's a young man."

"Uh huh." She put the second rook in its corner.

Daddy let out air through his nose. "Tell you what. I think it's time that you were white."

White always went first. So Daddy thought she was ready to make the first move.

He very, very slowly turned the board around so the pieces didn't fall. Marissa thought how it was so nice and quiet in this big room when it was light outside. Daddy was going to take her to the movies before it got dark. Daddy'd asked her if she wanted to spend the night that night but she'd said that HannahSophia was scared to. Daddy had said, "But *you're* not scared, are you? You can't be scared when you're with me." And she'd said no, but she couldn't help thinking about the grandma ghost. She'd dreamt about it once: it looked like Morgana, the skinny witch from *Return to the Sea,* and she'd slipped out through a key hole like the genie in Aladdin, but mean, and got into the rest of the house.

"Okay, Wissy," Daddy said. "Show your old dad what you've learned."

That meant she'd been taking too long to decide. She pushed a white pawn one square forward.

"H'm," Daddy said. "Don't you think you might want to push it two squares out?"

"But that way it'll be easier to catch him!"

"But it'll be easier to get your other pieces out, too. And you have to take a risk if you want to win."

She used two fingers to push the pawn to the next square. There was a rule that if you took your hand off a piece you couldn't move it anymore, but Daddy says the rule doesn't have to count for her, not until she's six.

Daddy pushed his own pawn forward, the one exactly opposite her, so that the pawns could have a stare contest, but neither could take the other.

"I'm glad Jack has a friend," Daddy said. "What's his name? What's he like?"

"Trevor. He's o-kay."

When Trevor wanted to get Jack's attention he would shout his name over and over. Maybe this was the kind of thing that Emma meant when she said Jack was weird, because other people didn't do that.

It was too bad they couldn't have Jason without Trevor. Jason set up the barbecue in the backyard to grill hamburgers and he talked to Marissa about HannahSophia and her new friends from first grade. The week before Jason and Trevor came over on a school night for the first time, and Jason helped both Trevor and Jack with their homework. Usually homework time was the worst part of the day, because sometimes Mommy got impatient and she even yelled, though she always apologized later.

But then later that same night, Jason asked if he could read to her instead of Mommy. Marissa thought, *No way, Jose!* She'd said that it was HannahSophia who said no, to be polite, but Mommy reading to her was their special time — the only really special time they had left!

"It's your move, Wiss." Daddy tapped the head of one of his knights. The knights were horses and they were the only pieces she still had trouble moving sometimes.

Marissa liked to keep her knights near the king and queen so they could protect them. But she took the knight on the king's side out.

"This boy ... Trevor? How did Jack meet him?"

"He came over with his dad."

"Not his mom?"

"He doesn't have a mom."

Daddy had a finger in his mouth. Sometimes he bit his nails but he wasn't supposed to. "Heh-heh-heh. Everyone has a mom."

"Trevor doesn't."

"So ... you've met Trevor's dad?"

"Yeah."

"What's he like?"

"He's o-kay."

"Is he mommy's boyfriend?"

"No."

"Are you sure?"

"Yes."

Marissa's tongue sought out the gap in her mouth where she'd just lost her first tooth. She wasn't sure at all. She'd never seen Mommy and Jason kiss and that was what boyfriends and girlfriends did, even when they were old, because her friends whose mommies and daddies had boyfriends and girlfriends told her. When daddies have boyfriends and mommies have girlfriends they kissed, too.

It was Daddy's turn but he didn't move. He always moved right away. Instead he was looking up at that high ceiling. He must have been thinking about a trip to the kitchen to the refrigerator that was so ginormous that it used to scare her. Thinking about an ice cream bar made her relax a little.

"I'm glad that Jack has a new friend." Daddy was still looking at the ceiling. "He hasn't had a lot of friends."

Daddy was right, but Marissa felt that it would be disloyal to Jack to agree.

"Tell me more about Trevor's dad."

"He's o-kay."

"Is he tall? Short? Blonde? Dark?" Pause. "What does he do?"

"He's a policeman."

Daddy took a very deep breath. Then he slid one of his bishops out through the hole he made when he moved his pawn before. He tapped the top of her knight to point out that he could take it if she didn't move it on this turn.

But she was mixed up again about where to move the knight. She stared at the board until her head began to hurt.

"Do you like him?"

"Who?"

"Trevor's dad."

She didn't want Daddy to think she liked Jason better than she liked him. But she'd learned the trick of changing the subject from him and Mommy. "Can we have some ice cream, Daddy?"

"That does sound good." But Daddy didn't get up. He rubbed his palms on his pants' legs. "You know the offer is still open. To come live with me."

"You said we could have ice cream."

"Sure, sure. But it's still your turn, Wissy."

"I need more time."

She wanted ice cream real bad, but especially this early in the game, every move counted, and even with Daddy stretching the rules for her, if she made a mistake now she wouldn't be able to undo it.

Fuck no, Ashleigh didn't want to come to this party.

But she'd promised her mother — though she didn't remember *exactly* when — so here she was, at the door of what could be Gatsby's mansion, mansard roof and all.

"Kimberly and Ashleigh Allen," her mother trilled when the man who must have been the butler — a *butler?* This was like what, *Jane Eyre?* — opened the door. How soon could she get out of here?

But she owed this, and more, to her mom. Since-she-had-to-be-a-single-mom, Kimberly didn't get to go to Stanford herself, and so now, like a lot of immigrant parents (for Kimberly, being from The Flyover, might as well have immigrated from another continent) needed Ashleigh to fulfill her dream for her. Ashleigh might never go to Stanford, but at least she could go to a party.

Ashleigh had asked Kimberly how it was that they could attend, when Kimberly wasn't an alum. "It's not *strictly* an alumni party," Kimberly had explained. "I know Hastings Whitfield through a friend. Real estate's a small world. But it'll be *mostly* Stanford people and you know what they say. It's not what you do, it's who you know!"

She had ended that speech with her trademark airhead laugh. Kimberly thought it was "ladylike." Ashleigh thought it was humiliating.

When they stepped into the two-story entryway, Kimberly started up with the laughter but directed at no one and nothing. The last thing that Ashleigh saw was the back of her slinky gold cocktail dress.

She must have been on the hunt for "the right people" to introduce Ashleigh to. Kimberly knew how to work a room, and Ashleigh would just be dead weight for this early reconnaissance.

One of the red-vested valets had followed Ashleigh inside. "There's another party on the lower level," he said. "For the teens."

Ashleigh bristled at the idea of being lumped with the teens, even if she did look like the All-American girl. Sometimes being judged by her appearance made her want to scream.

"I have a break coming up," the valet said. He looked like he was no more than nineteen, and his face was covered in pimples. "Maybe I'll see you down there?"

Ashleigh never wanted to be unkind. "Sure," she lied. And then, "I just want to catch up with my mom." Another lie to smooth over her abrupt entry into the "grownup" party.

It was crowded and noisy enough that she could be anonymous. There was plenty of laughter: louder, and far more obnoxious, than her mom's ever was. It made the sound of a band playing some Eisenhower administration crooner song less grating by comparison.

She'd never seen so many white people in one place, let alone in a place as large as the three hotel-lobby sized rooms that encompassed this gathering.

Three more dudes managed to hit on her: all of them over 50 and wearing wedding rings.

Waiters and waitresses passed with trays of hors d'oeuvres and flutes of champagne. The champagne was seductive: golden and with stray bubbles floating to the top. Ashleigh drank rarely anyway, and in the past year not at all, but even if she were a raging bottle hound, she wouldn't let her mother see her with alcohol in her fist.

Ashleigh *was* hungry, though. She took an hors d'oeuvre from the next tray that passed, without looking at what it was, but careful to say, "thank you very much." She tasted some kind of ham, maybe prosciutto, but when she bit down her teeth didn't sever it.

"I like to see a girl who doesn't worry about transfat."

Ashleigh was pulling the ham away from her mouth. It kept stretching, narrow strings of it breaking off, but one stubborn string remaining.

The young man in front of her broke it with a pinch of thumb and forefinger. "Are you having fun yet?"

He was college age, or older: straight blonde hair that covered the tips of impossibly tiny ears. He had the sleeves of a red cashmere sweater tied around an open collared shirt. His eyes were rich kid blue.

She held her hand in front of her mouth so he wouldn't see her chewing the last of the ham.

"I don't think there's transfat in — in whatever that was," she said as soon as she could speak. "Just regular fat, and no, I don't worry about it."

"You look like you hate being here as much as I do."

"I doubt it." She tossed her hair over her shoulder. "My mother made me come."

"Well, I'm glad she did," College Boy said. "Quite a crib, isn't it?" He indicated the enormous room with its terracotta walls and recessed lighting.

"Have you ever been here before?" Ashleigh asked.

"A few times. Wanna explore? Maybe there are secret passageways, like the Winchester Mystery House."

"The Winchester Mystery House doesn't have secret passageways."

"That they *know* about." He shaped his hand into a gun and pointed it at her with a conspiratorial wink.

They exchanged names: he was Dylan. She grudgingly admitted to herself that she was a little curious about the rest of the house, but also that Dylan was hella cute, the way his hair flopped over his forehead.

She followed him down some stairs into the kitchen which was almost the size of her house. There were two stoves with six or eight burners — she didn't want to count them — and a kitchen island with more trays of hors d'oeuvres and men and women chopping vegetables.

But Dylan led her through all this quickly and then through a small doorway that led to a different staircase: this one narrow and dimly-lit.

"You've been here more than a few times," she guessed.

"Well, more than a *few*."

Two levels up and they were on a floor that looked like a hotel, but here it was like the floor where they had all the meeting rooms when they have conventions. The hallway was super wide, the wallpaper had yellow stripes, and the rooms had double doors.

"I wonder if the doors are locked? They must be with the party going on."

Dylan shook his head. "I doubt it. My parents are trusting folk."

"You're the son! Dylan Whitfield. I knew it."

"Spell that 's-u-n.' "

He *was* sun-like: with his canary-yellow hair and the red sweater like one of those sashes that royalty wears.

"So can I see inside one of the rooms?"

"Sure." He turned the closest door knob. "This is my parents' room."

The room would have made her poor mother spontaneously combust from envy: the four-poster bed; the flat screen TV as wide as the far wall; the "conversation pit." And when Dylan told her, "Every room has its own bathroom," she thought of her mother again, but with pity, having to show houses all day long to entitled, never-satisfied yuppies who made offers and then took them back — sometimes at escrow.

Dylan showed her two guest rooms and a home gym ("when Mumsy can't be bothered to go to the one in the basement"), and his brother's room.

"Does he go to Stanford, too?"

Dylan had told her on their way upstairs that he was a first-year law student there.

Dylan's mouth twisted. "He's … out of town at the moment."

Ashleigh couldn't help but stick her head in a little farther, but Dylan gently closed the door. "He deserves his privacy."

Ashleigh put an end to the awkward pause that followed with, "After all this I've got to see your room."

Dylan shrugged as if to say, *it's nothing to look at,* but he led her to the very end of the hallway.

This time he let the door swing open wide. Ashleigh was stunned to see two — no, wait, four, *six?* — arcade games.

"Are those real?" she asked.

"Sure as shootin'. Try one. They work like the regular machines, except that you don't need to put money in." He winked.

Ashleigh sat in the nearest one. It was a raceway game, where you got points for outrunning other cars. You could pick from four different cities for your background, and one of them was San Francisco, so you could keep driving over the Golden Gate Bridge over and over. It dissolved, became a freeway, then reappeared and disappeared again....

"This is good practice for when you get your license," Dylan said. "Or do you have it already?"

"I ... have ... my ... permit...." Ashleigh breathed out one word at a time as she swung and swung to pass the other speeding cars, but then she crashed into the side of the bridge and her car plummeted into the Bay. It was the last life of her automobile. "Whew!" She put her head down on the fake steering wheel. "Driving is hard."

"You'll be an awesome driver. It's not like you have to pass every car on the road in real life."

Ashleigh had decided that she wouldn't get a license, because it was just more bourgeois bullshit. But then Parker had gotten hers and carried on like she was the first person in the universe to get a driver's license. It was a restricted license for the first 18 months anyway! But Parker's boasting had gotten Ashleigh thinking: what if there were an emergency some day and they needed a driver? Or what if she went out with friends, and they needed a designated driver? She could save someone's life!

"Unless you come riding with me. If I make law review I'm getting a Porsche."

Ashleigh's hands froze on the steering wheel. The images of landmarks and destruction on the machine's screen saver passed by until they blurred before her eyes. How could anyone spend money on a Porsche? She wanted a car, she'd admitted that to herself, but just something that ran.

"You look wiped," Dylan said. "You need a beer."

"No, thanks."

"You might as well. It's your one chance to drink and drive." He patted the top of the arcade game.

"Well...."

By the time she finished that one syllable Dylan was holding out a small, dark bottle with a blue-and-white label. It had a German name: two words that were each longer than any in the English dictionary.

"Where did this come from?" she asked.

Dylan pointed over his shoulder with his thumb to the widest flat-screen TV she'd ever seen so far. He must have meant that there was a mini-fridge behind it.

"Daddikins introduced me to these." He twisted off the top of the bottle, then handed it to her. "You could drink these all night and not have a hangover the next day."

"I don't know...."

Dylan seemed puzzled, and perhaps concerned, by her hesitation. "You're eighteen, aren't you?"

She was too flattered to correct him. "It's still not legal, you know."

"Seriously? You think that the drinking age should be 21? They could draft you and send you behind enemy lines."

She laughed. The drinking age *shouldn't* be 21. If you could sign binding contracts and vote, and yes, enlist in the Army, you should be able to drink. Did they expect kids barely older than she to fight the Taliban and not come back to the barracks for a "cold one"?

Dylan twisted off the top of a second bottle. "Only God and I can see you."

He winked again. His winks were like Gatsby's "old sport." At first she thought it was the supercilious tic of a WASP prince, but she'd come to see it as a sign of insecurity, a desire to be accepted.

So she felt like she was being generous when she tipped the bottle back into her mouth. It was far more bitter than any beer she'd ever tasted and she tried very hard not to grimace but she couldn't help it. She almost spat it out.

"It takes some getting used to," Dylan admitted.

"A little strong for me," she admitted in return.

She balanced the bottle on the edge of the driving machine. Then, afraid it would tip over, she took it back. And *then,* afraid she looked like a total wuss, she took a couple more swallows, squeezing her eyes shut against the taste.

"You've got to try one of the other games." He jerked his head twice toward the other side of the room. "Like the Star Wars fighter."

"Sure." But she didn't move. She hadn't forgotten what he'd said before. "Are you really going to get a Porsche?"

"Probably not."

"Good, because — "

"It's pretty damn hard to make law review."

"That's not what I meant. It's because — " *Urp.* She covered her mouth to muffle the belch. "I mean good because — " It had been so long since she'd had a drink, she could feel the alcohol swimming around her brain like a poor sad goldfish who couldn't remember that he'd just come around the same corner of the bowl — "it's *obscene,* that's what it is, to spend that kind of money on a car when there are hundreds of millions of people — "

Dylan looked as if she'd slapped him. "I just want to make law review to make Dad happy."

"Right." Indignant, she started to climb out of the driver's seat, but dizziness pulled her back down.

"You're so totally right," Dylan said softly. "It is obscene. But my father's love is so conditional."

Conditional. God, did she know what he meant.

"On my grades, on my clothes, on my friends...."

She didn't need to remind herself, *compassion begins with me,* because her feeling went beyond compassion: It was a bond.

She barely suppressed another belch.

"And making law review...." Dylan stopped. "I won't deny it. I want to achieve. But I want to achieve for a purpose, you know?"

She knew.

"My dad wants me to go to work for him," Dylan went on, "but I want to do something more important than that. Like give free legal services to people who need it."

"Really?"

"Yeah. Storefront law — that's what they call it, isn't it? Helping the homeless and shit."

"That's awesome," she breathed. "You know it's mostly mental problems that keep them on the street."

Dylan nodded. "Mental problems and substance abuse."

"There'd always be a place for people like that," she said, "if the earth were a loving family."

"'The earth a loving family,' " he repeated. "That's real nice."

The bond was unbreakable now. They were brother and sister. She quickly tipped the bottle into her mouth, which allowed her to tilt her head back so that he couldn't see her blink back tears.

But she was embarrassed, too. "Hey, can I play the Star Wars Fighter?"

"Thought you'd never ask," he said. "Let's nuke a few of those Imperial bastards."

After he'd settled her in the con he brought her a fresh beer. "I hate it when they get flat." When he took her still-half-full one away, she started to protest because of the waste but it wasn't like starving people needed beer.

THE EMPIRE WINS. TRY AGAIN?

She sucked at the game, really sucked, so bad that Dylan laughed at her and had to apologize for laughing. "Listen, I've been playing this game for years." He massaged her shoulders, which had gotten all knotted up. "So you'd have to be some sort of hashtag savant to get it on your first tries."

The massaging helped. She'd been taking this too seriously.

THE EMPIRE WINS. TRY AGAIN?

"I give up." She was feeling giggly. And a little dizzy. "I gotta lie down."

Dylan's shrug read, *be my guest.*

She collapsed on the bed. That was better.

Dylan brought her the beer and lifted her head so she could have a few more swallows. Something about the way he was holding her head up, like she was just in an accident, was very, very funny, so she started to laugh, and ended up with a splash of beer on the front of the "little black dress" her mom had made her wear.

Dylan laughed, too, then lay down on the bed beside her. "Why did your mother have to make you come? Are we that awful?"

"Yes, you are," she giggled.

"I'm not awful." He slid one arm under her shoulders. "I'm going to write appeals for prisoners who can't afford attorneys. The ones who are really innocent, you know."

"So you want to be a criminal lawyer."

"Yeah. Sure."

There was no reason this was funny but she giggled anyway.

He kissed her on the cheek. Even that was funny, but no more giggling. She hadn't made out with a boy in ages, and when his tongue went in her mouth her own tongue responded, seeking his. His arms slipped around her and hers around him, and for God knows how long — it was all a blissful blur — they made out.

When he reached to lift up her skirt, she pushed his hand away. He put his hand on her breast instead. It aroused her through the silk, and that felt good. But when he reached behind her for the zipper she pushed him away more firmly. "This is as far as I go."

"Noted."

He reached again, and though she pressed herself into the mattress he got his hand in underneath and pulled the zipper down. It scratched her back.

"No." She grabbed his arm. "I meant, no more than this."

"And I said that your protest has been noted. So now you can say that you tried to stop me."

"I *am* — Dylan!" Her hand was still on his arm and she tried to push it away, but it didn't budge.

"*Ashleigh.*" It was a taunting falsetto. "Don't be a cock-tease."

"I'm not — "

His laugh was short and harsh. "You ask to see my room, you practically spread your legs on my bed?"

"That doesn't mean — " She'd been wrestling with him, and she must have felt there was a point to that, but in the next moment she learned that there was no point. He hadn't been using a fraction of his strength, but now he did, and in a flash her dress was pulled down her arms, exposing her bra, and he'd pinned her down by both her wrists.

"Enough talking." He plunged his tongue into her mouth again. Just a few minutes before it had been erotic, but with her hands going numb and his body in a plank above her she was only scared.

"Stop! Get off me!" The effects of the beer had evaporated, leaving her nauseous.

"Baby doll, this is where we were headed, isn't it? I mean, how much longer was I supposed to wait?"

"No, I mean it, get *off.*"

"Just relax," Dylan said with something like a laugh at the bottom of his throat. He forced his tongue into her mouth yet again and it was like an animal had crawled in there. She kept trying to wriggle away but he had her wrists as tight as ever and she had almost completely lost feeling in them. "What are you scared of? You're not a virgin, are you?"

"Yes, I am!" Hopeless as it was, she still squirmed under him.

"You don't expect me to believe that."

He tried to kiss her again. She kept twisting her head away. After a few failed attempts he was angry enough to push her wrists deep into the mattress. "Stop it," he growled. "I'm getting pissed."

He wouldn't let her up, but there was only so far he could go like this. He'd have to beat her up, or knock her out. So it would happen when she was unconscious. She was unbearably sad as she waved good-bye to the dream she'd had for years that her first time would be special.

And then she remembered....

The woman who came to her Health class to teach about self-defense. "Women don't have the same upper body strength as men. Use your legs."

He caught her mouth again with his, and his tongue was inside again and she couldn't breathe and she was going to pass out. But then he raised his head to take his own breath, and she sucked in hers and she told herself....

Use your legs....

Use your legs....

She'd have one chance. She let him kiss her again, pretending that it was okay, and he whispered in her ear, "That's more like it," and he loosened his grip just a tiny bit and he raised up just enough.... *Now.* She pulled up her knees and then kicked him with both high heels as hard as she could, right in his junk.

"Ow! Bitch!"

When he hunched over she sprang into the air as if launched by a catapult.

She ran, pulling her dress down over her hips.

"Mom — " she started to call, but the word didn't come out.

These were the right boys her mother wanted her to meet, jerks like Dylan who'd let the African girl toting water hang herself before they slowed their Porsches down to 80 miles an hour.

The last ounce of pity that she'd had for her mother's life of hard work and lost dreams, the last ounce of gratitude she had for not being aborted, and every happy childhood memory of the time they spent together — all gone.

She ran.

Jack had been playing Game Boy worse than usual. "Dude, you suck today," Trevor said when the GAME OVER sign popped up.

"I do not," Jack said, though he didn't really care. He'd never thought he could be bored with *The Simpsons Road Rage.* He was so happy to have someone to play it with that it only bothered him sometimes that he usually lost. Almost always lost. But today....

"I'm going to kick your ass again," Trevor said in that voice that sounds like he has a cold. "*Again.*"

"Trevor?"

"What?"

"You said — you said you have a girlfriend."

Trevor had told him that the first time they met, but Jack had his suspicions now.

"Yeah. You wanna play or not?"

Not really, he didn't. But he picked up his controller.

"I like Miley Cyrus," Trevor announced. *"Miley Cyrus."*

Miley Cyrus was the star of the show *Hannah Montana*. Trevor had sent about 100 e-mails to her through the Disney Channel website, but none of them got answered and then they started bouncing.

"Wouldn't you like to nail some of that?" Trevor snorted. *"Nail."*

Jack pictured hammering nails into the wall, like to hang a picture, but he knew what Trevor meant. He was too embarrassed to say anything.

"Jack!" Trevor shouted. "Jack!"

Jack didn't want to think of Ashleigh that way. He'd only recently discovered the joys and horrors of masturbating. His mom had talked to him about it when he was 14. He was glad now because it would have been really troubling otherwise when he started, and he couldn't talk to her about it anymore. Now there was no one to talk to about things like that.

Jack and Trevor talked a lot about some things: Jack listened to Trevor talk about his fish, and about his running, and Coach Takanawa. Trevor listened to Jack talk about Crime Conquerors and about *Rugrats,* which Jack shouldn't watch because it was for little kids, but Trevor didn't care. They talked about other TV shows and they talked about school and baseball, because they both loved the Giants.

But Jack wished he could talk to Trevor about Ashleigh.

"Jack!" Louder: *"Jack!"*

"Yeah."

"Play the game!"

Trevor was beating the shit out of him already but it was hard to focus. He needed advice. Should he tell Ashleigh that he liked her? Weren't boys supposed to do that? If he and Trevor were like *Drake and Josh* it didn't help him because that makes Jack the Drake person and Drake had no trouble with girls.

"Miley is so hot," Trevor said. "I bet I could meet her."

"She lives in Hollywood."

"I could go to Hollywood."

"That's where Disneyland is."

"Jack! Play the game!"

"I am!"

Thoughts of Ashleigh didn't make him want to masturbate. He hated that "jack off" was the slang term. He learned that in middle school from other boys. The masturbation happened all by itself, even if he tried to stop it. But Ashleigh — he only wanted to hold her hand and to be with her.

Jack and Ashleigh talked a lot, too. Ashleigh talked a *lot* about her mother and the Peace Corps — as much as Trevor talked about fish and running. And she asked Jack a lot of questions, and she was really patient for him to find the English words, so now he did almost his share.

But Jack couldn't talk to Ashleigh *about* Ashleigh.

Jack knew that Trevor meeting Miley Cyrus was crazy. It wasn't like meeting the Crime Conquerors, which he still hoped to do, because they were only actors in those suits, but Miley Cyrus was really Miley Cyrus.

"Trevor." Jack was going to try one more time. "What about Ashleigh?"

"Ashleigh? She's not on *Hannah Montana*."

"No, she — she goes to school with us."

"I don't know her." *Zap, zap, zap.* Trevor angled his controller and scored more points.

"Yes, you do. She's — she's in our club."

Zap, zap, ZIIING.

"I don't know her. I win again!" Trevor raised his arms high.

Jack had hardly touched his controller during that game. But now he picked it up with new determination. "I'm going to win this time," he said.

Jason and I could hear the boys in Jack's room playing "Eviscerate the Mail Carrier," or maybe it was "Wipe the Floor with Grandma," shrieking with every successful shot, while we were in what had become our standard pose: facing each other in the middle of the sofa, one elbow propped on the back.

"If I can listen to over an hour of *Sweeney Todd*, you can listen to an entire George Strait album," he was saying.

I slapped his arm. "I listened to the first twelve songs. There are only three to go."

"Well, get on it." He leaned forward and said in a very low voice, "I'm heavily armed and dangerous."

"Oooh, I'm so scared!" I held my hand over my heart. "But there's so much Jesus stuff in country music."

"So? No one's asking you to go to church, just to listen. Maybe a little Jesus stuff would be good for you."

"Don't you be messing with me, *sheygitz.*" I pointed at his heart in mock threat. Then I giggled just like a woman who'd been drinking something more than French roast.

"No one is asking you to become a Christian."

"They damn well better not! Actually, my mother was kind of a frustrated Catholic. But anyway...."

"Excuse me, is this going to be a long story?"

"Maybe it is, Officer. *Deal.*" I straightened up and folded my hands in my lap. "So it's, like, I don't know, ten years ago, and Alex has to go to a funeral at a Baptist church in Oakland because it's for the father of one of his big donors, right? I go with him, because who can say no to a funeral, I mean, it's my idea of a rollicking good time, and everyone is singing and praising the Lord...." I swung back and forth to demonstrate. "He's walking with the Lord! He's gone to that happy shore!"

"You don't do Christian very well."

"Shut up!" I slapped him on the leg. "Anyway, you go to a Reform Jewish funeral and all you're going to hear is — " I pinched my nostrils closed — "he's not dead as long as we remember him." I let go of my nose and added, "Or her."

Jason laughed.

"So I said to Alex, 'if something happens to me, ship me over there.' "

"Nothing's going to happen to you."

He took my hand.

"I'm just saying," I shrugged.

"Nothing's going to happen to you," he repeated, and he kissed the hand he held.

The clatter of a key ring made us both jump back.

Then Marissa came into focus: standing before me with big accusing eyes, to the sound of Alex clearing his throat.

It is definitely time to change the locks.

"How was the movie?" I asked.

Both Count and Countess Buzzkill were staring at me now. I looked from one to the other and back to my partner in crime. "You've met Jason, haven't you, Alex?"

"Haven't had the pleasure," Alex said.

"We didn't go to the movies," Marissa said, adding darkly, "Daddy taught me to play chess."

Jason was still holding my hand. I suppressed my impulse to wriggle it away, while clinging in memory to the sound of our giggles.

"We went to the Pacific Islander-American Democratic Club dinner," Alex said sternly.

"Instead of the movie," Marissa elaborated.

"Really. Isn't she a little young for those things?" I wondered why he hadn't chosen an escort from his stable of Lady Long Legs.

"Why?" he asked. "Don't you think she can sit through half an hour of speeches?"

A moment of silence for us both to remember how much *I* hated sitting through half an hour of speeches, especially since it was more like *ninety freaking minutes* of speeches. Signifying nothing. I'd tried to pretend I enjoyed those dinners; I tried really, really hard.

"You always underestimate her. She made me proud," he said.

"My Misty makes me proud every day," I said, submitting my entry in the World's Corniest Nickname Contest. I reached out for her; she took a step back, and I spread out my arms as if that were the gesture I had intended all along. "Bedtime for Bonzette!"

"I'm not tired."

"Oh, yes, you are," I corrected her.

"Why not let her stay up a while?" Alex said. "It's not a school night."

Don't you have someone to indict for murder? Maybe even me, in about two minutes?

"Marissa, go to bed now and I'll come read to you in a minute."

"I don't want to."

"Let her stay up a while."

"*Alex.*"

Jason draped his arm around the back of the sofa; close to, but not quite, resting on my shoulders.

"H'm. Maybe your mother's right," Alex said.

God had spoken. "Ohhhhkaaay."

Alex bent down and Marissa stood on tiptoes to kiss his cheek.

I expected Alex to be gunning his Cadillac before Marissa's door closed behind her, but instead he collapsed into one of the armchairs. "Whew, I'm not as young as I was," he said. "Anna, any chance of a cup of coffee?"

Jason let his arm drop another inch closer to my shoulders.

"You don't drink coffee this late," I said.

"But you do."

"Um … not tonight — I've had five gallons or so. I swish when I walk."

"She does," Jason confirmed.

"Jason, I understand you're in law enforcement," Alex said.

"Yes."

"Chief Hsu's a friend. You met him?"

"Informally."

"Well, if you ever need anything, I can make a — "

"I'm fine."

I wanted to take Jason's hand again, in a show of solidarity, but wasn't sure if that would make things better or worse.

"Pretty late, isn't it, Anna?" Alex asked, not as casually now.

"My mommy said I could stay up 'til midnight," I said, doing Fanny Brice's Baby Snooks.

"I was thinking of Jack. It's pretty late for him." He tilted his head in the direction of Jack's bedroom, whence the noise of animals being strangled was being emitted. "When he gets overstimulated he has trouble sleeping."

Oh, so now *he's concerned about Jack.*

"But he and Trevor are having so much fun." I tilted my own head toward Jason. "Trevor is Jason's son."

"Really?" He drummed the arms of the chair. "Cozy."

"It can be," Jason said pleasantly.

"You married, Jason?" Alex asked, as if simply trying to hold up his side of the conversation.

"Divorced. You?"

Alex frowned in the exact same way as Marissa did: brows dipping into a V. But his version was in no way comical. "You sure about that coffee?" he asked me. "I've got a long drive."

"You live five miles away, dear."

And then:

"Eee-yah!"

"Eee-yah!"

It was the boys, screaming from Jack's room.

And above even those Aspie shrieks we all heard Marissa's plaintive, "Moommmeee, they're keeping me awaaaake…."

Alex heaved himself out of the chair, but now with a satisfied smile. "Looks like you two will have your hands full."

Then he left, without saying good-bye to either of his children.

ACTUALLY, we did not have our "hands full." Jason went to tell the boys to keep it down, while I read to Marissa, who fell asleep after only a few minutes, just as the cloud of grasshoppers descended to destroy the Ingalls' family crops.

Telling Jack and Trevor to "keep it down," was *pro forma,* and very much like asking the earth to rotate counterclockwise, but in fact they were unusually quiet after that.

When Jason and I returned to the sofa, though, I not only couldn't recapture the pre-Alex mood, I started to rant.

"Why does he have to act that way? I mean, he swoops in here for ten fucking minutes, gives them advice on how to get better grades, lectures me about everything I'm doing wrong, then *swoops* back out thinking he's goddam father of the year."

"Hey, hey. Don't let him get to you like that. Besides, all he did was drop Marissa off and sit down for a few secs. You can't blame him for that."

I fumed silently. I would never tell Jason what I knew Alex would say to me later. *Still a patrolman, after how many years? No promotions? Never wanted to be sergeant, a detective?*

"Alex always has an agenda. He came in here to see just how friendly — I mean, just how friendly Jack and Trevor are."

"I dunno. He didn't even go say hi to them."

"That's the point!"

I raised my fist. Jason caught it mid-air, and then unwrapped it finger by finger. "Hey, hey. Let's not let him spoil *our* evening."

"You're right," I said. "I'm sorry."

"After all," he crooned, "Can't a man and woman be friends in this day and age?"

"Politicians don't have friends," I explained. "They have ledgers where they keep track of who's done what for whom."

Jason laughed and I felt the thrill I always did. "You don't seem like the type to put up with too much shit, Annie."

That was the first time he called me "Annie."

"I just want to keep it nice for the kids, you know?"

"And that's exactly what you should be doing."

"I don't want them to see us fighting every time we're together."

"No."

Jason was tucking loose strands of hair behind my ears. He'd started on one side, moved to the other, and now, with no more loose hair to work with, was simply moving his hands over the tops of my ears and down my neck.

"But you know, the more I think about him the more I give him what he wants," I decided.

"So it's time to stop thinking about him, right?" His hands rested on my shoulders while his thumbs caressed the bottom of my neck.

I pretended to consider this. "Then do something to get my mind off it."

"Way ahead of you," he replied, right before we had our first kiss.

CHAPTER 8

On my thirteenth birthday I had awoken to find that I needed a D cup. After that I attracted the attention of men. I held on to my virtue for a few years, only to discover that most men — most of the men who had been slobbering over *me*, at least — lost interest after their Big Slobber.

Before you call me vain (though I am), let me say that any woman can get laid. Not every woman can get loved.

It made me cautious. Too cautious, perhaps. I'd had no more than six lovers throughout college and I married Alex while I was in graduate school.

But even an "N" of six, when combined with the stories told by my girlfriends, had provided me with a puzzle I had yet to solve.

Which was: after just one sexual encounter a man is either besotted or bored. If he leaves in the middle of the night, he's already lost interest.

Making it to the a.m. doesn't guarantee success. Comes the dawn, the guy has decided that you're either a Relationship or a One-Night stand. You don't have to know any fancy-schmancy positions from the Kama Sutra. My sister Darya once said that the key to making a man attached to you is not what you do but how much you make him believe you're enjoying it. I didn't look to Darya for advice in many areas, but she'd had enough men following her around like the rats following the Pied Piper since her own thirteenth birthday, that I trusted her on this.

In the morning, sunlight would have streamed through the lace curtains, except there was no sunlight and I had pleated drapes that needed a good dusting. So instead, a wan gray sky clued us that it was time to get up.

And things had changed for me. I remembered waking up at 3:15 a.m. and seeing the back of Jason's head, recognizably blonde even in the near-darkness. But it was the sound of his snoring that made me feel that he belonged to me, at least for the moment.

Forget about the wan gray sky. What really woke me up were the shrieks from the other room.

"I did so win!"

"No you didn't!"

Jason yawned and stretched. "That's-a my boy," he said. "Trev's always up early."

We'd made the boys promise to go to bed by midnight. Jason thought that Trevor would conk out before then. Jack suffered from insomnia. On weekend nights I didn't fight him and he was usually up until 2 a.m.

"Oh, God." I sat up, fully aware that as the comforter fell it revealed my (ample) bosom. "I'm a slut." I had had no intention of letting him stay the night, not with the kids in the house. Yet I'd ignored the opportunity to ask him — politely — to leave when he'd mentioned that his car was safe because there was no residential parking enforced on Sundays.

"Don't take this the wrong way," I said now, ignoring the fact that any sentence that begins with "don't take this the wrong way," inevitably ends badly, "but don't you think you should leave?"

"Now, how could I possibly take that the wrong way?" he grinned, propping himself up on one elbow.

"There's bus fare on the dresser," I muttered.

"Marry me."

"Oh, right," I said. I flung the comforter all the way back. "If you think that's going to get you another roll in da hay, you be wrong-o, my friend." I had planned for that first gesture to extend into a quick-change operation into jeans and t-shirt, or anything that would look as if I hadn't just had intercourse. Instead I lost momentum, and sat on the edge of the bed without moving.

I felt Jason stroke my naked back, and I jumped. It got me standing up, at least.

"I mean it," he said softly.

He was joking, but it wasn't funny. "All right, fine," I said, punctuating my reply with the closing of a dresser drawer. I was pulling on those jeans I'd been thinking about. Snapping them closed required some effort. Then I remembered, with a great flood of relief, that they were fresh out of the dryer and therefore would need a little stretching. "Marissa can be a flower girl. She'd love that. What about the boys? Can we have two ring bearers?"

I turned around expecting him to look deservedly ashamed. Instead his expression was contemplative. "I thought we'd do something simple," he said finally. "It *is* a second marriage for both of us, Annie."

With a mix of rising to the challenge and a slight bit of irritation I said, "You know it has to be a Jewish ceremony."

He frowned a little. "Does that really matter to you?"

Did it? I hadn't been inside a synagogue since Jack's modified Bar Mitzvah. But since we were being silly, why stop now? "Of course. An Orthodox ceremony, with four *chuppah* holders."

"What's a hoopah?"

"Think tent with no sides." As if I knew anything about tents.

"Unitarian?"

"Oh, Uni*tarian,*" I said lightly. "Why do, ge — Christians think that's so all-inclusive? How welcome would a Hindu feel? I know, I know," I added, "I sound like an ecumenical panel discussion on PBS, right? I can't find a clean t-shirt."

He was still resting on his elbow. Even in this grim daylight, I could see how well-developed his shoulders and pecs were. "We can have a Jewish ceremony, as long as we keep it simple. Just family." He rolled his eyes. "Actually, one thing — we can have a Jewish minister, if *you* deal with my mother."

Before I could tell him that there were no Jewish "ministers," my brain registered the word "mother."

Was he serious?

"She's not really a church-goer anymore. But she had trouble with me marrying a Protestant."

"I've known you a month," I said.

"I didn't mean get married next week. I wasn't even thinking until after the first of the year. Wouldn't it be fun to have an anniversary on Valentine's Day?"

"You need to get dressed," I said. "Quickly." I turned my head in the direction of Marissa's room. "You know, I once heard someone describe second marriages as the triumph of optimism over experience."

"That's why I suggested a long engagement."

"On what calendar is five months long?"

"We don't have the same time to waste that we did." After a pause: "We both married when we were way too young." Solemnly: "I think that was the deal-breaker."

I never had found a clean t-shirt, and now I had a red turtleneck half-pulled over my head. On the outside I must have looked like a monster with a red knit head and webbed claws. Inside this red skin I could hide from all the possibilities and problems of the world. But after a moment I poked my head through the neck hole. "Tell you what. I'll think about it."

Suddenly from the other room: "I'm really good at this game! That's why I never lose!"

I recognized what I'd come to think of as Trevor's "argument voice." Followed by Jack's milder but firm, "I — I won that time."

"You never win. You must have cheated."

I'd been aware, but not quite conscious, of this black noise in the background while Jason and I talked, but now the voices were too loud to ignore.

"Jason," I hissed.

The urgency struck him suddenly, and he leapt out of bed with the same speed he might have had giving chase to a suspect.

"I didn't cheat," I heard Jack insist. His honor was at stake.

"That's my cue," Jason said. He pulled his clothes from a pile where they were wrinkled from a night spent on a chair.

"Mommy!" It was Marissa shouting, as loudly as the two adolescents. "Why is Trevor still here?"

Another day in paradise.

"You cheat, you cheat, you're just a fucking cheater!"

"I do — do *not*. You — *you* cheat. Cheat! Cheat! *Fucking* cheater!"

I'd never heard Jack use the F-word before.

Jason opened Jack's bedroom door first, and so he largely blocked my view. What I could see in the gaps surrounding Jason's body were mostly piles and piles (and piles) of discarded wrappers from potato chip bags, candy bars, Hostess Cupcakes and Twinkies.

Where there are wrappers and empty bags there are potato chip crumbs. Chunks of chocolate. Spilled sodas. Melted ice cream.

The two black handheld devices used to slaughter digital beings lay on the floor. One was broken in half, exposing the wires inside.

"Cheat!"

"Cheat!"

They looked pale; their eyes were bloodshot and swollen. Their arms trembled as they shouted.

When they fell on each other I was too stunned to move.

Jason was on them both before another half second had passed, with a hand on either side, pulling them apart.

"Liar!"

"Liar!"

They wiggled in his grip. He held on more tightly. "Stop it right now."

"But he — "

"But he — "

"You were up all night, weren't you?"

Jack and Trevor both sagged. Jason shoved them in the direction of Jack's bed, not very hard, but they both fell backwards onto it.

"Look at this mess," I said hollowly. It would take hours of mopping and vacuuming and laundering.

But they weren't fighting any more, at least. What would I have done if Jason hadn't been here?

If Jason hadn't been here Trevor wouldn't have been here either.

Then I saw the two knocked-over cups of coffee with the logo of the nearby convenience store, the 24/7.

"Oh, shit." I picked one up, and sent up the selfish prayer that Trevor had drunk both. Then I entered the bargaining stage of grief and decided that the coffee was okay as long as they hadn't stolen the junk food from the 24/7. Because they either stole the junk or the money, unless Jason let Trevor carry around more cash than I entrusted with Jack.

Either way, they obviously *had* been up all night. And I knew at a second glance that Jack had been into the coffee. I'd always known that caffeine and Jack would be one notch shy of mixing ammonia and bleach, but I hadn't been able to hide my own addiction from him: I drank enough to support a Starbucks franchise in my garage.

At least Jack was calming down a little. Thank God it wasn't a school morning. He lay back on his bed, still shaking, and reciting the script of a Crime Conquerors show.

But Trevor was not collecting himself. He'd rolled off the bed but righted himself and was now whirling like a dervish, arms flailing, and moaning. The faster he whirled the louder he moaned — and the wider and harder his arms flew out.

"Oh, boy," Jason muttered, "here we go again." He pantomimed rolling up his sleeves, since all he was wearing was an undershirt, and with a short lunge, wrapped himself around Trevor's torso.

Alex used to do the same thing. Jack's first therapist had advised it, and it usually worked. Eventually. It wasn't unlike Temple Grandin's now-famous hugging machine. The all-round pressure from a big guy such as Alex or Jason gave the Aspie in question a sense of security, often protecting him from the overwhelming stimuli. Back when Alex threw his big arms around Jack I would fall in love with Alex again for a few minutes.

I heard Marissa wail from the next room: "What's happening? I'm scared, Mommy!"

I thought she was more pissed than scared, but maybe that was wishful thinking. "I have to go to her."

But I stopped at the door.

Trevor still wasn't calming down. He fought Jason like a demon. Jason was big but Trevor, though sinewy, was of almost equal height and now fueled by the overwhelming distress of a nervous system gone haywire.

Jack, by comparison, though still strung out from coffee and sleep deprivation, almost seemed relaxed, though I knew it was more like a stupor. His *Crime Conqueror* recitation continued *sotto voce.*

The battle went on between Jason and Trevor. The steady solid pressure that had apparently worked before wasn't helping, though Jason was huffing and puffing enough to blow the house down.

"Let me," I said.

"Just stay away," Jason barked.

I did not like being barked at, but I pleaded again, "Let me try."

"You're going to get yourself hurt," and it was the voice of a policeman speaking through his car-mounted bullhorn, commanding the driver, "Pull over!"

"Give me a chance," I said, as softly as I could while still being heard.

I didn't know what was going through Jason's mind right then. Maybe *I'm not getting anywhere* or perhaps even, *I don't trust myself with this kid any longer.*

"All right." He warily loosened his hold. Passing by me he said, "I'll be right outside, understand?"

"No. Marissa's freaking out. Can you deal with her? Jack, go with Jason."

Jack was too exhausted to protest with anything more than a little foot-dragging.

When Jason released Trevor, Trevor collapsed to the floor. His head landed on a half-full Ruffles bag, making a loud crunch, and his knee knocked over a bottle of ketchup. He lay twisting and moaning.

As I crouched next to him, I was struggling to overcome a slight revulsion. Trevor was a young man, not a boy. He smelled of grease and coffee and sweat.

But when I pulled him up to sitting, using the legendary strength that mothers have when called upon, I saw tears coating his grimy cheeks.

At the sight of those tears my chest ached. I plunked down onto my ass, and drew him close, guiding his head onto my shoulder. His twisting had miraculously subsided. So had the groaning. He was just sobbing now. Gradually I held onto him more tightly, and we began to sway together.

After all the time he'd spent in my house, after all the time he'd spent with Jack, I hadn't connected with him. I was so happy and that he and Jack had fun together. That was all I cared about.

But he was a stranger. And Jack, even when he hadn't showered, even when he reeked, was mine. He smelled like me, underneath whatever repulsive odors he might have acquired. Just as my own stench didn't bother me, Jack's didn't.

Trevor had the flesh of a young man. Yet it was a boy I held in my arms, and as I did, an unexpected tenderness entered me. Inside that big sweaty body was the same small vulnerable heart as Jack had.

Trevor pulled away. "I want my mommy," he said.

I bit down on my lower lip. He was looking right at me with big brown eyes that he must have gotten from his mother Denise. What idiot said that autistics didn't make eye contact?

I put a hand on his shoulder. "Can I be your mommy, just for today? Maybe just when you're here, hanging out with Jack? You know — " I squeezed his shoulder. "You know, I always wanted another son. Always wanted Jack to have a brother." I got ready to lie. "I'd love to go places and show off my three kids."

When I said it, it didn't feel like a lie.

He sniffled. "Okay."

I knew that I was no substitute for Denise. You get one Mommy and a woman has to go *pret*ty far to lose that place in a child's heart. Even those severe autistics abandoned to bang out their lives in head-knocks against the walls of state hospitals — might they be banging a code for, "I want my mommy"?

"Just when you're here," I repeated softly.

"Ok," Trevor said.

Marissa sat on her bed, holding HannahSophia tightly in her lap. Up until now Trevor had mostly just been annoying, but this….

Jason came in with Jack and closed the door behind them. It didn't do much to soften the noise, and now Jack was there, wandering around.

"I don't like Jack in my room."

A long time before, Jack had started taking stuff to use in his Crime Conqueror games, where he repeated what happened in the show that day. He took things from all over the house, like Mommy's coffee cups and her earrings, and forks from the drawer, but Marissa didn't care about that until he took the Fruit Loops necklace she made at pre-school and lost it. Maybe he ate it.

"I'll keep an eye on him," Jason said. He knelt down in front of her so that they were face-to-face. "How's HandSoap doing?"

"Don't call her that."

"Okay. HannahSophia." Jason didn't say anything for a minute. "Trevor can be scary, can't he?"

"No. Just he scares HannahSophia."

Jason sighed. It sounded like the way Mommy sighed sometimes. "He's difficult, though."

Marissa looked over at Jack. He was wandering around, tapping things like her books and the pictures on her wall. "The galaxy needs you, Crime Conquerors... Crime Conquerors...."

Sometimes the stuff that she thought Jack took from her room showed up again and then she felt guilty for being a tattletale to Mommy. But when she couldn't find Astronaut Barbie, and Mommy said maybe she would turn up, and then Marissa found her in the bathtub, drowned, Marissa screamed until her throat hurt.

What might Trevor do if he came in her room?

"You know that Trevor can't always help the things he does."

"Then why can I help the things I do?"

She'd wanted to ask this for a long time. Just last week she'd gotten in trouble because Mommy told her to put her paints away, and Marissa kept saying, "Just one more minute," and then she spilled the cup with the water and the paints on the carpet.

Mommy said she couldn't watch TV the rest of the night because she hadn't listened. She ended up letting her watch TV anyway, but not until Marissa missed *SpongeBob*.

"We can't let Mighty Quarko down ... down...."

"Well...." Jason rose to his feet and sat next to her, but not too close. "Their brains are different."

"How are their brains different?"

Jason patted his knees. "I don't know," he said finally. "But no one knows yet."

Marissa thought that Jason wasn't very smart, not like Daddy, who knew everything. She shifted HannahSophia from one arm to the other.

"Can you shoot Trevor if he's really bad?"

"I don't shoot people."

"Daddy said you do."

"He did, did he? H'm." Jason reached out as if to push her hair off her face but quickly withdrew. "If I ever have to shoot someone, it's only to protect someone else, and I do it in a way that hurts them the least."

Marissa was curious about what "hurting the least" was but she didn't want to ask.

"A policeman is supposed to protect people," Jason said. "Not hurt them."

"Unless they're bad guys."

"Unless they're very bad guys who are going to hurt someone else."

"Can't Trevor hurt someone else?"

"Deathtania is out for revenge … revenge…."

"He never has. He's only ever hurt himself."

Marissa heard a rolling sound, and she looked over to see that Jack had just opened her underwear drawer. She couldn't even speak: She just gasped and pointed.

Jason was already leading Jack away. Jason could move very quickly. "I wouldn't do that, Buddy. Private stuff." He closed the drawer.

Marissa shouted, "Don't ever look in my drawers again!"

"He won't," Jason said, but then added, "we'll do our best to keep him away."

Because there was no making Jack do or not do something.

He wasn't a bad brother. Olivia's brother told Olivia that she had cooties. Jack wouldn't do that.

Jack was a good brother. Sometimes.

Trevor had stopped screaming. The silence was very loud, but in a good way. It was comforting silence. Maybe that was why they called blankets "comforters."

"I wish it could always be quiet this way."

"I like quiet, too," Jason said.

"I will rule the galaxy…."

Daddy's house is always quiet.

I knew that Trevor and I were not about to walk off into the fog of a Casablanca night, looking forward to a beautiful friendship. Trevor had his own version of Jack's, shall we say, challenging habits. Since he was not my son, those habits were both easier and more difficult to live with.

But that morning I was not thinking very far into the future. I was back on the sofa, my French roast on my thigh and coming from a new position of strength. The fact that Jason and I had made love did not add to my confidence. The fact that he had proposed did. I was pretty sure that if I had said yes that he would have fled with both his son and his shoulder mic. But for now, at least, all hesitation I'd felt about asking him personal questions had evaporated.

Jason, returned to his own position on the sofa, was a far humbler version of the man who had shouted orders at me a short time before. I rapped my fingernails against my coffee mug and asked him, directly and without fanfare, to tell me what led to his divorce.

"You know how it is with kids like this," he began, and I inferred an apology in his words for yelling at me earlier. "Stress on the marriage."

"Yes, I know," I said — smugly, because I was experienced in such matters.

"So ... Denise left us."

"Oh." Not so smug this time around.

"She was a paralegal. There was a lawyer in the office. Separated, not divorced, but she moved in with him."

"I'm sorry," I said, then quickly stuck my nose into my mug for the sake of hiding my guilty expression. I was the one who had left Alex. Not willingly, and not until the end — but still. That was why I put up with so much from him now: I deserved his treatment.

"It was partly my fault," Jason said. "I spent too much time away from home. And then I'd come home so tired and ... and just not wanting to make any more decisions. She'd ask, 'what do you want for dinner?' and I'd say, 'I don't care.' " He paused. "I can see how you start to feel neglected after a while."

"M'mmm," I acknowledged vaguely, remembering Alex's long hours at the office. Though after a certain point, I hadn't wanted him around anyway.

"When I look back — I went into law enforcement to provide for my family and that's what tore it apart. If I'd already been a cop, or waited 'til Trevor was older...."

"Well...." This time I began with the hope of saying something that would relieve him of some responsibility but I went blank.

He defended himself a little: He worked more overtime, to pay for all the therapies. Then he admitted: Sometimes it was to stay away.

Denise was a fighter. She had battled the school district until they surrendered and paid for 40 hours a week of Applied Behavioral Analysis, a miracle treatment that was as much of a miracle as Linda Bartlett's Garden. That was going to fix Trevor. Read the testimonials on the Internet!

It didn't fix Trevor.

Denise became depressed. Which was natural enough. All of her friends in her support group were taking anti-depressants, and she decided to try: Doctor gave her Prozac. Then more Prozac. Switched to Wellbutrin. Combined Wellbutrin and Prozac. Tried Wellbutrin and Lexapro instead.... Was this right? So many names, most of them the generic equivalents on the prescription bottles. A lot of Xs and Zs on the brand names, had I ever noticed that?

Doctor finally got it right. Denise got cheerful. Kind of creepy cheerful — but he only saw that looking back. Jason was finally at Richmond Station, which policed "good" neighborhoods: plenty of domestic abuse, he had to say, and auto break-ins, but no gang violence. And then Trevor, still in elementary school, discovered that he could run, run like the Devil himself was after him. There were track meets and Trevor was always winning, winning for a change, and going on to the next level, even the citywide meets.... His real gift was for cross-country. He had that kind of persistence.

Two almost-peaceful years.

Then the fire in the microwave. Denise only left Trevor alone to get the mail, but it was enough time for a fork to meet its end.

Then Denise's half-hearted suicide attempt with a bottle of Tylenol.

Jason got a call one afternoon not long after. No one had picked up Trevor. Jason went to get him, took him home.

Denise was gone. Trevor called out for her. Jason dashed around the flat, looking for forced entry, looking for a struggle. But he didn't call the police, not because he was the police, but because he knew that no one had hurt her. No one had taken her. She'd blown that popsicle stand.

Which he confirmed shortly thereafter, looking at the nearly-empty closet. What she'd left behind: the blue nightgown with the lace top. The thick pink pullover sweater. The scarf with the flowers on it. All three had been gifts from him.

He didn't know how long he stood at the open closet door, but it was until Trevor wailed. He'd found the note: *CLEAN CLOTHES IN THE DRYER. MOM.*

Denise and the lawyer — he was one of the partners — only lasted six months. Maybe it was only five. The lawyer went back to his wife. Denise didn't go back to work. She didn't come back to him. Not that he was so eager ... but he would have taken her back for Trevor's sake. Of course, for Trevor's sake.

He tried to get her to come visit Trevor. She said that would make things worse. That they all had to move on.

One day she said she was moving to Japan. Another day she confessed that she had stayed in bed.

Then they stopped talking. How long ago now? In March it would be seven years. Or eight. He wasn't even sure where she was living.

"She's bi-polar," Jason concluded hoarsely. "You treat that differently than regular depression, I understand. And — " he cleared his throat — "it usually appears in someone's mid-twenties."

My left leg had gone to sleep.

"I should have told you about this sooner," he said.

"No, no! I mean … I mean…."

I was trying to say that he'd been under no obligation to tell me his secrets. We were friends — not even friends, just casual acquaintances! He hardly owed me his entire past.

Even if we had made love the night before.

Even if he'd made a facetious proposal that morning.

Besides, there were stories about my marriage that I hadn't told him. That I still wasn't going to tell him.

CHAPTER 9

Ashleigh was waiting for Mr. Takanawa to finish talking to another student. She had her purple binder, the one with the big gold peace sign embossed on the cover, balanced on her knees, and she was trying to focus on the presentation she wanted to make to him, but she was so nervous that she caught herself chewing on a clump of her hair, a terrible middle-school habit that she thought she'd broken for good.

Ashleigh hadn't spoken to her mother since Saturday night. Kimberly wanted her to meet "the right people," did she? Like, a would-be rapist whose father probably had a mistress who was invited to the same party?

Kimberly was never going to guilt-trip her into anything again. Because obviously the only reason that Kimberly *did* fight her family and give birth to Ashleigh was because Young Kimberly could see how the baby could be of use to her someday.

Ashleigh had almost run away that night. After she and her mother had gotten home, Ashleigh thought about packing a couple of pairs of jeans and heading over to Sue's house.

But things were still tense between her and Sue's best friends, Parker and Blake…. Besides, anywhere she'd showed up the mom or dad would have busted her.

Kimberly hadn't believed Ashleigh when she told her what happened. First she'd said, "You always exaggerate," and then, when Ashleigh had given her a more detailed account, she said, "You went into his room alone? You might as well have said, 'have your way with me.' "

What happened to "no means no"?

"Boys only do that kind of thing when they get encouragement," was Kimberly's conclusion. "Sometimes the signals are unconscious, I'll grant you that."

Ashleigh had always thought that at least Kimberly wanted the best for her, even if they didn't agree on what "the best" was. But now….

"Sorry to keep you waiting, Miss Allen." Mr. Takanawa slipped behind his desk. He was so graceful; she wondered if he was ever a dancer. "Are you all right?"

"Yes." She saw that her hands were shaking. She gripped the edges of the binder to stop them.

"You'll pardon me, but it doesn't seem so."

Jack was a good listener, sometimes Freddie, too, but she needed an adult now. She decided to take the chance. "It's my mother."

"Yes?"

"She — she put me in a dangerous situation."

And then it came spilling out: from the sweater around Dylan's neck to the massage that turned into a brush with rape.

"And you think your mother knew this was a risk?"

Ashleigh dug her fingers into the edges of her binder. "Maybe not. I guess not. I know she doesn't want me to have sex."

Mr. Takanawa shook his head as if to say, *what a piece of work is woman.*

"I want to move on." Ashleigh suddenly felt very uncomfortable talking about this to Mr. Takanawa. He was a man, too, after all. She wondered if she'd ever be able to trust any man: gay, straight or autistic.

"I hope you can put this behind you," Mr. Takanawa said, opening his slim leather briefcase. "Of course, you know you can come talk to me any time."

But he snuck a look at his watch — was it gold? was it a *Rolex?* — and she could tell he had lost interest.

"I'm okay," she said. "I have a plan for something the One World Club can do for the, uh, full-inclusion kids."

Since that awful night, Ashleigh had thrown herself entirely into research on autism. She'd thought she was such an expert already, but actually she was really ignorant. It was, like, *humbling.* Sure, she knew there was an epidemic, but it was almost a *pan*demic. Some sites said that as many as *1 in 68* kids had some sort of autism. There were a lot of theories about why: better diagnoses; more pollutants in the environment; vaccinations.

Heredity loads the gun and environment pulls the trigger. That seemed to be the latest and greatest when it came to scientific knowledge. The problem was that no one knew what in the environment that was.

But even if Ashleigh's science skills weren't the best, nothing in her research contradicted her intuition.

When had this epidemic started? Right when e-mail was just starting. And it had just gotten worse since the Internet and Facebook and Flickr and Pinterest and Instagram.... The air was so full of signals going back and forth, and babies' brains weren't fully formed, so it must have had something to do with that. Not everyone her age was on the spectrum, so some babies must have been more vulnerable than others, and that was where heredity came in.

"The full-inclusion kids?" Mr. Takanawa asked. "Do tell."

"Not the full-inclusion kids exactly ... the ones 'on the spectrum.' " Would he know what that meant?

"Like my star runner," Mr. Takanawa nodded. "Trevor."

Her face got warm. Of course he knew Trevor, who almost became president of the club instead of her. Why did Mr. Takanawa always make her so nervous? She didn't have this problem with other teachers. Maybe because he looked so sophisticated, like today in his shirt with the button-down collar and the silk burgundy tie. (Never mind the freaking watch. She hoped she was mistaken, and that it was something he bought off Market Street.)

So she fumbled through, first explaining her theory, and then her current idea: "If we can, like, just get them out of the city for a few days, on nature hikes, and away from the computers.... it'd be like a cleansing fast." Ashleigh herself had never done a cleansing fast but Blake was always doing them to lose weight.

"Just you and a dozen or so kids on the spectrum?"

It was a secret smile, a knowing smile, and it was all for his own amusement. It pissed her off. Would *no one* take her seriously?

He would. She would make him. "No," she said emphatically. "Me and other NTs." There. She hoped that would show him. She'd only learned the term "NT" last night from the Internet. It stood for "neuro-typical." Did he know that, too? "Other NTs from the club, for starters," she said, when he kept smiling at her, unruffled. "There's a place in the Marin Headlands that's really isolated, the Marin Headlands Nature Center and Retreat. They have accommodations for — "

"I'm familiar with the Center," Mr. Takanawa said. And after a pause, "It's an admirable plan."

Her heart beat a little faster. The MHNCR doubled as a hostel and a place where visitors could explore the surrounding, as yet untouched, flora and fauna of the coast.

"But also very ambitious. You know the Nature Retreat gets booked up very far in advance."

She practically interrupted him, "But probably not over winter break! I mean, I bet not. It's cold and people are going places for Christmas."

"There's also likely to be rain."

"That's why God invented umbrellas." She wasn't usually a smart-aleck. She wouldn't tell him that she'd made a pact with God to help her autistic friends if He wouldn't let it rain.

Mr. Takanawa took a fountain pen from the pencil holder on his desk. The rumor that he was gay was easy for Ashleigh to believe. But if

Mr. Takanawa was gay, why wasn't he out? It was almost cooler to be gay than straight, though the parents hadn't gotten the tweet.

"I don't think a few nature hikes are going to be a cure." He wrote something on the folder on his desk, as if it was the only thing that could keep him from laughing out loud at her.

"Of course not!" How stupid did he think she was? Besides, she didn't want to "cure" Jack. *He* was good without expecting a reward. Like when he wanted to carry her book bag for her, and she let him until she saw how it was dragging him so far to one side that he nearly fell over. So she told him, "My yoga teacher says I need to carry it as part of my practice," even though she hadn't taken yoga for two years now.

She just wanted to help Jack, and the other kids like him, fit in better. Aren't a lot of the things they do, like screaming for no reason, the same as bad habits that a lot of people have, like when she was a kid and used to bite her nails?

"I'm not sure you really know how much work this will involve."

He sounded kinder now.

"Oh, but — " But maybe she didn't.

Mr. Takanawa shook his head. "It'll cost money."

"Everything does."

"Miss Allen, you sound a bit cynical."

"I didn't mean to." That was exactly what she had to stop herself from becoming: cynical.

How could she tell him how much she needs this — needed this more than Jack or Trevor or any of the autistic kids? How much she needed to prove to herself that she was more than something for construction workers to hoot at? Than a photo for a porn site? Than a way for her mother to get in with those "right people"?

Kimberly had a career. *Kimberly* took pride in her success as a realtor. But she must have decided, when Ashleigh turned into a hot teenager, that she was just a dumb redhead who wasn't good for anything except being a rich man's wife.

"Well," Mr. Takanawa sighed, "the money is the hardest part, but there's an awful lot of planning that goes into something like this. You'll need health forms from all the kids who are going. You'll have to bring your own food."

Food? No, she hadn't thought of that. Jesus. Could everyone bring their own — ?

"And you'll need chaperones. Maybe some of the parents — "

The word "parent" was a wasp sting.

"*No*. The last thing we need is the parents." She hated the thought of parents in general and the whole point was to get the kids away from their normal environment.

"Did I say that money would be the hardest part? The chaperones are going to be the hardest part."

"I guess." Whenever he spoke, the self-doubt crept in.

He propped his elbow on his desk and leaned his head against his hand. "Is there anything I can do to talk you out of this?"

I am committed to my plans, I am committed to my plans....

"No."

Mr. Takanawa slipped a stack of papers into his briefcase and closed it gently.

"Well, then, I'll sign on as your faculty sponsor and first chaperone."

Indian summer in San Francisco surprised me every year: Late in October we still had sunny days that were warmer than any single day in August.

That October Saturday we, the New Fab Five, were going to Golden Gate Park for a free concert.

Getting everyone out the door was the usual hassle: Trevor couldn't find the "right" earphones, and Jack was anxious that the timer be set on all three TVs for reruns of Nickelodeon's parade of bizarre animation. (*Invader Zim* was weird, while *Cat Dog* raised troubling questions.)

But eventually we were all outside with the Armstrong family cooler full of sodas and sandwiches. Jason marshaled the boys into a kind of military formation behind him, leading Jack as the green Crime Conqueror Morgan, and Trevor as the blue Crime Conqueror Maxwell, across the desert of the planet Gorgatron. Marissa followed, dragging one foot behind her, when — stupidly, it turned out — I stopped them. "Hang on just a sec?" I asked. "I want to get the mail." I'd finally started paying bills online but I still received them in their dead tree form.

There was a huge pile that day: so much that I needed both hands. I put my purse down on the porch and started shuffling through.

As per: offers for credit cards, the opportunity to borrow money on cards I already had, department store and cable and phone bills (those I plucked out and put in my purse), requests for donations, advertisements for cruises (which I wouldn't have gone on when I was *rich*)....

I heard Jason slam my cargo hold door. I looked up to see that he'd retrieved the basketball he'd been keeping there and started a four-way game of catch. Jason and Trevor were natural athletes, but Marissa was too little to keep up with them and Jack no better than Marissa. Somehow Jason managed to level the playing field, metaphorically as well as literally, catching awkwardly-hurled balls before they hit the ground. *What a mensch,* I thought, and returned to the mail, taking my time now, not wanting to interrupt their game.

Suddenly one of the ads made me stop to look more closely. A weirdly familiar face stared back at me. Then I saw the name to the right of the photo, in big red letters against a white background: KIMBERLY ALLEN. On the left was the name of the brokerage firm, MONTICELLO REALTY. I'd seen their signs around town occasionally, though their logo resembled its namesake in ambience only: It was a generic plantation house with five columns nearly obscuring the façade.

Allen was a common name, but I knew that this woman must be Ashleigh's mother, and the same lady with whom I'd had the very dubious pleasure of speaking on the phone. After that phone call I'd asked Jack about Ashleigh. At first he didn't want to talk about her, but when he did open up it was to show me upwards of twenty pictures of her on his cell phone. She'd posed for most of them, but others appeared to be candid. Jack had the newly-acquired habit of taking people's pictures in public places. So far the worst that had happened was that I had to apologize (profusely) to a large and heavily tattooed bald man who looked as though his picture might already be hanging in a post office. It was handy to have Jason around, in or out of uniform, at such times.

"There ya go, Jack, that's it, just keep your eye on the bouncin' ball...."

Thump.

"You never catch it, Jack," Trevor laughed.

"Trevor," Jason warned.

No one seemed to need me for the moment.

Back at the postcard: To the left of the picture of Kimberly Allen was the picture of a roomy Edwardian home. Photoshopped on top of that was a banner with the word SOLD in red letters.

I turned the card over. How had I gotten on her mailing list? Had Ashleigh given her our address? Was this the beginning of a subtly unnerving campaign to remind me that she was out there, keeping an eye on me and Jack, watching for him to touch her presumably virginal daughter?

You are being totally paranoid, I told myself. It was just a coincidence. I might have gotten cards from her before and just not noticed. I looked over at the foursome once more: Trevor was now too engaged with the game to notice Jack; Jason was lobbing the ball gently so that Marissa could catch it.

I decided to forget about all the mail, including the bills, until Monday.

But when I propped the mailbox lid open with my elbow, planning to stuff it all back in, I saw that there was another sheet of paper, this one white and folded into thirds. I freed one hand by pressing all the other mail against my chest, and pulled it out.

I'd assumed it was a homemade ad for yard work or a housecleaning service; I got them regularly, and always felt a stinging mix of admiration and pity for the struggling entrepreneur behind it.

"Meadowlark Lemon, eat your heart out!" I heard Jason cry.

When I pulled the sheet out I saw that, on the side that had been facing down, ANNA KAGEN was printed in clumsy block letters.

The background noise of Trevor and Jack and Jason and Marissa faded as I read the note inside, also written entirely in crooked capital letters.

YOU AND YOUR RETARDED SON ARE A MENACE TO THE NEIGHBORHOOD. THE NOISES HE MAKES SENDS THE NEIGHBORHOOD CATS INTO HEAT!!! WHY DON'T YOU MOVE SOMEWHERE HE CAN'T HURT ANYONE WITH HIS OFFENSIVE BEHAVIOR?? OR BETTER YET, YOUTHANIZE HIM AND DO THE WHOLE WORLD A FAVOR!!

I folded up the page very slowly. When I looked over at Jason and the kids again, the ground swayed. In the past 60 seconds what had been an advertisement for the joys of family life sponsored by the Church of Latter Day Saints had been nearly blotted out by an unscheduled total eclipse of the sun. I hadn't realized how loud they were being — especially Jack. I wondered who on the street they might be disturbing: who was sleeping in because it was Saturday, or who was just trying to read the paper.

Suddenly Jack whooped. He'd caught the ball.

"Look, Mom!" he cried, holding it over his head.

"Get in the car, everyone!" I tried to make myself heard without raising my voice.

"Mom, I caught — "

"Get in the car!" This time I shouted. I would have plenty of time later to feel ashamed.

Marissa was teed off. The ball game with Jason and Trevor was unfair. They were both almost 10 feet tall, so of course they could catch the ball better! And every time Trevor caught it he whooped, "I rule! Girls drool!" and even though Jason had told him to stop, he kept doing it until Jason put him on a time out.

Trevor was "sexist." Mrs. Persons said that it meant you didn't think girls were as good as boys.

Marissa hadn't wanted to play the dumb game anyway. She had already been upset when she came out of the house, and things hadn't gotten any better, because these days, since there was five of them instead of only three, she had to sit in the third row of seats, all the way back, where you could hardly see out the windows.

They were on their way to the park to listen to some dumb woman sing. They always had to do what the boys and the grown-ups wanted to do. Mommy said their family was a democracy, but a democracy wasn't fair when there was more of them than there was of you. Jason understood this and he didn't always take Trevor's side, the way that Waimea said her dad always took her sister's side just because she was in a wheelchair. You were supposed to treat people with disabilities the same way you treated everyone else. Mrs. Persons explained that if you gave them their way all the time it showed that you felt sorry for them.

So Jason said that they had to let Marissa choose sometimes, but when they did what she wanted the boys complained all the time, so it still wasn't fun like it was in the beginning when Jason and Trevor first came over.

"Jack!" Trevor called out. "*Jack!* I'm going to get really close to the stage. *Really close.* To the stage. The stage."

"Not too near, Buddy. We would've had to sleep in the park to get that close."

"Sleeping in the park would be fun!" Jack said.

Marissa waited for someone to ask her what *she* thought about sleeping in the park, which didn't sound fun at all.

But all this was nothing compared to what happened in the bathroom.

The bathrooms at the park were called port-a-potties and they were more gross even than when Scott Benchley threw up in the hallway at school. So she always went pee right before they left.

She'd always shared that bathroom with Jack. He made a huge awful mess but Mommy always went in right after him and cleaned up.

When Trevor was at her house, he used that same bathroom. Jason cleaned up after him. But since Trevor came along *someone* had been getting sloppier. Marissa found hair in the bathtub drain and lumps of toothpaste on the washcloths.

She complained to Mommy who said, "I'll be more on top of it. You know they can't help it, right?"

They can't help it, they can't help it. Until Trevor it was "*Jack* can't help it." That was bad enough. And Trevor was even sloppier than Jack.

Mommy said she'd be more on top of it, but today when Marissa went into the bathroom she slipped. One second she was walking and the next second she was looking at the light in the ceiling. And her butt hurt really, really bad.

It turned out that there was a wet towel on the floor, a *soaking* wet towel, and Marissa was afraid that there might be Jack's or Trevor's pee on it.

Mommy told Marissa there was no way it could be pee because no one but an elephant could pee that much. Mommy was trying to be funny.

So Marissa stomped her foot and said, "It really hurts, Mommy!"

She showed Mommy the place where she fell. Mommy said it was her tailbone, but that she'd be okay.

Before Jason and Trevor, Mommy would have put Marissa in bed and got her a plate of cookies and read more *By the Shores of Silver Lake.* But today Mommy said that it was just a bruise, though if Marissa didn't feel better later they'd go to the Emergency Room.

The thought of the Emergency Room made Marissa's butt hurt a lot less, but Mommy made everything worse again when she said, "Let's not let it ruin our afternoon."

There was a time when Mommy would have said, "We don't have to go out if you don't feel up to it."

A time before Trevor. A time before Jason.

When they had to get in the car Mommy was really cranky. Marissa asked if they couldn't put her booster seat in one of the pilot seats and make Jack or Trevor sit in the third row and Mommy said, "Please don't give me a hard time. Not today."

That wasn't like Mommy.

Mommy wasn't like that before Trevor. Before Jason.

Trevor and Jack were arguing about what music to play on the radio.

Marissa couldn't take it anymore. Things had to change.

"YOU'RE THE police. Can't you do something about this?" I shouted.

It wasn't fair to be angry at Jason, but I was angry at everything: at the people sitting close to us, who were taking more than their just share of space, at the woman performing, who was screeching like a latter-day Janis Joplin and didn't deserve the adoration that radiated from the audience, and most of all, at the migraine-inducing noise that would have forced me to shout even if I had achieved enlightenment. We were far away from the band stage but there were speakers hidden all around the field, so there was nowhere to hide.

I was also angry with Jason for not noticing how upset I was, though I'd been doing my best to hide it during the inevitable logistical nightmare of driving, parking, walking, and tripping on other people before we could find a tiny patch of grass to call our own.

The boys were standing next to us, facing the stage, and screaming so loudly that I could feel their voices knocking on my eardrums. Both Jack and Trevor clenched their fists tightly while they yelled; then, when they were out of breath, they exchanged glances, half in solidarity and half as challenge, to outdo themselves and each other with the next scream.

Jason removed his sunglasses and pulled up a little closer to the letter I was holding out.

"Well?" I demanded. The letter shook in my hand.

Far more than angry, I was hurt. And scared. What would be waiting for us when we got home? My *nebbish* house tagged with "Aspie Go Home"? A yellow star of David just for history's sake? The house on fire?

"I can't arrest someone for this," Jason said, "even if we did know who wrote it. There's no actual threat and it doesn't rise to the level of hate speech."

The last thing I wanted from him were quotes from the criminal code. "Aren't there clues, like fingerprints, or like ... DNA or something?" I never watched those crime shows that were so popular. I didn't need to see women held prisoner in boxes under beds or dead infants dredged out of New York Harbor.

"It's not that easy, Annie," he said, as if I alone were affected. Trevor was loud, too!

"But who do you think sent it?"

Jason took the letter into his own hands. "I don't know."

I fumed silently.

He had put his sunglasses back on and now he looked at me over the rims. "You know that I'm on your side, right?" he asked quietly.

The concert in the park was awesome. The sound hurt his ears so that he couldn't hear the music, or anything else, but he was having fun.

The only thing that could make this day better would be if Ashleigh were with them. He'd tried to get Trevor to talk about girls some more but the conversation always turned out to be about Miley Cyrus again.

He had a new good memory now, though: He gave Ashleigh candy. He bought it at the 24/7. There was a man who worked there named Mohammed who always gave him free slushies.

Jack had eaten some of the candy before he gave it to her, but there was still a lot left. He kept it in the same bag that Mohammed gave it to him in. It was true that there was a black spot on the side of the bag. He only noticed it because Ashleigh ran her hand over it, and when she did, he wondered if he should have put it in something else.

She put it in her book bag and said she'd eat it later. She also said that it was the best gift she ever had, and he believed her.

But anyone could buy candy. He really wanted that driver's license. Trevor kept talking about the red sports car that *his* dad was going to buy him. Jack saw a commercial back on August 24th where a man and his girlfriend were driving in a red car with the top down, and the girl's hair was all messed up in the wind. He couldn't see the faces but that was all the better for imagining himself at the wheel with Ashleigh at his side.

Jason did go door-to-door that night, in uniform, displaying the letter and asking for help, while looking for any "tells" of guilt.

Before Jason had come into our lives, I hadn't been friends with any of our neighbors, beyond a nod and a hello, the latter more a mumble than a greeting. On the day that I moved in, Jack had had a full-blown Trevor-size tantrum on the sidewalk. It was a weekday and many of the residents were at day jobs, but I saw more than one woman peeking out from a crack in her drapes. Another woman came to offer help, but there was nothing for her to do.

That wasn't the only time the neighbors had an opportunity to see Jack thrashing on the ground, while at other times he displayed less disruptive but equally odd behavior.

So I was self-conscious, and shy, around my fellow Highland Street residents, even after Jack not only outgrew his tantrums but made his own attempts to be friendly, and Marissa turned into Little Miss Sunshine, eager to show off how polite and articulate she was.

Then along came Jason, Jason Big and Tall, with the outgoing smile and the handcuffs on his belt. With one arm around my shoulder and his free hand waving, he introduced me and then himself to the Kapjians, with their twin teenage daughters, and the Campbell-Carsons who were both nurses at SF General, and Robbie the Reclusive Retiree.

Now we were all pals and it was a good feeling — or at least it had been.

When Jason returned home that evening I asked him specifically about the family — I'd forgotten their names — with the teenage son who went to Lick-Wilmerding, the most exclusive private school in the city. They lived around the corner but I sometimes saw the son tooling down the street on his bike with the orange flames painted on it.

They were the Van Ambergs, Jason reminded me, and they knew nothing. Neither did the Carrs, or the Nzeogwu-Okafors, a gay couple who had just adopted twins of their own, or the Wongs or Huangs, or Isabella Ortega, whose family had been in San Francisco since it was called Yerba Buena by the first Spanish settlers.

We made love that night and during the time we spent in each other's arms I forgot the letter.

CHAPTER 10

I was awakened by the slamming of the front door, a noise so sudden and loud that I sat up clutching my chest.

"Anyone home?"

Alex.

It was Sunday morning and Jason was asleep beside me.

"For God's sake," I whispered to the back of Jason's head, "it's 8 a.m."

Then I heard Marissa's voice, "Hi, Daddy!"

She must have rushed out to greet him.

"Is your mom here?" I heard Alex ask. "Heh-heh-heh. She must be here. She wouldn't leave you alone, would she?"

Marissa giggled. I pictured Alex tickling her.

"Eight a.m.?" Jason yawned and stretched. "Shouldn't The Enforcer be at work by now?"

I didn't answer because I was eavesdropping on Alex outside my door: "I had a flash of insight on the way to work this morning. Why don't you bring some of your stuffed animals to my house, so they'll always be there for you?"

"Not HannahSophia."

"No, of course not HannahSophia. But you have so many. That I bought you."

I jumped out of bed. I had no robe, no slippers, and I was wearing a t-shirt with plaid pajama bottoms. To be fair, the pajama bottoms tied with a pink satin ribbon. To be extremely fair, my costume made me appear as though I were half of a real couple, not a woman who had just entertained a one night stand.

"Mommy, Daddy wants to take some of my stuffies to his house."

"Maybe some extra clothes," Alex said.

I pulled my pink ribbon-belt tighter. "Why would she need extra clothes?"

"I think she'll feel more comfortable. You never know where or when ice cream might melt, do you, Wissy? Why don't you grab a few things for me to take with me now?"

"Keep it down, now," I warned her, being as quiet as I could myself. I didn't want her to wake the boys, though I doubted she would even if she broke out into the Hallelujah chorus, the way they slept —

once they did sleep, anyway. (We hadn't had a repeat of their midnight foray to the convenience store.) And I guessed that Jason, once he heard Alex's voice, would stay in our room. He was a peace officer, after all.

The moment Marissa turned into her room, Alex growled, "So, he's staying the night, is he?"

"That's none of your business," I retorted, then — damn! Alex hadn't known that either Jason or Trevor were here. I'd given it away with my answer. "It's time for you to give me my keys back," I declared, extending my cupped palm, "since you can't stick to our agreement."

Alex jammed a hand into his pocket. But left it there. "Just what kind of example do you think you're setting for your daughter?"

"Did I miss it when you turned your house into a monastery? You have women over!"

"Not when she's there." Alex's greatest weapon was his ability to keep his temper. No matter how calm I remained — not that I was calm at the moment — I appeared hysterical by comparison.

"I happen to know that he's been sleeping here since September. Marissa is very upset about it."

"He has *not* been sleeping here since September!"

"Can you try to control yourself?"

I remembered why I was so against having Jason bringing his service revolver into the house.

"I can sue you for custody over this," Alex said matter-of-factly.

"The hell you can." Alex getting custody of a child because his ex-wife from five years before had a boyfriend was ludicrous — except that this was Alex, San Francisco's answer to Boss Tweed. "And you do so have women sleep over! Do you think you've made me such a pariah that none of our old so-called 'friends' will even talk to me? Let me tell you, dear, they come running to me to tell me about all your amorous adventures." Let him deny those "amorous adventures." I'd always suspected those reports were greatly exaggerated.

His shoulders, starting to hunch ever-so-slightly, shoved themselves six inches back. "I have never had a female guest when Marissa or Jack are in my house."

"Well, we know you haven't had one with Jack in the house," I retorted. "You haven't had Jack in the house at all for a year. So you do the math."

He skipped the math.

"You're a tramp," he announced.

Behind me I heard the rattle of the doorknob I'd closed behind me. I knew *he* was coming. My breath came fast. Alex's composure, so solid a moment ago, suddenly seemed brittle.

Thud, squish. Thud.

No bare feet here. This was the sound of boots in the jungle.

I turned. Jason was in a white undershirt, sweat pants, and those ugly black policeman shoes. They weren't exactly jack boots, and you can be only so intimidating in sweat pants — nevertheless, his weather-exposed face and large shoulder muscles bespoke someone who subscribed to *Soldier of Fortune.*

Alex clenched and unclenched his fists.

"How're ya doin' Alex?" Jason asked, his words half-swallowed by a yawn. At the same time he dropped his arm lightly around my shoulder. He must not have heard Alex's final words, or he certainly would have come out with that weapon I'd been looking for a minute earlier.

"Not well," Alex growled.

"Really? It's such a beautiful day. We've got to get out soon, don't we, Annie?"

"Uhh…."

"I don't like what you're doing here, Armstrong."

"You've got it all wrong." Jason took my hand with his free one, laced his fingers into mine, and smiled — yes, beatifically. "This isn't some sleazy one-night stand. We're like the Brady Bunch here." Looking straight into my eyes he began to sing, "It's the story of a love-ly la-dee…." Then, mangling the phrasing, "and a policeman busy with a kid … of his ow-own…."

"The Brady Bunch weren't shacking up." Alex squinted at Jason, calculating what favor he could trade in exchange for getting Jason's name on the next round of police lay-offs.

"Nooo," Jason began, but he didn't sound so pleasant now and an alarm bell went off in my brain.

"We aren't shacking up either!" I announced. "We're getting married."

Jason gave my hand a short, very tight squeeze. "That's right," he said thickly, and I felt happy and terrified at the same moment, the way people who ride roller coasters must feel as the car climbs at almost 90 degrees to the top.

"You are," Alex said.

"Yes. Soon." Jason squeezed my hand again.

I hoped he wouldn't say anything about Jewish ministers.

Marissa came to the rescue, skipping from her room, her arms in front of her chest, enclosing several second tier stuffies. "Here, Daddy." She glanced at me ever-so-quickly and I wondered if she'd heard me announce my marriage plans.

Alex took lions and tigers and bears into his arms. "Why don't you come help me put them in the car? To make sure they're comfortable."

"Put some shoes on," I said, happy that I'd thought of it first.

The moment Alex and Marissa got outside, Jason hugged me. "Whatever it takes," he said in my ear, "to get you to say yes."

The roller coaster car plunged.

The first time Jason had said "marry me," I'd thought he was kidding, or at most, that it was the impulse of a man who saw a way to get laid regularly. But he'd reminded me of the proposal twice more in the weeks that followed.

Jason was not Val, the man who had hurt me those many years ago. While hardly noticing, over the past months I'd moved the "Val" file farther and farther back in the Drawer of Pain, so that I came across it rarely.

But the more secure I felt with Jason, the more urgently the practical aspects pressed themselves on me: If we married, would we all live in my house, which felt cramped with the three Kagens, and downright claustrophobic when Jason and Trevor were over? The two of them took so much *space*. With Jason it was only physical space, but with Trevor it was psychological space: He encouraged Jack to even louder "laughter" and more than doubled the mess: Just last weekend Trevor had had a nosebleed and left a pool of blood at the bottom of the kitchen sink. I was monstrously grateful that I'd been able to clean it up before Marissa saw it. What I couldn't hide from her were his full-scale tantrums.

"Why don't we talk about dates?" Jason said. "Let's try to do it before the Christmas craziness."

Oh, shit. Christmas. "I don't really celebrate Christmas," I said, even while knowing what a buzzkill that would be.

"Why not? It's a national holiday. It's for everyone."

I looked into his weather-beaten face and at his crooked nose and couldn't get mad at him, though I could feel how I was trying my best to find fault.

"Jack and Marissa would love it," he promised.

My heart split in two, thinking of how they *would* enjoy it, how Marissa had pouted the two previous years when I wouldn't get them a tree. But my mother, who hadn't been inside a synagogue since I was a baby, drew the line at putting up Christmas decorations.

"Let's not worry about that yet," I said.

He was running his hands up and down my arms, and now I was thinking how sweet he was, how modest, how affectionate toward Jack, and how — especially as his hands moved more slowly down my arms — how much more natural our sex life had become. Even better than sex (for me) was lying in bed with him, someone I actually liked, his arms around me while I made a cave out of his arms and his big, hard chest.

Still. "We just made it official. Why don't we wait to check with the kids' calendars." I added cunningly, "We don't want to pick a date and then find out that Trevor has a race that day." Trevor's races were always on Saturdays, and Jewish weddings were never on Saturdays, but I had a feeling that Jason wouldn't know that.

"Shit. You're right. Let's at least tell the kids, though."

I held him at arm's length. "Have you thought that they might not be happy about it?"

"Why wouldn't they be happy?" One corner of his mouth turned up. Then he continued the Brady Bunch theme song: "That this group must somehow form a fam-i-ly."

"You have a haunting baritone. Like Len Cariou on the original cast album of *Sweeney Todd.*"

"And to think I gave up show biz for law enforcement."

"Let's wait a day on the kids."

"Why?" He stopped moving his hands. "You weren't lying when you said we were engaged, were you?"

"Of course not!" I protested.

Alex and Marissa re-entered, hand-in-hand and both smiling. Any remaining fears I had about marrying Jason were swept away by the far greater, though nameless, dread that engulfed me at that moment.

"I'm going to move in with Daddy!" Marissa announced.

A few hours later I left Jason and the boys watching football. They were a picture of Norman Rockwell male bonding, circa 2009: popcorn everywhere and the television almost as loud as their shouting.

Marissa was playing with HannahSophia in her room. "Tomorrow I'll see Emma at school," I heard her say as I passed.

Alex had agreed to meet me at my own local Starbucks. He was coming to gloat.

I was coming to beg.

Starbucks was entertaining the usual Sunday afternoon crowd: men in t-shirts with two day's growth of beard at their MacBookPros, and young mothers with double strollers.

I arrived before Alex, which gave me time to stoke my optimism with half of a venti mocha.

"You drink too much coffee," was how Alex greeted me.

"You eat too many carbs." It slipped out. "I'm just kidding, dear. Let's talk about this calmly." I squeezed my cup, causing the remaining gray liquid to slosh. "Neither of you really know what you're getting into." The venti had done its work. "Marissa worships you, we both know that — " I was perfectly happy to kiss his ass if that would help my case — "but she sees you on weekends and special occasions and she's going to expect every day to be a holiday. You know, hot fudge sundaes...."

The only two things that Alex and I actually had in common were our love for ice cream and See's candy.

"Disney on Ice...." Alex had never taken her to Disney on Ice. "She'll expect to eat dinner out every night — and I know you want her to eat a healthy diet."

"That's true." Alex looked past me to the pastries in the case. "Now I'll be able to make sure she gets it."

Alex had never acknowledged his formula to himself: *I* was the one who was supposed to provide the healthy diet so that he could guiltlessly ply her with garbage when he had her to himself.

No use telling him that he'd have to be the "bad cop" now, especially since it would give him an opening to say something snarky about Jason. *My fiancé.* I allowed myself the first real moment of pleasure at the title.

But only a moment.

"I'm thinking of you, too, Alex." I called on all my powers of self-delusion to make myself believe it. "You see her when she's in a good mood and rested and eager to please. You don't see her when she's too tired to want to go to bed or doesn't want to take a bath — "

"That's her way of acting out with you," Alex explained.

" — or do her homework — "

Alex interrupted me again, this time with a derisive snort before I finished the "H" word. "Of course she doesn't want to do her homework. She feels guilty about surpassing her brother and now there's — "

He cleared his throat suddenly, thus leaving unsaid any unkind remark concerning Trevor. That was luck for both of us, because I would have thrown what remained of my venti in his stony face. We could discuss Jack's limitations dispassionately: he was *our* son. For the moment, Trevor was off-limits.

"Look." It was time to be more direct. "She's going to want you to read to her. She's going to want you to *play* with her, for God's sake. Are you going to get down on the floor and have a tea party with HannahSophia? There are some things you can't delegate to a nanny."

His response: "You managed to do it with Jack."

The background noise of hissing espresso machines and one-sided cell phone conversations, which had dipped below the level of my consciousness, rose to a roar.

That's what I did. I let the nanny take over.

The nanny was Mairead, an Irishwoman of phenomenal ability who had helped me raise Jack without killing him and/or myself.

Alex's face was as expressionless as ever but I could hear him thinking, "checkmate."

CHAPTER 11

Marissa was not with us for dinner that night so when Trevor announced, "I want Marissa's room. *Marissa's room*," I froze with a dripping forkful of Jason's spaghetti halfway to my mouth

"We'll talk about it later, Buddy," Jason said in a very policeman-like voice.

"But I want — "

"Wait until you hear this story!" Jason boomed. "I was down at the Embarcadero today and guess what? Some guy put on a white coat with his name embroidered on it — " he drew a circle over his heart — "and started parking people's cars for them."

"But — "

"Later, Buddy. He'd take their keys and drive the cars into the Financial District then come back for more."

I laughed. On an ordinary evening it would have been a real laugh.

In bed that night Jason assured me, "Of course Trevor's not taking Marissa's room."

"No, but...." I stopped for fear of revealing the extent of my self-pity. Each time I passed Marissa's room, while Trevor and Jack were next door, quarreling over which Game Boy to play, the sight would re-open the same wound. For now, the Armstrong men only spent the night on weekends but once they were here fulltime....

"Besides I have an engagement present for you."

I sighed. "I wish you wouldn't spend money on — "

"You'll be surprised how little this will cost."

"So you don't have it yet." I sounded ungrateful, and hated myself for it. This was not turning out to be a good day for my self-esteem.

"No, and it's not something I can wrap, either."

"If it's a three-way with my sister, you can forget it."

"Annie, don't talk like that."

He paused so I could feel the shame, but he rescued me quickly.

"I'm going to build us a third bedroom."

"What?"

"A third bedroom. I've been taking measurements. There's plenty of room to put a third bedroom in the basement. It'll be a little small — "

"Can you *do* something like that?"

He propped himself on one elbow. "I would have thought that by now you'd appreciate the full extent of the talent of these hands."

He drew a line from my breasts down my stomach.

"I'm beginning to," I said.

Whatever (deeply) hidden good qualities Kimberly Allen might have had, timing was not one. The very next morning she invited me over for a "coop off tea" — her faux British accent having descended a couple of rungs on the class ladder.

My first and passionate instinct was to say no, and without further explanation.

Still no clue as to the author of the nasty letter. I didn't dwell on it except when I had to pick up the mail: I seized up until I'd shuffled through the stack and assured myself that it was just the usual waste of trees.

Neither did I receive any more postcards with Kimberly Allen's face on them, but I was feeling paranoid about her nonetheless. Just a few days after that one first postcard, when I was at the grocery store, I'd looked down and been horrified to see Kimberly's face staring back at me. It was on an insert in the fold-out kid seat of the grocery cart.

I had never registered that the shopping carts had advertisements on them. But in fact, they were covered in advertisements. It was one of those things that once you do notice, you wonder why you didn't before. I was sure that I wouldn't have noticed it that day either, except that I recognized Kimberly from the postcard that had arrived in the mail on the same day as the hand-written letter.

The shopping cart ad was different from the postcard: To the right of her picture was the logo of her real estate company, Monticello, and below that, in quotation marks, "This is the only time I get pushed around."

An encouraging message to her clients, I supposed, but I wasn't a client.

"I said yes," I told Jason after I received Kimberly's invitation. I was scrubbing a saucepan: Jack and Trevor had been experimenting with making s'mores. "But I can call her back and change my mind. I've got enough to worry about with getting Marissa ready to move." I scrubbed harder.

"Let me do that."

"Okay." I handed it to him. "You're stronger than I am," I added, so it wouldn't just be laziness on my part.

"Did she say why she wanted you to come over?"

"She said she wanted my help with something."

"Well...."

I knew what he was leading up to. Jason had told me more than occasionally, though gently, that I didn't give people the benefit of the doubt often enough. "You assume they don't like you. You assume they're going to be mean. Try it the other way," he had said.

"And if you see someone running out of a liquor store at 3 a.m. wearing a ski mask and carrying a large green garbage bag, do you give him the benefit of the doubt?"

"Or her."

"Or her."

"Of course I would. I'd stop her and talk to her with a completely open mind." He applied the Brillo pad with additional force.

"She did sound propitiatory," I said. "I mean, you know, like she wanted to make up."

Kimberly had in fact sounded very different from the angry woman with whom I'd spoken early in the school year. This time around she had made a couple of references to Ashleigh's time with Jack in a way that implied that she was no longer disturbed by their friendship.

Jason held the saucepan up to the light from the window. "Annie, honey, I think this is ruined."

"It could be worse," I said. "They could have been cooking meth."

"That's my girl." He kissed me on the neck. "Always think positive."

I was already on my way when Kimberly called me on my cell. "You won't believe what happened."

"Try me."

"I forgot that my open house was starting at noon instead of one this afternoon! There's been so much interest in this home — a contemporary classic on a traditional street. Can you meet me thair?"

"I'll meet you *thair* if you tell me *whair*." I imitated her. *Keep an open mind,* I admonished myself. *Like you promised Jason you would.*

"I'm so looking forward to seeing you," she said. Then she gave me an address in St. Francis Woods, a neighborhood of narrow streets that was one of the priciest in the city.

Exclusive neighborhood or no, as the first decade of the 21st Century came to a close, there were few places where you were more welcome than at an open house. The Great Recession had hit bottom, and home prices in San Francisco had dipped at much as 25%.

No matter the discount, the first thing I thought when I saw the house was, *this is going to be one tough mother-fucker to unload.* It was a glaring white, as in white elephant, with ridiculous Corinthian pillars framing the entryway and a three-car side-by-side garage at the top of the driveway.

Perhaps Kimberly wished to intimidate me. *Look at me, successful single parent with a job!* I wasn't going to let it work. I threw my shoulders back (which threw my bosom forward), and climbed up the drive.

At the door, though, Kimberly's evil scheme almost took hold. Both sides of the double front doors were open but people were squeezing to get through: middle-aged men with millennial-aged wives; late twenties couples (men with women, women with women, and men with men) wearing jeans stamped with designer names above the derriere pockets, and a multitude of strollers, many of them double strollers to accommodate the exploding twin population.

The doors may have been open, but when I saw the crowd, my mind slammed shut.

But…. But maybe she wasn't trying to intimidate me. Maybe she was trying to *impress* me. Maybe she thought I would be good for wealthy referrals; she might not realize how far out of the society loop the centrifugal force of separation from Alex had thrown me.

Maybe my reputation as stylish dresser had spread and she wanted me to be her personal shopper. Or join her in her real estate business.

Maybe I'd finally lost my reason completely.

"You're blocking the doorvay!"

It was a stout woman in a navy dress, a little tight in the waist, plain enough to look like a uniform. She thrust a flyer in my hand and commanded, "Take von."

German accents made me nervous in the same way that policemen did. For policemen still did, unless Jason was around, even though I'd met many of his buddies and most were friendly and clearly good people. Most of all, I was impressed with their strong loyalty to one another. There were a few, though, who seemed tense, as if a sniper might have them in his sights, and the only way to relieve that tension would be to find someone who deserved to be thrown as roughly as possible into the back seat of a cruiser. Or worse.

"Move on," the woman in navy ordered, and I obeyed.

"Will you sign the guestbook please?"

This dulcet request came from a snub-nosed twenty-year-old with wispy blonde hair and a skim-milk complexion. She sat behind a writing desk with spindly legs and marquetry trim that belonged in design, if not in reality, to an Empire or Louis. In the corner, a single lily tilted over the top of a tall, slim vase.

"I'm just here to see Kimberly," I begged off, seized with paranoia about committing my name to print.

"Please. Ms. Allen would appreciate it."

She handed me a white pen with the logo of Monticello Realty. It triggered memories of the postcard and the shopping carts.

I signed the book, "Emma Goldman."

"Your e-mail, Ms. Goldman?"

"Sure." I wrote EMMA4U@GMAIL.COM. I was so edgy that when I noticed a plate of butter cookies next to the guest book my stomach lurched. "Where can I find her? Kimberly?"

"She's everywhere at once." The girl's eyes were wide. "Is she a force of nature or what?"

"Hurricane Kimberly! That's her."

"I think she might be on the lower level."

In the Realtor Universe there are no basements, only lower levels.

At that moment I heard the slapping of feet coming upstairs. A white-painted door was flung open and Kimberly emerged. "You just don't see that in the city, do you?"

The couple behind her looked dazed, blinking in what may have been the sudden light, but otherwise my eyes were fixed on Kimberly. This was the first time I'd seen her *punim*-a-*punim*. The effect was very different from that of her headshot. She was beautiful in the way of such 21st Century ideals as Nicole Kidman or Gwyneth Paltrow, with small, slightly angular features. A nose not found in nature.

At the sight of her I thought of other reasons she couldn't talk to me on the phone. Ashleigh had run away, but Jack knew where she was. Jack was sexting Ashleigh. Jack was turning into a werewolf at the full moon. Ashleigh was pregnant and she and Kimberly were going to put the blame on Jack.

I wish.

"The floor plan on the upper level is very versatile," Kimberly was saying. "You could have five bedrooms, or four bedrooms and a home office, or three bedrooms and a home office and a second guest bedroom, or — "

Then she saw me. "You are Anna Kagen! I know it. And don't you look lovely! Thanks for being so flexible. Let's — what's that word? — smooze."

"*Sch*mooze," I corrected her.

"Oh, ha ha." I recognized her wind-chime laugh from our phone conversation. "I thought it came from the word 'smoothie,' like to 'smooth' things over.' " She put air quotes around the word "smooth."

"I have a couple who wants to see the upstairs!" The woman in navy made it sound like an order.

"It's okay, Magda, why don't you show them?"

Magda *hmmph'd.*

"We'll go in the kitchen. I wasn't expecting such a turn-out! Lily, can you hold down the 'fort' for few minutes?" Again she used air quotes, this time for "fort."

For a moment I wondered if Kimberly were talking to the flower, but the girl behind the desk fairly squealed, "Oh, if you'll trust me with that!"

Kimberly motioned me to follow her with a crooked finger. I was a little calmer now: calm enough, at least, to study her outfit from behind. She wore a tight-fitting jumpsuit in crinkly gold taffeta, as though she had just returned from the International Saks Fifth Avenue Space Station.

The long, narrow kitchen provided a cramped alcove with a round smoked-glass table with four elaborate place settings: bone china with a black-and-white op art pattern, sterling silver utensils and crystal glasses. It made me ashamed of my melamine plates and plastic tumblers, and angry that it made me ashamed.

"You like espresso concoctions, I understand." Kimberly seemed delighted with her inside track.

"How did you know that?" A little of my paranoia returned.

"Because it's my business to know what people need. And one of my clients just gave me the LaserCaff 5000. It's from Europe — it has the same engine as the Mercedes."

"German engineering at its finest." There was a theme here. "How could I say no to that?"

Just at that moment, Magda stomped in on black clogs. "Zey say that the master suite is too small."

Kimberly sighed. "Some people are hard to please, aren't they? Magda, will you bring us the cookies from Lily's table out front?"

Magda put her hands on her hips. "Those cookies are stale now," she said.

"St. Francis Bakery will deliver more," Kimberly reassured her. "Do you mind giving them a call? But the ones out front will be fine until then."

"Please don't bother." I didn't want to feel any obligation to stay, but Magda had already *hmmph'd* out again.

"Oh, look it's ready!"

Kimberly slapped two cups on the table. The cappuccino looked watery but I was ready for a fix. "You said you had a problem I could help you with."

"Well, yes." Kimberly pulled her chair in. "By the way, have you seen the art show on Maiden Lane by that darling autistic girl?"

I managed to swallow. "Have you?"

"No, but I'm going next week. Perhaps we could go together, if you have time?"

I wasn't sure how to answer. Was it possible that Jason was right? Was it possible that Kimberly had spent some time with Jack and warmed to him? I *did* want to see the art show. I'd been planning to go alone since Jason wasn't big on museums. He was interested in this exhibit, but was willing to wait until he could view the paintings on the Internet.

I sipped cappuccino to postpone answering. Kimberly had done nothing but be sweet since I arrived. I had just assumed it was an act. Maybe, just maybe, underneath that crinkly jumpsuit was a woman I could be friends with. I didn't have many friends, and the problem went deeper than Jason knew.

It turned out that I didn't have to answer, because Kimberly leaned forward and said in a low voice, "I hope you take heart from this girl — the artist? Your son — he could be another Bill Gates."

I sighed. There was a persistent rumor on the Internet, and among Aspie parents, that Bill Gates was actually autistic. To me, the notion was ludicrous, but also sad: It was the last ephemeral hope of a mother or father on the floor, trying to get his or her child to "touch the blue car."

But Kimberly was looking at me expectantly. Other moms of Asperger's kids had given me that same look. *Another Bill Gates, another Temple Grandin.* I couldn't expect Kimberly to know more than they did. And it seemed as though she *was* trying to connect in her own patronizing way.

Magda plunked the plate of cookies between us. "Klaus says zey are out."

"Aw, really?" Kimberly put her hand on Magda's arm. "Did you tell him it was for me?"

"He's sending the *liebe Scholokade.*"

"Good." Kimberly picked up a cookie, examined it from several angles, then put it back on the plate. "You know — " she leaned forward to deliver another confidence — "Jack has been good for Ashleigh. He's helped her expand her horizons. She was confining herself to her studies. Now, she's brilliant — " Kimberly adopted a British accent again, but for some reason it didn't sound as phony this time around — "so she doesn't even need to study that hard to get into an Ivy League school. To tell you the truth…. Well, I know that Ashleigh has her eye on Cornell, or maybe Harvard, but Anna, in all sincerity, those things aren't important to me. *I* went to a Seven Sisters school — "

"Really? Which one?"

"Oh, you know, the one in Pennsylvania."

"You mean Bryn Mawr?"

"That's it. But I want her to be a com*plete* person. A good, loving person. And Jack has helped her with that. He's inspired her to focus on the less fortunate. Before him…."

Magda returned, this time with a couple who wanted to see the double oven. Kimberly was up like a Jack in the Box, describing not only the double oven (two more ovens than anyone needed, *IMHO*), and pointing out features on kitchen appliances that I'd never heard of.

I absently chose a cookie and nibbled at the edge. I didn't like Kimberly's condescension, but for once I was trying to put that aside. As for bragging about Ashleigh, hadn't I been guilty of that, when Marissa walked at ten months, said her first sentence at fourteen months? And now I'd told plenty of people that she'd skipped kindergarten.

And was I to go through life expecting everyone to consider my feelings as the mother of a disabled son, tiptoeing around me like a live grenade?

I took a much larger bite of my cookie. It certainly didn't taste stale to me: It was all butter and sugar, with just enough flour to hold it together.

Kimberly had her attention back on me. She tasted her own cookie and wrinkled her nose. "You are not leaving 'til you get one of the *liebe Scholokade.* Fresh. Now, let me ask you something. Is Jack really ready to be away from home?"

"He's been away before," I said.

"Really!" Kimberly clapped twice. "Good for him! Where? How long?"

Jack had only ever been to Disneyland with Alex. The other times he had traveled outside of San Francisco had been to see specialists when we were looking for a diagnosis.

"Oh, gosh." I waved my hand. "I can't think of them all right now. Why do you ask?"

"Because I'm concerned. I don't know if 'this trip' " — "this trip" in air quotes — "is right for him."

This trip. I put my cookie down. "What trip is that?"

"Don't tell me you don't know!"

"Mmm," I said evasively.

"My Lord!" Kimberly raised her head to the ceiling. "Why, these teachers have the most bizarre thing planned. They're going to take all the, um — they're going to take a wide variety of kids out into the middle of nowhere and leave them on their own. It's some kind of survival test."

I almost laughed. "You make it sound like *Lord of the Flies.* It's just a couple of nights at a hostel in Marin Headlands — "

"But it's going to be dangerous, isn't it? There's poison oak, there are poisonous — "

"Oh, for God's — " But I stopped. *Give peace a chance.* "I know they've been calling it a 'camping trip' " — I made my own air quotes, curling my fingers deeply — "but that's a misnomer. They're going to be sleeping indoors in a building with plumbing and a fully-equipped kitchen. I've seen it. I was there when — "

"No!" Kimberly looked panicked. "I know I can trust Jack with Ashleigh, but...."

"But — ?" I prompted.

Kimberly delicately plucked a crumb from among the crinkles in her jumpsuit. "But Ashleigh doesn't realize how attractive she is and...." She trailed off, seemingly preoccupied with finding more crumbs.

"Yes?" I tried to slip into therapist mode, but it had been a long time and it was a bit like riding a unicycle.

"Ashleigh and I are very close," Kimberly said finally. "When her father died I made a commitment, right then, that I would remain single until she was eighteen. Not even dating."

"That's a very serious commitment," I observed.

She spun her empty cup by flicking her finger against the handle. "I know not everyone has the sense of self necessary for it."

I imagined Kimberly saying aloud, *You didn't have the sense of self to put your own daughter first and now you're losing her.*

Lily dashed in at that moment, her pale skin flushed, and her fingers gripping the roots of her hair as if about to pull it out. "Kimberly? There's a couple here who says that the sun will come in through the second-floor skylight — "

"That is what skylights are for, yes."

"But the husband says that in the winter, when the sun is in the south? That it will shine right on his computer monitor late in the day?"

Without looking up, Kimberly took a second bite of her own cookie. "Tell him...." She pondered as she chewed. "Tell him that the sellers consulted with a prominent astronomer before installing the skylight."

"But — " Lily looked terrified. "Doesn't the sun set in the west?"

Kimberly's annoyance showed in the appearance of tendons in her neck. "Just tell him what I said."

"Yes, Ma'am."

The honorific "Ma'am" caused the tendons to pop out farther, but Lily was already gone. Kimberly dropped the cookie. "These *are* stale," she said in disgust.

I struggled to retain the impassive façade of the all-accepting shrink while I imagined putting air quotes around the word "strangle" in "I'm going to 'strangle' you."

"So you see," she went on, "since I've created this rather *shaltered* environment for her...."

"Yes...?" I prompted again.

Suddenly Kimberly looked up, wild-eyed, and exclaimed, "She has no idea what men are like! She's too young to understand. She thinks you can be yourself with them and nothing will happen. But they can't control themselves, so you have to control them *for* themselves. They're animals! They have one head and it isn't on their shoulders."

She pounded the table with the heel of her hand. The cups rattled in their saucers, and I jumped an inch backward in my chair. Still attempting to sound shrink-like, I asked, "Have you discussed your concerns with Ashleigh?"

It took Kimberly a moment to compose herself enough to speak, and the tendons in her neck bespoke the effort. "I *said* that I'm not worried about Jack. It's that some of those boys ... well, you know," she repeated.

"Pretend I don't."

"You know that some of those boys don't know right from wrong!" She pounded the table again. "If normal boys — boys from good families — can't control themselves, then how can — how can — "

"Differently-abled is the word you're looking for."

"And that boy you know — what's his name, the runner?"

"Trevor."

"He's the size of a gorilla! Ashleigh wouldn't stand a chance against him. Anna, I'm thinking of your boy, too. Jack wouldn't stand a chance either, if that was the boy's ... uh...."

"Proclivity might the word in this case." Had I really been thinking of this woman as a friend a few minutes before? I looked at my watch. "It's been real, Kim, but I'm half an hour late for an appointment to donate a kidney."

"You've got to help me!"

I had an inspiration. "Why don't you talk to Trevor's Coach? David Takanawa. He knows Trevor well, and he might be able to reassure you...."

"Takanawa! Is he the same irresponsible — is he the same Takanawa-teacher who's behind all this?"

"Well, they might be identical twins."

Kimberly stood, suddenly eerily self-possessed. In an almost believable British accent she said, "I will talk to him. I know how to protect my dawghter, and exposing her to sex is hahdly the way."

I winced, but otherwise remained calm.

"I doon't like to do it this way, Anna. But we all have to be true to ourselves."

"Indeed we do, Kimberly." I reached for my purse. "Indeed we do."

Jack stopped at the doorway of Marissa's room as soon as he saw his Mom there. She was helping Marissa pack to move in with Dad.

He didn't think this would really happen. "You can't go!" he cried.

Marissa was jumping on her bed. She didn't hear him. Neither did Mom. Either that or they were both ignoring him.

"Why don't you leave your Barbies here?" Mom asked.

"But I might want them!"

"They'll be safe here."

If Marissa left then they couldn't all be the *Drake and Josh* family, with him as Drake and Trevor as Josh and Marissa as Megan. Megan was really Drake's sister, but they never talked about whose sister she really was, because they were a family.

It wasn't just because they needed to be Drake and Josh that Jack didn't want Marissa to go, but he didn't know another way to describe his feeling about how her room was going to be empty. The problem wasn't that English had too many words, it was that English didn't have *enough* words. He loved Marissa but he also loved root beer, and how was that the same thing?

He had to think of a way to keep her at home. Maybe Trevor could help him.

Mom was looking in one of Marissa's drawers. "You'll need more underwear." Then she went on in that growly voice that she used to talk about Dad, "I can just picture your father in the girls' underwear department." She didn't think anyone else could hear her, but Jack did.

"You can't let Jack or Trevor in my room when I'm at Daddy's," Marissa said.

"Of course not!" Mom said. "You need this room for when you come back to visit."

"I probably won't," Marissa said. "You come visit me. Just you."

"Like I'd set foot in that Museum of the Damned," Mom said in the growly voice again. "But what about Thanksgiving? You have to come back for — "

"Thanksgiving!" said Jack as loud as he could, to make sure they paid attention. "We'll have the best Thanksgiving ever! Turkey and cranberry sauce and gravy and mashed potatoes and stuffing and...." That was all he could think of for now. However many things "love" meant, Jack knew he loved the holidays. On Halloween he was the red Crime Conqueror and Trevor was a policeman, wearing one of Jason's old uniforms. Trevor and Jason had a fight because Trevor wanted to carry a gun and Jason said no way was that going to happen ever.

They had fun trick-or-treating, but Mom said this was the last year because they were getting too old; she said they could go out and act like they were babysitting Marissa, who dressed up like a lawyer. Mom put her in Jack's own suit, the one he had when he was a little boy, and gave her one of her own big purses and said that that was Marissa's briefcase.

"We can't have Thanksgiving without you!" Jack persisted. "There has to be five of us!"

"No, there doesn't," Marissa corrected him. "Daddy might take me to Disneyland for Thanksgiving."

Disneyland. Another thing Jack loved was Disneyland. Dad would never take Marissa to Disneyland without him ... would he?

When Dad started spending all this extra time with Marissa before the summer Jack thought that he was making up for all the time he spent with Jack before Marissa was born, and that was fair.

So maybe Marissa had to live with Dad the same number of years that Jack lived with him before Marissa was born. Maybe that was why she was moving in with him.

The thought didn't make him feel better. Because they couldn't be a family in two houses. There was no family in two houses on TV.

Mom bent her arm and rubbed the front part over her forehead. That meant she was tired, and maybe even about to lose her temper. So Jack asked, "Can I help?" He didn't want to make it easy for Marissa to leave but he didn't want Mom to get mad, either.

"Of course!" Mom said. "Come help! Um, what can Jack do, Marissa?"

"I don't know."

"Stop jumping on the bed. You'll hurt yourself."

"I — I want to help."

"Well...." Mom tapped her lips. "Um ... I know! Why don't you fold the clothes in the pile over there?"

"Ok." Jack bent over the pile.

"We're giving those clothes away," Marissa said.

"They still need to be folded," Mom said. "Please stop jumping on the bed."

"But I'm the little monkey jumping on the bed!" Marissa said. She sang, "Three little monkeys jumping on the bed...."

Jack knew the song. "One fell off and broke his head!" he cried.

"That's right," Mom says, "he broke his head. And if there's one thing that Daddy can't buy you, it's a new head."

"Jack is making a mess of my clothes!"

Jack had been folding, but the jeans and sweaters looked the same as they did when he started.

"But we're giving those clothes *away*, remember?" said Mom. She stacked a big pile of Marissa's dresses on the chair. Marissa had a lot of dresses. Jack didn't care about clothes. Ashleigh said she liked that about him.

"Marissa, sit down," Mom said. "I want to talk to you."

Marissa jumped once more but then she sat.

"Don't let your father ... make you do homework all the time."

"I won't!"

Jack hated homework. In school they were reading a book called Mockingbird, but it wasn't about a bird at all. He could read all the words

— that part was easy — but he couldn't tell what the story was about. Ms. Ling said that he could read the summary on Wikipedia, but he couldn't understand that very well, either. Then Mom sat at the computer and talked to him about it. When she *told* him the story he understood just fine, about Scout and Jem and Boo Radley. So he had no trouble helping her write the paper.

"You know this doesn't have to be a permanent move," Mom said. "You can see how you like it."

Marissa leapt up. "Two little monkeys!" she cried.

"Stop jumping on the goddam bed!" Mom yelled.

"You'll hurt yourself!" Jack yelled, too.

Mom had her hands over her face. "That's right," she said through her hands. "I just don't want you to hurt yourself. I'm sorry I shouted. But you have to listen to me when it's for your own safety."

"From now on I just have to listen to Daddy," Marissa said.

That made Jack's stomach hurt. "You have — you have to listen to Mom, too," but once again it seemed as though neither his sister nor his mother could hear him.

CHAPTER 12

"It's T-309. Do you know it, Miss Allen?"

"I'll find it." Mr. Takanawa still treated her like she was a total airhead. He'd have to come unlock the door, but he wouldn't stay there for the planning meeting. "This is your vision to fulfill," he said.

It was raining that Saturday afternoon, and Jack was waiting at the bungalow. He looked like one of the pictures of homeless kids she saw on the St. Elizabeth's Dining Room website. He didn't have a raincoat or an umbrella, his hair was matted down, and he was clutching a grocery bag to his chest that was so wet it looked like the bottom was going to collapse any second.

"Trevor showed me where to come," he said happily.

The bungalow was meant to be an office for all the coaches, so there were desks in every corner but not enough chairs. The walls were covered with pictures of the different sports teams: everyone in their jerseys with the porcupine logo. There was a single shelf running against the back wall, displaying a butt-load of trophies.

"We'll have to sit on the floor!" Jack wailed.

But she knew he didn't really mind. The first thing he said when they plunked down in the junction of the cross-shaped space was, "This will be the best trip ever!"

"I hope so," Ashleigh said. "We'll need to raise a lot of money."

"We'll have a bake sale!"

"Yes, we could do that." He was so sweet and enthusiastic, she didn't point out that there was a bake sale going on in the cafeteria pretty much every day.

"Or we could have a raffle!"

"But what will we raffle off?" she asked.

"A trip to Hawaii!"

"That's a fun idea," she said.

"That was the prize at the Mayfair at my last school." Jack often spoke highly of his K-8 school. *Her* mother sent her to a Catholic school for grade and middle-school, but Ashleigh was sure that Kimberly was as happy as she was when she got into George Takei, the "smart kid" alternative school you had to apply to specially, even if you wanted to get in as a full-inclusion or "diversity" admission. Takei was a public school and tuition-free, while Our Lady of Keep Your Legs Together, though significantly cheaper than the secular private high schools, still would have forced Kimberly down from the Mercedes S-class to the C.

"How did they get the free trip to raffle off?" Ashleigh tried to stretch out. The floor was hard, and the space was cramped.

"They — they found it!"

His grin told her that he knew it wasn't true. Also that he didn't have the answer to her question.

"I thought I was going to win!"

"We always think we're going to win," she sighed, "don't we?" Looking out the one window, she added, "It's still raining."

"Maybe we'll have a flood!"

"No, we won't. But where's the rest of my committee?"

"They're not coming!"

"They'll be coming," she promised, though she had her doubts.

They did. Parker, Blake and Sue arrived together, only fifteen minutes late, and about ten minutes after that, Freddie and Edward, all wet, all bitching about the weather.

Ashleigh asked the five of them to be the planning committee because they were all members of the One World Club, and officially this was a One World Club project, though they never took a vote on it. She could count on Freddie to support her and he'd drag Edward along.

As for the Unholy Trinity.... She asked them because she wished they could put that stupid shit about Nicholas behind them all. Also, whatever those did a lot of the other girls wanted to get in on. The nastier you were the more people wanted to be your friend. Seriously? No wonder the world was so fucked up.

Everybody looked uncomfortable: Sue was squeezed between two desks and Freddie and Edward were crouched beneath the window. She'd take them outside except for the rain.

"Okay, well … I have an agenda to pass around."

She came to this Saturday afternoon meeting prepared to the Nth degree. She brought her lucky pen, the one that wrote purple ink and had a purple feather at the end. The agenda was printed out in a cool, Tim Burton-ish font and all the main points were bold-faced.

Everyone took it, most of them grumbling, but not Jack who stared at it so hard that he got cross-eyed. The page rattled in his hands.

"If you'll all look at the first item." Why did she sound squeaky? "I'd like one of you to take charge of putting the packing list together."

She wanted to delegate, because once they put their own time into this, they wouldn't want to back out.

"Don't forget condoms!" Edward shouted.

That made Jack laugh, that shrieky, cover-your-ears laugh. Ashleigh glared at Edward. Then she turned her glare to Freddie, sending the message, *keep Loverboy under control, will you?*

Sue raised her hand, just shy of shoulder-level. "I could try it." She hesitated. "You know, my family goes camping every summer in Russian River."

"Isn't that special," Edward said in falsetto, fanning himself with his hand.

"So, at our next meeting, a week from today, you can bring a proposed packing list and we can all go over it." If only there were room for her to uncross her legs, and if only the corner of some coach's desk weren't sticking in her back.... "Next is the health forms. I have that taken care of." She paged through her binder with increasing speed but when she didn't see the forms she just flipped her hair over her shoulder. "You don't need to worry about that. We just have to make sure they're in the packet when we send it home."

"Dude," Edward said to Freddie, "you said we could go see *The Hangover*."

"There's a showing at 5:20," Freddie said.

"Let's get this over with!" Blake snapped. She was always edgy. Ashleigh didn't like gossip, but she'd heard a rumor that Blake got into her mother's diet pills last year, and she believed it because Blake was either hyper or depressed most of the time. All to lose five freaking pounds.

"Don't you have some dick to suck?" Edward fired back.

Then Jack shouted, "Time for snacks!"

And out of the sodden Cal-Smart bag he brought out those ruffled potato chips he liked and a tub of onion dip and — though he had to wrestle with it — a 2-liter bottle of Coke.

Everyone fell on it like they'd spent a month in Somalia. Jack didn't bring cups but there were paper cups for coffee in one of the cabinets. Coach Whoever wouldn't care.

Ten minutes later everyone was chill. There were crumbs all over the floor and onion dip smeared a few places but Ashleigh could clean that up later. Over the crunching and munching she went through the rest of the agenda as quickly as she could: transportation (a tough one), chaperones (tougher), and money (probably impossible).

When Edward made a paper airplane out of his agenda and flew it straight between two of the trophies she knew she had to wrap up. "Participants" was the last item.

"That's a good one," Parker sneered. "Who are the fucking losers who are going to come on this lame trip?"

Ashleigh realized only then how quiet Parker had been. She hadn't been taking notes. Of course, neither had anyone else except Sue. Jack had been trying, but…. "Are you okay, Parks?"

"I wondered when you were going to ask." Parker's voice was haughty as usual, but there was something different, too.

Sue turned a frightened look in Blake's direction. Blake took out her gum and whopped it into a nearby wastebasket where, thank God, it landed. "It's about time one of you guys paid attention to what Parker is going through."

Everyone was silent. Even Jack. Periodically he checked out, and right now his head was lolling to one side.

"My parents are getting divorced," Parker announced. She was twisting a Kleenex.

Parker's dad had had an apartment downtown for a while. The story had been that he was too tired to drive all the way home after work, but how pathetic was that? Ashleigh used to go to Parker's house but she'd stopped, telling herself that she and Parker were drifting apart, but really it was because the atmosphere was major tense there. Parker's mom was — probably still was — a drunk who bought organic produce and vodka.

Sue stroked Parker's back.

When the silence continued another few seconds, Ashleigh took a chance. "Do you see how that's a First World problem?" she asked, trying to sound gentle. "The best way to not feel sorry for yourself is to find out about how many people are much worse off than you are. In Zimbabwe — "

"Fuck Zimbabwe!" Parker exploded.

At the word "divorced," Jack had snapped to attention. "My parents are divorced!" he declared, as if happy to find common ground with Parker.

"That's right," Ashleigh said, "and you see, he doesn't sit around feeling sorry for himself."

"He sits around enough, though," Edward said to the ceiling.

But that wasn't the point. The point was that no matter how much Parker was hurting, she could survive out in the world. While Jack, with his never-ending optimism and willingness to think the best of people, would have to depend on the whims of brats like Parker.

"You don't know what it's like to lose your dad," Parker said.

"My mom has a new boyfriend!" Jack interjected. "She says we have an extra dad. And he's a policeman and he always carries a gun!"

"That's the way to look at it," Ashleigh said.

But Parker stared her down. "Your dad didn't even want you to be born."

Ashleigh gasped so hard that she felt cold air rushing all the way down her esophagus. Parker was Ashleigh's first friend at Takei and in their freshmen loneliness they confided in each other. Ashleigh told Parker about how Kimberly had to fight to keep her. Parker swore on the life of her cat Willow that she would never mention it to anyone.

Compassion begins with….

"My mom doesn't have any DUI's," Ashleigh said.

There was a lot of shouting, a lot of F-bombs, none of which Ashleigh could pay attention to because she was so pissed off at herself.

Parker stormed out with Blake and Sue. At the door she said, "Count me out of this cray-cray plan," which kind of went without saying, didn't it?

Ashleigh sat with shoulders slumped. If she only had one of those ten seconds back buttons on her life.

She hardly responded when Freddie and Edward politely took their leave. Or when Jack asked, "Can we go now?"

As soon as Daddy came in Marissa was afraid that he and Mommy were going to have a fight, because he was late picking her up. He said he'd get there at 2:00 but it was 4:00.

She heard him mumbling something to Mommy about an emergency. Then they both looked over at her and shuffled into the kitchen, walking sideways at the same time.

They didn't really have a fight but Marissa could tell from the sounds of their voices they weren't happy with each other. She bit her lip hard until they came out.

When they did come out they looked mad but they weren't going to do any more arguing, she could tell.

Finally Daddy put the big suitcase into the trunk of his car. Marissa looked behind her and Mommy looked sad. Marissa didn't want to leave Mommy then. She didn't even want to leave Jack, not really.

But now Jason and Trevor were here all the time. Marissa couldn't even watch TV because Jack and Trevor made too much noise for her to hear, or Trevor and Jack would be watching separate shows and Marissa would have to watch the really small TV in Mommy's room.

Daddy said that Jason wouldn't marry Mommy, and Daddy was always right, but Marissa was still nervous, because if Jason did marry Mommy, then he would turn mean the way that Natasha's mom's boyfriend turned mean after he became her stepdad.

"Climb on in," Daddy said.

"You'd better put her in that booster seat," Mommy said.

"When do I not put her in the booster seat?" Daddy asked and Marissa didn't say anything because she knew it was a secret that Daddy used to not do it. "Ridiculous," he mumbled so that only Marissa could hear. "In my day we stood up in the back seat."

Marissa twisted around as far as she could (the booster seat wouldn't let her go very far) so that she could see Mommy as Mommy got smaller.

After a while she couldn't see Mommy anymore and her neck was starting to hurt so she turned back.

She'd been in Daddy's car a zillion times but being in Daddy's car to go out and being in Daddy's car to move in with him … it was like there were two different cars.

Daddy was whistling. Marissa waited for him to put on one of the "story tapes" that were so boring. She asked if they could listen to Radio Disney once and he asked back, "Don't you like hearing stories about how our country was born?"

Marissa did *not* like the story tapes. Mommy had taught her to tell people what she wants. She called it "standing up for yourself." But Mommy had also told her that she should be polite. She called that a "white lie." Mommy had admitted that it was often hard to know which one to use. With Daddy, Marissa usually chose the white lie.

"Are we going to your house now?" Marissa asked.

Daddy stopped whistling. "Ohh … after we make a couple of stops."

Marissa knew for sure that one of those stops would be for ice cream. She spent a lot of the rest of the ride thinking about what kind of sundae she would get.

But instead Daddy took her to one of the big, big stores downtown. She'd been there before with Mommy. It was called Saks. She remembered the name because she'd asked Mommy if they called it that because they put what you bought in a sack and Mommy said that she was just adorable, and then said no, the store was named for the person who owned it first.

Daddy took her to the part where they sold clothes for girls her age. Was Daddy going to pick out clothes for her? Even though Daddy was a lot smarter than Mommy Marissa thought that maybe one thing he didn't know more about than Mommy was clothes.

"You need a lot more things for school," Daddy said, right before he started talking to a strange lady.

Marissa got scared, wondering if the lady was Daddy's new girlfriend and if the real reason they had come here was so that Marissa could meet her. Emma also told her that her dad would introduce her to girlfriends like this before he married one she'd never met. Now she had a baby half-brother that her stepmom wouldn't even let her hold.

But it turned out that the lady was there to help Marissa pick out clothes! Daddy said that the lady's name was Sinead Pham and that Marissa should call her Ms. Pham but Ms. Pham said, "Sinead, please."

"Sinead is the expert on what's fashionable."

Marissa was so really excited. She'd rather go shopping with Mommy than Daddy, but she and Mommy sometimes argued about what was ok to wear to school. Now she could finally pick out some nice stuff on her own.

But it turned out that she was supposed to sit in the dressing room while Sinead brought in all the clothes, and she brought in really stupid clothes, almost all dresses and the rest skirts with ugly blouses. No t-shirts, and no jeans — and no leggings. *Everyone* wore leggings under their skirts!

When she asked Sinead about the other stuff, Sinead said, "Your Dad has told me what you need," in a teacher voice, and then in a cartoon voice, "And besides, you look so beautiful in these!"

Most of the dresses had flowers on them. Mommy hated clothes with flowers on them and Marissa did, too. And the skirts were so long!

Whenever Marissa tried something on she had to go out and show Daddy and at first she thought that he would see how ugly everything was, but instead he asked Sinead what *she* thought!

And Sinead kept saying, "fabulous!"

When Marissa came out in a dress that was barf green with puffy sleeves and Sinead said "fabulous!" Marissa knew there could be no more lies.

"I don't like it," she said.

Daddy coughed and said, "Maybe we'll skip that one," to Sinead and Sinead laughed like it was a joke between them.

"I don't like any of them," Marissa said.

"She's had a very long day," Daddy said to Sinead. "I don't think she knows what she wants. She's tired."

"I am not."

"I understand," Sinead said.

"We'll just take the ones we've already picked out."

Marissa was afraid she'd be in trouble now but back in the car Daddy said, "We'll have to try a different personal shopper next time. Maybe at Neiman's."

After Saks they went out to dinner and after she finished eating her hamburger Daddy said she could have that sundae because it was a special occasion, "You're finally moving in where you belong."

When Daddy pulled into his garage Marissa got nervous.

She was going to sleep at Daddy's house for the first time since Jack used to come with her. She almost wished that Jack were coming that night, but she didn't think that she'd feel safer with him there anymore.

Daddy's garage was awfully dark. She wasn't scared of the *dark*. She was scared that she couldn't see all the way into the corners of the garage, and there was a humming that could be anything and there was a door at the back with chipped paint that she didn't know where it went.

The wooden stairs that led up to the real house were creepy, too, because they looked like they could come crashing down. But there was a light at the top, and Daddy was behind her, dragging her big suitcase and grunting, so once she got halfway up she felt okay.

And now they were in the kitchen, the big beautiful kitchen, where the counters and the cabinets were so shiny it was like *they* were the lights.

Not very long before when she came to visit Daddy he told her to look for a surprise in the refrigerator. It was a big cake that said HAPPY HALF-BIRTHDAY, WISSY 5½ . It had six whole candles on it and then another one broken in half. Lots of times Daddy had another surprise, not always a cake but sometimes a cherry pie because she really liked those.

So she went to the fridge like always, and there was a surprise all right. Just not a good one.

There was nothing. Nothing except vegetables like broccoli and lettuce and a whole bunch of green stuff that she didn't know the name of. There was yucky yucky yogurt. *Mommy* bought yogurt.

While she was staring at the inside, though she knew you weren't supposed to keep the refrigerator door open because it makes the hole in the ozone layer bigger, Daddy said, "You see, if you're living here you have to eat healthy food."

"You don't eat healthy food."

"Heh-heh-heh," Daddy chuckled. "It's too late for me."

Marissa kept staring inside the refrigerator, waiting for the cake to walk out on two little cartoon legs with a big smiley face drawn on the side and to say, "Hi, Marissa! I fooled you, didn't I?"

Behind her, Daddy coughed. "Wissy, there's someone, I mean, two ladies I want you to meet."

Marissa turned around. Out of nowhere, two nurses had appeared. So this was all a trick to take her to the hospital! To have an operation!

"This is Leonora," Daddy said, "and Dania."

"*Bienvenudo a su casa,*" one of the nurses said.

"They're going to help me take care of you."

They "take care of you" at hospitals. And every hospital had needles and big machines and sometimes people died there.

"*Hola, Marissa,*" said the other nurse. She pronounced it "Mar-*ees*-sa."

Marissa knew that they were speaking Spanish and she even knew that they said welcome to your home and hi. Everyone knew that much Spanish, and *gracias* and *por favor.*

"Are we going to the hospital?"

"What? No." Daddy reached down for her and started to lift her up, but when she got a little off the floor he put her down again. "I'm just going to work."

"But it's Saturday night."

"I'm not going to the office, Wissy. I'm only going upstairs. But I probably have to work until after you go to bed."

Marissa wanted to ask if he was going to read to her. She brought the book that Mommy had been reading: *The Long Winter.* It was a sad book because everyone was hungry, and now Mary was blind, but it made Marissa really want to see snow.

"You three get to know each other," Daddy said.

"But Daddy — "

"Yes?"

"Do they — " She pointed.

"It's not polite to point," Daddy reminded her. "And they have names." He pointed. "Leonora. And Dania."

"Do they speak English?"

Daddy looked hard at her, almost like a mean teacher. "Marissa," he said firmly, "that is a rude question."

"But — "

He lowered his voice. "No, not very much. But this is the best way for you to learn Spanish."

Marissa wondered why he was whispering since Leonora and Dania didn't understand English anyway.

"Parents leave their babies with nannies who don't speak English all the time," Daddy said, "and that's *babies.* You're a big girl and you know how to use the phone so you just call me when you need anything."

"I'm not a baby!" Marissa declared.

"Okay, that's better," Daddy said.

Then he disappeared, almost *poof.*

The nurse named Dania opened the refrigerator again. She smiled and pointed inside.

Leonora said, "Dinner? *Comes?*"

"I don't want dinner," Marissa says. "I'm full."

Leonora and Dania spoke Spanish to each other.

Marissa said, "I need help to go to my room."

Leonora and Dania talked some more. In between talking they kept looking over at her, and smiling and nodding. Dania had braces and Marissa had never seen a grown-up with braces.

Marissa pointed to the big suitcase. "It's heavy." Daddy forgot to take it upstairs with him.

"*Muchos vestidos bonitos,*" Dania said knowingly.

Marissa flogged the air with her finger because it wasn't the same as pointing. "I need help."

"Yes, yes," Dania nodded. Everyone knew the word "yes" in English just like everyone knew the word "si" and those other words in Spanish.

Marissa stabbed at the ceiling to make them understand "upstairs." Then she tapped her suitcase.

Leonora and Dania talked to each other.

Then Leonora said, "Suitcase?" and tapped it, too.

So Leonora knew the word suitcase! This was progress.

"Papa upstairs," Leonora said. "No go."

Marissa was very tired. She sat down on the suitcase because she knew it wasn't going anywhere for a while.

Jack often had trouble sleeping, and when he did he turned on the TV. If he kept it soft enough his mom wouldn't hear. When she did, she'd come turn it off and take the remote away, but he could turn it back on with that side button. If she heard the TV a second time, she'd unplug it.

His dad got him the TV in his room as a present for his Bar Mitzvah. Mom was happy for him then but sometimes now she said that it was a mistake. When she got really mad she said that she was going "to leave the goddam thing out on the sidewalk and anyone can have it!" but he knew that she'd never do that.

When Trevor slept over, on non-school nights, he had to watch the TV in the living room.

Usually when he couldn't sleep he started thinking about all the things he did wrong that day. But tonight he was looking back and feeling happy.

He was a big help to Ashleigh today. She told him so when he was helping her clean up. The refreshments were his idea. And he had lots of other good ideas, too, like the Hawaii trip raffle, and doing Secret Santa on the field trip since it'd be so close to Christmas.

He felt something changing. The other kids talked to him a few times but they weren't talking to him extra slowly or extra loudly. They talked to him like he was one of them. They weren't nice but they weren't that nice to each other.

In the beginning, when they first knew each other, Ashleigh talked that extra-slow, extra-loud way but she hadn't for a long time.

The field trip was still 27 days away, really 26 since it was after midnight. That was a long time to wait, but he was sure that something special was going to happen there.

CHAPTER 13

The day after Marissa left I almost walked into her room to pick up her laundry when I remembered that there wouldn't be any.

She didn't even call the first night. I called her the second night and was informed that she was already asleep. Alex and I tossed the hostility ball around for a while and then, under duress, he promised to have her call the following afternoon. Which she did, though just to tell me that Emma was over and she couldn't talk.

I replayed each word of her side of the conversation for the rest of the day, hunting for signs of remorse, ambivalence, longing, anger. I could find nothing. She was a Rorschach ink blot spilled on black paper.

Or perhaps I didn't want to admit how much happier she must be. That big, clean, beautifully furnished house. No blaring TVs. No Jack or Trevor shouting. Alex would have hired a housekeeper, probably even two, to serve hot (but not too hot), balanced meals at the same time each night. To pack lunches with cheerful notes, signed with smiley faces.

To follow her around and smooth out the depressions her shoes made in the carpet.

I was always a little depressed that time of year: short days, lots of rain, and the Big Holidays were bearing down on me. Never mind Christmas — first I had to deal with Thanksgiving.

I knew that Jason would spend it with his mother. Apparently, Jason's Ex, Denise, had been Cook of the Century and had hosted lavish holiday banquets that included Jason's parents and other assorted, if distant, relatives. Not long after she had decamped, Jason's father had died and his mother had moved into an assisted living facility. Since then Jason and Trevor had driven across the Bay Bridge to Grandma's for Thanksgiving. Sunnyhill Towers in Pleasanton was neither sunny nor pleasant, nor even a tower, but there they went, and were thankful.

I wasn't quite ready to meet her (or to introduce myself and Jack, or to explain Marissa's absence); it was preferable to tackle yet another sequel to my childhood Thanksgivings, or *Nightmare on Arnold Avenue,* as Darya and I had called them.

The year before there had been three of us, at least. Alex was always previously engaged. That year he had joined in a protest staged by

PLEAD (People Lending Enormous Aid to the Desperate) who were among his most left-leaning supporters. Alex must have told me *twenty freaking times* about this "meal" in which attendees sat in front of empty plates, while *I* knew that earlier in the day he had made the rounds of the homes of the City Attorney, the President of the Board of Supervisors and the Mayor, as a *pre*-dinner guest, so that even before he reached Vegans Against Bird Murder, where they were serving eggplant turkey, he would have consumed half his own weight in fey yuppie hors d'oeuvres, from shrimp wrapped in bacon to green pea hummus.

With Marissa to display, he'd probably have a catered dinner at his own house, and let his constituents come to him.

On that same evening, Jack, Marissa, and I sat around the table snapping at each other, each of us feeling in our own way the stinging loneliness of living on Gilligan's Island, if everyone except the Howells and Ginger had been rescued.

And this year Jack and I would have to muddle through without Marissa.

Then one night in mid-November, Jason said, "My cooking skills don't really extend to barnyard fowl. So, what can I buy — I mean bring?"

"But what about your mom?"

He shrugged. "She has a new dude in her life. Big 'Mario Savio' guy." He put "Mario Savio" in air quotes. "Whoever that was. Remind me to google him. Anyway, he thinks all policemen are pigs."

"Well," I said, trying to disguise my joy that Jack and I would not be alone, "if you think you can handle turkey Lean Cuisines, then by all means."

Thanksgiving morning I called Marissa. She didn't have much to say.

"How are you? What are you doing?"

"Fi-ine."

"I was hoping you'd come home today. For dinner with me and — "

"Daddy says this is my home."

My stomach lurched. "Are you happy?" I blurted, "at your father's place?"

"Yes!"

That was Marissa in don't-fuck-with-me mode.

After I heard the click of her hanging up I held onto the receiver, because once *I* hung up then the call was *really* over.

Just before I detached the phone from my ear I thought I heard breathing.

Jason was watching the football game — whichever "the" football game was — on TV, with Trevor and Jack, one boy on either side of him, and his arm on the back of the couch, though not touching either of them.

I watched them from the kitchen door. The only thing I would have changed would have been to take Trevor out of that neon orange t-shirt, a color that made everyone look like a CalTrans worker.

That, and to have Marissa with us.

I was not the only woman in San Francisco who didn't know how to cook a turkey from scratch. No, there was an upscale market in my old neighborhood where you could get upscale food that only needed to be heated, though exactly how "heating" is different from "cooking," remains a mystery to me to this day. We would have turkey, stuffing, cranberry sauce, glazed sweet potatoes, mashed potatoes — for God's sake, who, outside of Wicklow County, had two kinds of potatoes? Who were the people — I meant, besides Alex — who were eating so much food?

And who had the pots and pans for all of this? I'd really thought I was prepared.

But every time I called into the living room to ask if we could leave something out — the string beans, maybe? — someone called out "No!"

Yes, I was a stranger in a strange land — and an illegal alien to boot. Could I serve the stuffing in the same pan as I heated it in? I was pretty sure that I could, but since I didn't have a pan to heat the stuffing in to begin with....

I didn't even have an apron. I'd had one made of white linen that Marissa and I had decorated with fabric marker together at a pre-school Mommy and Me day. But I couldn't find it. I wondered if Marissa had taken it with her.

For the next half hour I dug out grease-stained baking sheets and tried to turn them into baking pans by building a wall of aluminum foil around the sides; I heated the sweet potatoes in the microwave and splattered half of them against the top; discovered that the gravy bowl I'd so clearly pictured in my cupboard was a screen memory.

Occasionally I'd hear the yee-haaah! or the *Noooo!* From the living room that could have come from any one of the three.

I peeked at the turkey, which had required a full two hours of heating. With the oven door open it emitted a smell that was a little too turkey-ish even for a turkey. And just *how* brown was the skin supposed to be? I checked my watch. Uh oh.

Hoping for the best I shouted, "Dinner is served!"

They came to the table like the Three Stooges, bumping each other on the shoulders, with Jason offering "Yuk! Yuk! Yuk!" as punctuation. When they sat, Jason leaned over to Jack and said, "Let's fool your mom and pretend we're not hungry."

"No way!"

"No way!"

I took up two tea towels and started to lift the turkey from the oven. It was heavier than I expected. *Call Jason. No, you can do it without help.*

And I did. I got it up on the stove and looked at it with pride. The meat was separating from the bones, but I *thought* that was good.

Wait! The cranberry sauce. No cooking *or* heating involved there. I'd put the plastic container atop the stove when I unpacked the box, tired of bending over to grab items one at a time. I could do a *little* better than that, at least. I grabbed a cereal bowl, then reached for the cranberry sauce....

The lid came off in my hand. The carton slipped out from under and took a swan dive down over my blouse and skirt.

I couldn't move at first. Then I looked down slowly. The blood-red sauce splattered all over my white blouse turned me into one of Alex's murder victims. It dribbled down my gray pencil skirt and then — no, no, please, Lord, no! — it ended in a great gob on the toes of my black suede pumps.

That was when I sat down on the step stool, held my head in my hands, and came as close to a good cry as I had in years.

I'd really wanted to make this a good meal for everyone. I hadn't meant to dash it off as if I were too good for the kitchen, but it sure looked as though I had. Turkey dry as the Sinai desert, half the sweet potatoes left behind in the microwave, and just a few dabs of cranberry sauce at the bottom of the tub.

"Food! Food! We want food!"

Jack and Trevor were banging their silverware on the table, prisoners in the dining hall about to start a riot.

"Calm down, boys." But Jason was laughing. Big help.

I wiped the corner of my eyes with the cuff of my ruined blouse. Little paw prints of mascara came off on the sleeve. "Just a minute!" I called with a mix of feigned cheer and firm motherly hold-your-horses.

Then I went into my bedroom and changed into what I should have worn in the first place: an oversized t-shirt and my plaid pajama pants. The boys kept up their silverware banging, and it sounded as though Jason had joined in.

A few minutes later I came out with the turkey. They all three turned around at the same time. And I knew, not just from their faces but from my recent glance in the bedroom mirror, what they saw: a woman who looked like she just rolled out of bed, her hair, so recently piled into perfectly tousled waves and fastened with a butterfly clip, now falling down over her face.

And I saw they didn't care. They didn't care that I had put out paper towels instead of cloth napkins. They didn't care that the salt and pepper were in their original Morton's and McCormick boxes. They all three smiled at me with an expression I couldn't identify at first — but finally acknowledged as love.

Ashleigh was finally old enough that she didn't have to go with Mother to one of her stupid society friends' houses for Thanksgiving. She liked doing that when she was little because it made her feel grown up, but now she saw it for what it really was. "Rich white men protecting their property," was how Mr. Takanawa once described the authors of the Constitution, and now the privileged weren't *all* white, and they weren't *all* men — but it was still the same old same old.

So Ashleigh volunteered to help at St. Elizabeth's Dining Room. She kept putting off telling Mother about it because she knew it would be all like, WTF? She had just about gotten up the nerve when there was the night with Dylan Dickhead. Since then she hadn't spoken to her mother. Maybe a sullen, "yeah," after Mother asked her like twenty times "Are you really wearing that?"

Ashleigh had finally erased her debt with her mother. If Kimberly wanted to embarrass herself by pretending to be Ashleigh's sister (because Kimberly *was* only 34), then sing the hallelujah chorus.

Early Thanksgiving morning Mother came into her room and announced, like she was Angelina freaking Jolie, "I hope this afternoon you'll wear something decent for a change."

Ashleigh was on her bed reading *Bleak House* for AP English. It was a really thick paperback and hard to hold open.

"Ashleigh, I'm talking to you."

"This is me not answering."

"You have so many lovely dresses in your closet."

This was worth answering. "Clothes made in Bangladesh by eight-year-old sex slaves."

Mother rubbed her hands together in the circular way she did when she was putting lotion on. "That is not the issue."

Ashleigh switched the book to one hand and held it a little higher. It hurt her wrist a little but she could picture herself in this pose and it was the model of indifference. She was aware of her long jean-clad leg stretched out, the other leg raised at the knee and she knew that she looked like a flamingo. *Suck on it, Mother.*

"Ashleigh, listen to me." Mother sat down on her bed, and took Ashleigh's other hand. Mother's palm was cold and slimy, like a reptile's. "I know I haven't always done right by you."

"Seriously? This insight dawned on you when?"

"You can help me. I know you want to, um, help people."

"That's right." Ashleigh let her book drop. She *should* have thrown it across the room. "I want to help *people,* not...." What should she call her mother? She wouldn't stoop to Mother's own level and call her a bitch, let alone a cunt or something. "Not money-making machines."

"Honey, tonight means a lot to me."

Mother didn't know that Ashleigh had never planned to go with her. That she was wasting her time trying to get Ashleigh out of her "lesbian clothes" (which is what Mother has started calling them), and into something that would make her look like Princess Diana, her mother's heroine.

"I made my special sweet potatoes with the marshmallows," Mother said.

Ashleigh frowned. She thought she smelled something before. Sweet potatoes with marshmallows was what Mother made when Ashleigh was little and they ate Thanksgiving together just the two of them. When was the last time they did that? When Ashleigh was eight?

"So, can you do this for me?"

"Do you believe me about Dylan now?"

"I do," Mother said quickly, "and I'm very, very disappointed in him. I've already spoken to his parents."

"How come you didn't believe me before?"

Mother took a very deep breath and held it for a moment before she let it go. "I guess the truth is that I didn't want to believe it. Dylan looks so good on paper, like the kind of boy you should be getting to know."

Ashleigh wanted to believe her mother. She didn't; not quite. But why not give her one more chance? She was stuck there for almost two years and she sure would have liked to feel comfortable in her own house, even if it wasn't really hers anyway. *I could go to St. Elizabeth's extra early and leave in time to stop by the society client's house later.*

Mother actually leaned down and kissed her on the forehead then. Ashleigh shivered, thinking that it was like being kissed by a frog, except that that meant that Ashleigh would turn into a frog instead of Mother turning into a princess.

"Ashleigh, I'm grateful."

"So whose twelve-story mansion are we going to?"

"The Whitfields."

"*What?*" Ashleigh truly almost fell off the bed.

"Yes, isn't it exciting? It's a bit of a drive so we'll have to leave pretty soon. Now you see it's important to wear something nice and be polite. Mr. and Mrs. Whitfield will be so happy to see you." Then Mother smiled. Ashleigh could have sworn that her teeth were all pointy. "I think I've got the j-o-o-o-b." She sang the final word.

"Job?"

"With Dombey and Whitfield!"

Ashleigh only stopped to put bus fare in her pocket and to grab a sweater. She got to St. Elizabeth's way early, but they were glad to see her. Sarah was the lady in charge of the kitchen and she got Ashleigh an apron. "A shame to put your hair in a net, but that's the health department rule." She smiled. "And no one wants to see a hair in their gravy, even beautiful long red hair like yours." Sarah's hair was red, too, but that crimson-red that older women dyed their hair sometimes.

Ashleigh got lost in all the final preparations: stirring huge metal pots and carrying heavy, hot containers, and now, just as the first people in the line were coming through, her face was damp from the steam rising from the hot creamed corn, the stuffing, the carrots — even the turkey, all the way at the other end of the counter. It all smelled good, too, though there was the tang of metal in the air. Her legs hurt, her feet hurt, even her arms hurt, but in a totally good way.

This was where she belonged.

"ISN'T THIS nice?" Daddy asked.

Marissa would have said yes two weeks before. Usually when she and Daddy ate at a fancy restaurant like this, with big glasses and extra silverware, a whole buncha people came over to slap him on the back and ask if they can call him at work. The men always sounded like a grown-up version of the other kids in her class when they forgot their homework. The women sometimes kissed him on the cheek, which made her nervous.

But tonight was Thanksgiving.

Nobody knew Daddy here.

When Mommy called, Marissa had to act like she was happy. She was the one who wanted to come live with Daddy.

The restaurant was The Magnolia Room, and it was on the top floor of one of the tallest buildings in the city (Daddy said), so they could see the tops of other buildings nearby, but mostly they could see the buildings below them and, just barely, the cars moving on the street. Daddy said they got a seat by the window because she was special.

"Where do you usually go on Thanksgiving, Daddy?"

"Heh-heh-heh. I have friends."

Marissa looked down at her plate: three thick slices of white meat with a little creek of gravy flowing across the middle. A mound of stuffing. Cranberry sauce. And some vegetable with some other little red things on top that could only be described as gross. She wouldn't have been surprised if one of them started to crawl away.

She'd never thought about Thanksgiving at home very much. She really only remembered last year. That had been fun, though. Mommy wanted her to help as long as she didn't go near the stove. She wasn't going to let Jack use the stove, either, but Marissa said, "You treat Jack too much like a baby," so Jack got to stir the gravy while Marissa watched from a little ways off.

What were they doing now, without her, Mommy and Jack? She could have gone home with them. But Trevor would be there. And Daddy said that he'd be lonely without her.

"Wissy!"

Daddy's voice made her pay attention.

"You're crying."

"No, I'm not!" she protested. She was ashamed when she heard herself sniffle. But she didn't want him to know what she was thinking about so she said, "I was crying about the animals. I want to become a vegetarian." It was true that she'd been thinking this ever since she saw on TV about how calves are kept in little cages, even though she hated every vegetable except corn. She'd have to live on bread and bananas.

"Ooooh…." He stretched it out. "Well, now, let's see. You know that all life on earth is divided into plants and animals, right?"

"Right."

"Well…."

She listened at first while he described the food chain again. Then the beautiful lights of the bridge across the velvety Bay got all her attention.

"Herbivores only eat plant life, and carnivores only eat animal … animal products."

She wondered how high up they were. She heard about the planes that flew into the highest buildings in the world. A girl at school, Xi Ying, told her how she was scared of tall buildings, but Marissa wasn't scared, not of tall buildings.

"So you know what an omnivore is."

Marissa decided to eat a few bites before she answered, because she *didn't* know what an omnivore was. When she tasted the turkey — she cut right into the part that had some gravy on it — she discovered that it really was super good. The gravy wasn't thick or sticky. Then she tasted the stuffing and that was even better. They probably made it with chicken broth, though. She only knew that because Franklin brought his grandma's recipe to school on International Recipe Day. If she became a vegetarian she wouldn't be able to eat this anymore, either.

But she could worry about that later. "Can I have more gravy?" she asked.

"Of course." He raised his hand with his pointer finger in the air. "So what do you think it means? Om … ni…." he prompted.

Omni….

Before she moved in with Daddy she always liked being the one who got the answer first. Daddy would pinch her nose in that way that meant that he was proud but couldn't say so in front of Jack. Only lately she'd wondered, if it was something to be proud of then why did they have to keep it secret? And if it wasn't something to be proud of, then shouldn't she feel ashamed?

"Omni…." Daddy tried again. Then: "People who believe in God say that God is 'ominiscient.' That means He knows everything."

She tapped her fork against her plate. How did Daddy manage to eat so much while he was talking? Sometimes, just sometimes, he ate with his mouth open a little. She had to look out at the view then. Where was the gravy?

"And they believe that God is omni-present. That means He's everywhere. So an omni-*vore*…."

"Means that God is always with food?"

"Heh-heh-heh."

That meant she was wrong but for once she didn't care.

"Daddy, I don't like going to Linda's."

She had to go see Linda Bartlett every day after school. Linda called her apartment The Greenhouse and Marissa was supposed to call Linda "Violetta," and she did when she was with her, but in her mind she always called Linda "Linda" and Linda's apartment her "apartment."

"You don't?" He sounded surprised. "Her feelings would be hurt. She likes having you so much."

"Oh." Marissa used her fork to make her stuffing into a mound, and then patted out a little hole in the top. If she could ever get more gravy she would put it on the top and it could be a volcano.

At first working with Linda was kinda fun. They planted a lot of seeds that Linda said would grow into flowers, and Linda showed her pictures of the flowers they would be. But then days passed and nothing happened, it was just dirt. Linda told her to be patient, that being patient was the most important part of learning. But sometimes Linda looked at the dirt and said, "I don't know what's wrong."

"You told me I only had to go for two weeks."

"Has it been two weeks already?"

"Yeah."

Daddy had been looking down at the plate and scooping food into his mouth. Mommy said that he ate like someone was about to take it away.

"Why can't I tell Mommy about it?"

Daddy put his fork down. "You know we don't keep secrets from Mommy."

"Right."

"But we don't want to hurt her feelings, either."

"N-no...."

"And this would hurt her feelings."

"Why?"

"We never got you some more gravy, did we?"

No, they didn't, and she did want some. She watched how Daddy raised one hand, with one finger up, and a determined, teacher-face. She heard the scrape of his chair back.

The next thing she saw was a hand pouring gravy onto her plate.

"That's better," Daddy said. He cleared his throat. "Did I tell you about my friend's daughter?"

"No," she said automatically, while thinking that she knew what the story was about: a girl who didn't pay attention to her teacher and who now worked mopping the floors in the same school where she didn't listen.

"I had a nightmare about Linda," she interrupted. Interrupted Daddy! And she was lying, too. Her nightmare was about the calves in the cages. Did they keep turkeys in cages before they killed them? She didn't think so. The pilgrims killed them in the woods, right? So it would be fast.

Still, she didn't want to eat any more turkey. Just the gravy would be enough.

Ashleigh was bursting with the joy of knowing she was giving happiness as well as food. Her arms were really, really tired now, but she could go the distance.

From the second St. Elizabeth's opened the doors the dining room had been packed. The big space filled so quickly that it reminded Ashleigh of the last concert she went to with Freddie, at the Bill Graham, to see Kid Cudi.

In spite of all the ugly accusations about priests that had been in the news, Ashleigh wished at that moment that she had been raised a Catholic instead of some dumb no-name Protestant, though of course Mother said they were Episcopalian now. She'd even have thought about becoming a nun, except she'd probably end up in a convent that had the Mother Superior version of Kimberly. And in spite of Dylan Dickhead, Ashleigh didn't want to stay a virgin all her life.

The first man who came down the line said, "Thank you, miss," when she spooned creamed corn onto his plate. He was black, and had a salt-and-pepper beard, and his hand was shaking so bad that she was afraid that he'd drop the tray as soon as he got his pumpkin pie.

She had to look down. Why was she young and healthy and beautiful, while this man probably slept in a doorway?

She tried to say something to everyone who came by. She noticed their clothes, and took a solemn vow that from now on she would dress not just inexpensively like she had been, but *really* shabby, as a show of solidarity. There was plenty of inspiration for her new look. Nothing matched: one woman had on a dark red blazer with hot pink jeans. Now that was making a statement. And nothing was clean: many clothes had dried mud from the recent rainfall.

Another woman wore a newsboy cap covered with political buttons: Ashleigh only had time to read I LIKE IKE on one and MANGE MERDE ET MORT on another before the woman passed by, talking to herself.

A few of them had been drinking.

But Ashleigh didn't judge. She'd drink, too, if she were out on the streets.

A lot of them had missing teeth. None of them had *good* teeth: They were all dark yellow and crooked. But so many of them had gaps. A *lot* of gaps.

Ashleigh knew that tweakers lost teeth, but that wasn't necessarily what happened to these people. Did any of them have dental insurance? Not hardly.

Even sadder than all the missing teeth were the families. There were even some two parent families, which was ironic, since that was more than *she* ever had. Sarah told her that she should expect that, that a lot of people who come to St. Elizabeth's weren't homeless, they just couldn't afford to buy food.

The parents looked ashamed, but the children looked so happy. Over at one of the tables there was a little boy holding a pink plastic cup and blowing bubbles into it. His mother told him to stop but while Ashleigh couldn't hear her, she could tell that the mother was doing it in a nice way. That little boy had a better mother than she did.

"Can I have some more?" the man in front of her asked. Right out of *Oliver Twist*.

"Oh, I'm so sorry." She'd only dribbled a little of the corn onto the plate.

As soon as she gave the man a really big serving of corn she looked up again. Just like in the Takei cafeteria, there were The Tables: the family tables, the African-American tables, and the veterans' tables, the last divided into elderly veterans (Vietnam?) and middle-aged veterans (Afghanistan?) and she couldn't help smiling to herself for a second, because she hadn't seen so much facial hair since Mr. Takanawa showed that documentary about the Summer of Love.

She was treating everyone like a human being, so when she saw that the woman in front of her was about to let her tray fall off the rack she spoke very respectfully. "Ma'am, your tray — "

"Mind your own business, bitch," the woman said. "Can't you see I'm talking to my husband?"

The two people on either side of her were female.

"Don't mind her," one of them said. "She's cuckoo-bird. C'mon, Patty...." The woman took Patty by the elbow. "Let's get some cranberry sauce."

"Bitch!"

The woman spat at her, and Ashleigh told herself not to take it personally, but she did feel better when another woman said, "You're really pretty."

Ashleigh knew that she had to keep the line moving, but after that compliment, she quickly asked, "Do you have a place to sleep tonight?"

"Oh, yes," the woman nodded. "The Palace Hotel."

"That's wonderful."

"I've been staying there a month. In a suite."

Ashleigh had just started taking driving lessons and she had the same feeling now that she did when she swung too widely to make a turn.

"With Kevin Costner."

Ashleigh didn't know who Kevin Costner was, but she definitely knew then that the woman was mentally challenged. They'd been talking too long and the man who was next in line barked at the woman to move along.

That was when Ashleigh had to sit down for just a minute. She hadn't known her feet could hurt like this in sneakers. And her forearms were starting to cramp up.

Sarah said, of course, hang out in the kitchen for as long as you need.

"I just need a minute," Ashleigh said.

When Ashleigh sat down even her ass hurt. The kitchen was so steamy that within a minute her hair got as wet as if she'd taken a shower. It didn't smell good there any longer: it was more like *old* food.

"Channel 2 is here!" someone shouted.

"What, the TV people?"

"Oh, yeah," one of the cooks said. "They'll do a segment tonight, you know, like thirty seconds on 'we be cool 'cause we feed the hungry.' "

Ashleigh jumped up. She didn't care about being on TV, but ... if she *did* appear on the clip then she might inspire some of the lazy dweebs at school who thought they were so cool just by recycling.

It was just one guy and a cameraman and they were walking out by the time Ashleigh got back to the creamed corn.

"Where've you been?" the woman next to her asked.

I HAD ASKED JASON TO BRING A CAKE, and he had: a glorious ice cream cake from Baskin Robbins, Trevor's favorite. Jack had never met a meal he didn't like, let alone dessert, and I already had big plans for a 1 a.m. clandestine meeting with whatever remained of this heavily iced confection.

I brought it out on a real cake plate made of Waterford crystal that had belonged to my mother-in-law.

The table looked like Dresden, and I didn't mean the china: There was more food *on* the table than on anyone's plate, and several glasses of soda had spilled.

Trevor and Jack were whispering to each other as I lowered the cake, my hands gripping the side. My mistake, I saw a moment later, was the way I reached across the table to do so, instead of walking around to the other side, where I would have been protecting cake and cake plate from what happened:

Jack and Trevor each grabbed for the platter, one on each side. Jack, I was sure, was trying to help me, and perhaps Trevor was, too.

The road to hell. Etc.

The cake slipped to the floor. The cake plate *fell* to the floor. The hardwood floor. I had time to hope that it would only snap off at the stem, that it would be something I could repair. But no, it shattered into countless shards.

That was why I liked dishware from Target. Kohl's, too.

Jack and Trevor both yelped delightedly, while Jason and I rushed around the table at the speed of parents. "Just leave it!" I cried. "Don't touch the glass! I'll clean it up!"

"But it's melting! We've got to eat it!"

"Here's a spoon, Jack," Trevor offered.

Jason pulled Trevor up by the collar and I took Jack similarly in hand.

"But our cake!"

"Our ice cream cake!"

By now Jason had both boys by the collars and I had brought out broom and dustpan. I was amazed that he could restrain the two of them.

"Don't, Mom!" Jack cried, almost breaking away, as a mountain of mushy pink slid into the dustpan.

"Don't!" Trevor echoed, and it came out a sob.

"Now, now," Jason said, releasing them after my second trip to the kitchen garbage can. "We just have to rethink dessert, that's all."

ASHLEIGH SHOULDN'T have noticed it, but so many of those people hadn't taken showers in a while. And now it was as hot in the main dining room as it had been in the kitchen.

How long had she been here? She was wearing a watch but she couldn't get to it because her sleeve was covering it and she was holding the serving spoon in her other gloved hand.

She wiped her forehead with the back of that hand which didn't help because of the latex gloves she was wearing. The gloves were making her hands sweat, too.

"Yeah, it's hard work, isn't it?" Ashleigh heard someone say. It was the woman serving next to her.

Sometime during the last few minutes there had been a shuffling of volunteers, but Ashleigh was just concentrating on staying upright. A couple of times she'd spilled creamed corn onto the diner's tray instead of getting it all on the plate.

The new volunteer was older than Ashleigh, maybe early 20's, and the first thing Ashleigh noticed was that she was really beautiful, in a fashion model way. She had to be nearly six feet tall, and flagpole-thin. Her eyes were dark blue, almost violet, and her cheeks were hollow in that I-only-eat-raw-veggies way.

Ashleigh knew that looks weren't important. It was just that she was used to being the prettiest girl in the room. People were always saying to her that she should go to Hollywood when she graduated.

"It's not bothering me," Ashleigh said.

"Is this your first time volunteering?" the woman asked. Then she asked the man in front of her, "Did you get enough?" She'd just dished out a serving-spoonful of carrots.

"I don't even like carrots," the man said. "But don't you worry, I'll eat 'em." He shuffled sideways so that he was in front of Ashleigh, who doled out her creamed corn, which suddenly looked like pale yellow glop.

"This is my third year here," the woman said to Ashleigh. "It's great, isn't it?"

"I know, right? Is that enough, Ma'am? Did you just get here?" she asked the new volunteer.

"No, I've been washing dishes," the woman said. "I'm Lauren. I guess we can't shake hands. Are you still in high school?"

"Yeah."

"I'm a sophomore at Berkeley. Did you get enough?" Lauren asked another man.

Did you get enough, did you get enough? Ashleigh mimicked Lauren in her mind.

There was a loud moan.

"I don't want to hurt anymore!"

Ashleigh reflexively looked down to the beginning of the line, next to the turkeys, where a man who looked younger than most of the clientele was looking at the ceiling. It was obvious that he wasn't talking to anyone who was *there*.

"Please!" he cried, "I'm so lonely already!"

The clatter of silverware and the buzz of talk paused for a split second, then rose louder than before. Different diners called out, "It's all good Gene!" "Pull it together, dude!" "C'mon over, here, Gene, eat with us!"

Gene, a tall skinny man, was still crying to the ceiling. "Just let me alone!"

Ashleigh imagined rushing to his aid.

Kitchen staff emerged in a group. Ashleigh heard someone say, "He stopped his damn meds again."

In another minute it was over. The staff, Sarah among them, formed a small circle and escorted Gene through a door that led ... somewhere.

"It's sad, isn't it?" Lauren said. "There just aren't enough services for people in need."

Duh, Ashleigh thought.

"Did you get enough?" Lauren asked her next customer and Ashleigh decided that even Berkeley students could be total airheads.

Jason and I took the boys to Mel's where there was no ice cream cake, but plenty of ice cream, mounds and mounds of chocolate and vanilla, great rivers of hot fudge and caramel sauce flowing down the sides, and all of it topped with giant swirly peaks of glistening whipped cream.

"I'm sorry about that, uh — dish, Annie," Jason said sometime between bites. I could almost feel his belt getting tighter. "Was it valuable?"

Alex's mother had received it as a wedding gift. "Not at all."

"Mom!" Jack interrupted, loudly enough to stop traffic.

"Yes, dear." There was ice cream splattered across his cheeks and chin, the shape of a heavy beard, and a smear of whipped cream on the tip of his nose.

"I wish Marissa was here."

"So do I, Boychik."

"But this is still the best Thanksgiving ever!"

Jason and I were finally in bed.

No moon tonight and the street light was still burned out. The darkness held Jason in its arms. He held me in his.

"That was nice, wasn't it?" he asked.

"Do you mean dinner, or…." I ran a crooked finger along his arm.

"Hey, I know *that* was good," he boasted. "San Francisco's finest are here to protect *and* to serve."

"They also have rather high opinions of themselves."

Sex had been getting better and that night … well, I trusted him more. Could relax more. That was the way it was for me. I'd been with men who couldn't wait to show me their many tricks with their tongue and the positions they'd learned from the Kama Sutra, when what I needed was for them to laugh at a few of my jokes.

Jason gave me a quick squeeze. "We'll do it again next year," he said.

"It's a date."

"I have an idea," he said. "What if we talked about another date?"

CHAPTER 14

There were many ways in which Jason improved my life but there was one area in particular that would have made him worth marrying even had he been an unemployed transgender cat.

One word: hygiene.

Jack's personal hygiene was … to avoid giving too much information, I'll go for understatement and just say, "disturbing."

Until he was thirteen, I could help him shower. Then one night he said that he didn't want me to be in the bathroom with him.

I was glad, because such modesty was normal, but Mom-free showers made for challenging logistics: me shouting on the other side of the closed bathroom door, "get *under* the water, Jack, *under* the water!" — while I pictured him standing a foot back from the spray. He rarely got his hair wet. So I'd do my best to wash it in the sink, which became a tug-of-war with his head substituting for the rope. As for the rest of his body, it was in God's hands.

To brush his teeth I had to get him in a headlock and, under his determined protests, shove the toothbrush onto as many surfaces as I could. He'd probably need implants before he was 30. I might not even be dead yet, more was the pity.

Right here I have to explain the problem, which (sometimes) helped me keep my temper during these daily World Wide Wrestling matches. It was called "sensory defensiveness," and it was common among people on the spectrum, although many NTs have some degree of it as well. *I* hated itchy clothes, such as tweed, though I'd wear it (or spaghetti in my hair, for that matter) if it was on the cover of *Vogue* that month. Jack was ultra-sensitive to the feeling of the toothbrush in his mouth, to the sensation of water pouring down his scalp, to the pressure of a washcloth on his face.

I told myself that most teenage boys didn't care that much about accumulating dead skin or just a *little* body odor. I'd always judged him too harshly, I told myself, because I had no other reference point for boys his age.

But the older he got, the stronger he got, and the harder it became for me to force cleanliness upon him. But Jason could. Jason was just another guy in the locker room. It wasn't noticeable that he was the guy holding the soap. When all three men squeezed into the bathroom, they could even snap towels at each other (though Jack never quite got a "snap" out of a towel).

So now in the evenings when I heard Jason singing "Don't Ask Her on a Straight Tequila Night," or "Seminole Wind," while he hosed Jack down, I could relax. Neither Jack nor Trevor turned into Calvin Klein models or ads for Irish Spring, but Jack could now pass as the typical teenage boy of my imagination who didn't care much about wearing clothes fresh from the dyer.

Right after Thanksgiving weekend, Jason took me to buy an engagement ring. I asked him to meet me at the store during his lunch break so that he'd be wearing his uniform. Then I chose a silver band with a tiny sapphire, which was my birthstone.

"I know I'm not Bill Gates," Jason said, "but I can afford to buy you something larger than the head of a pin."

I tapped my fingernail on the display case to confirm to the salesman that this was my first choice. The sound was not the sharp *click* of former days: I'd given up acrylic manicures. "I wouldn't make any pin head jokes if I were you," I said. "Besides, my first wedding ring was so heavy it almost dislocated my shoulder, and look how that turned out." I'd returned that four karat diamond to Alex without prompting; it had been in his family for four generations.

Outside the store Jason got down on one knee and put it on my finger and I looked around to see who was watching Anna Kagen become an honest woman.

Once I had the ring Jason felt more comfortable coming over during the week. On those nights we sat down to dinner together, and though it was sometimes take-out, it was still family dinner. That's why on all those old black-and-white TV shows the mom says, "Be home for dinner," or "you'll spoil your appetite for dinner."

Dinner was not meant to be eaten alone in front of the TV.

I had nothing against TV *qua* TV. We often watched together, though it required a certain amount of compromise for the four of us to find something to agree on. Jason and I drew the line at *Crime Conquerors,* though *SpongeBob* could be entertaining and we all loved *The Simpsons.*

I made the greatest sacrifice a mother can make and actually sat through football games. It was the least I could do to repay Jason for getting Jack interested in televised sports, though I found I had to spend a lot of the time running to the kitchen to make invented emergency phone calls.

We continued our weekend outings: to the park, to the beach (weather permitting), to the movies, to the bowling alley. (We tried miniature golf, but clubs in the hands of Jack and Trevor were not a good mix.)

Our foursome was obviously not a chronicle of bliss: Jack and Trevor needed space from one another. Jason's friends were helping with the third bedroom, but they could only spare a few hours on weekends, so progress was slow.

Meanwhile, Jason and I pulled the boys apart when we felt the tension rising — ideally, before we felt the tension rising — and sent them to other spots in the house: the living room, or the postage stamp of the backyard, weather permitting or not. At least there was a basketball hoop there now, thanks to Jason.

While Marissa's room continued empty. We could have put a velvet rope across her open door and called it "Little Girl's Room 21st Century." Visitors could look in at her white furniture and the Barbie collection which in the end she had left at home.

Did she miss me at all? I missed *her* like a limb. I missed how she would climb in my lap. I missed how she would hold my hand when we walked down the street. I missed how damn smart she was, how every day she told me something new that she'd learned, but how she retained her perfect naïveté.

I missed her uncorrupted smell, the inimitable softness of her hair, the even softer sensation of the skin of the back of her neck.

Her precocious brain was still embedded in childhood and so she'd asked me, when she was not yet three, "when I was in your tummy, was HannahSophia there, too?"

In ten years — in nine? — in seven? — I would be useless to her as anything more than a yardstick of measuring stupidity. Mothers and daughters survive that phase and reconcile — usually. If we missed these intervening years, though, what foundation would we have to return to?

But how could I bring her back into my loud, chaotic home?

The only way was to get rid of Jason and Trevor. And how could I do that to Jack?

Keep telling yourself that. Keep telling yourself it isn't just because you want a man in your life.

MARISSA WAS in her room alone. She could hear the slightly muffled sound of Leonora running the vacuum.

Her room reminded her of the ones that they stayed in when Daddy took them to the Disneyland Hotel, except for the shiny silver laptop on the desk, and no room service. She would never jump on *this* bed.

She had a headache.

School wasn't as much fun anymore. Mrs. Persons was such a nice teacher and she had the prettiest clothes ever. But then she got pregnant and she had to leave because she had to be on bedrest. The new teacher wore plaid pleated skirts and taught them rhymes like, "It's less about skill than it is about will," and "Make your best better than the rest."

When school let out, Leonora took her to see Linda Bartlett, oh right, "Vi-o-let-ta."

Leonora picked her up after that and brought her home.

Working with Linda was one of the things that gave her headaches. It had gotten worse since Thanksgiving. There still weren't any flowers yet.

When Marissa finally got home she ate dinner with Leonora and Dania. Dania came to fix dinner and Leonora was supposed to leave then, because Leonora was the day nanny and Dania was the night one, but Leonora and Dania were *primos* (cousins), it turned out, and they sat at a different table talking for a long time before Leonora left, while Marissa ate alone.

Then she was allowed to watch TV for an hour, before she did her homework from regular school.

Every morning Daddy said he would see her at dinner and then every night when she got home from Linda's Greenhouse, Daddy called on the phone and he was very, very sorry, but he couldn't come home 'til later. He would say something like, "An elderly man was run over by a car in a crosswalk. We have to see if we can find the driver of the car that hit him." Then he would say, "I'll be home early tomorrow night," and for a while she believed him.

The first week was the worst. Marissa sat eating the yucky salad and the gross white stuff called pissotto, fighting back the tears that pricked the corner of her eyes, because only babies cried. But Leonora and Dania would stop talking long enough to call over to her, "Eat! Eat!"

Most of the words they knew in English were bossy words like "go to bed" and "clean up," and of course "no," but that was the same in

Spanish so it didn't count. Marissa complained again to Daddy about how hard it was to talk to them but he chuckled and said, "You don't give up that easily, do you?"

Marissa *was* understanding a lot more words. She knew that *deberes* meant homework, and *jefe* meant boss. Now, too, she listened to the *way* the nannies talked, and she noticed how Leonora put her arms around Dania when Dania started to cry sometimes. Marissa heard the words *novio* and *amorio* and she could tell that it had something to do with a boyfriend, and whatever it was was going badly.

She'd picked up enough Spanish, in fact, that, the week before, she tricked Leonora into taking her to Emma's house for a playdate after school instead of to Linda's.

Daddy found out and he was *maaad*. He sat her down in the room Mommy called the Batcave.

"Do you think that was a nice thing to do?" Daddy asked. "You hurt Leonora's feelings very badly."

"But you wanted me to talk to Leonora in Spanish, didn't you?"

He answered her with another question. "Do you know why donkeys don't go to college?'

"No."

"Because no one likes a smart ass."

She could tell he wasn't so mad anymore.

"I hope you'll treat both Leonora and Dania with more respect in the future."

"Yes, Daddy."

"Good."

"But Daddy — "

He was half out of his chair already but he settled down again — slowly. "This isn't about 'the grandma ghost' is it?"

Daddy had said that first, his mother was a very nice woman, and second, that when you died there was nothing left of you, so you couldn't even be a ghost. He was going to take her to the third floor to prove it, but Marissa wouldn't go unless it was light, and Daddy was never home when it was light.

"When can I see Mommy?"

"Do you miss Mommy?" Daddy looked confused.

"I think Mommy misses me," she said, really carefully. "Maybe I should visit her on the weekend."

Daddy looked sad. "I thought you wanted to come to the office with me. I don't get to see you otherwise."

On weekends Daddy took her to the office and when she got bored, there was always someone who would take her out to lunch or for frozen yogurt.

On Saturday nights he took her to those dinners at hotels where there was chicken like sponges and the desserts were really tiny. Daddy introduced her to everyone and bragged about how smart she was, and everyone said, "No wonder your dad is proud," and "won't you make a great politician someday," but they didn't talk to her after that.

The vacuum had stopped, but that wasn't a good thing. It meant that Dania had come to take over.

The problem was that Marissa wanted a snack, and a good snack, not one of those dumb carrot sticks that the nannies were always shoving under her nose.

Marissa swung her legs off her bed and sat up, but too fast, so that it made her feel dizzy.

Marissa had figured out ways to sneak junk food. Daddy wasn't nearly as good at hiding as Mommy was, and it only took her a few days to find some. He had chocolate in a white box with a picture of an old lady, just like Mommy did, only his was hidden behind the Cuisinart. The problem was knowing what candy to take. Some of them were gross inside. If she bit into a gross one she just sucked the chocolate off and threw the rest away.

She found Daddy's ice cream the second day she was here. She dragged a chair over to the giant refrigerator and she found it in the back part of the freezer. It was funny that Daddy thought she was so smart but didn't think she was smart enough to pull a chair up to the refrigerator.

The trouble was that both the chocolates and the ice cream were downstairs. That wasn't usually a problem, because either Leonora or Dania was vacuuming almost all the time so they didn't hear her creeping into the kitchen. And it seemed like as soon as they finished vacuuming the house they had to start all over again.

But now that Dania had arrived, Marissa could be sure of not being able to sneak into the kitchen. The two nannies would be making dinner, and when Leonora finally left, Dania would load the dishwasher and clean the kitchen until it was Marissa's bedtime.

Maybe it was time to try out her idea, the one she'd had for a while.

She had only been in Daddy's study that one time when he was mad. Because when they left, though he wasn't mad anymore, he said,

"Wiss, I don't want you coming in here. I have confidential material on my computer. Do you know what 'confidential' means? All right. I trust you, so I won't lock the door."

But she wouldn't look at his confiden-shul stuff. She only wanted to see what treats he had in there, because that's where he would hide his *good* junk. She imagined a whole Walgreen's shelf full of bright colors: the yellow of peanut M&Ms, the red of Skittles, the green of the tropical fruit-flavored Starburst.

She got up from her bed slowly. She still hadn't watched her hour of TV. She wanted to save that for after dinner. Daddy said he'd be home early tonight, but she knew that meant late anyway "because something came up."

She tiptoed on the carpet in the hall. She had to be careful because if she let her shoes slide on it too much then she'd make it be static electricity.

She stopped when she thought she heard a noise. What if Leonora was bringing the vacuum upstairs? Marissa thought she should run back to her room, but if Leonora did bring the vacuum upstairs, Marissa would be trapped in there for Who Knows How Long with no way to get to Daddy's study.

She put her weight on her heels. If she was going to get trapped, let it be in the Batcave.

So she resumed sliding, sliding. Finally she took the last quiet slide to the door.

She reached for the doorknob.

Zap.

She got a shock when she touched the metal. It hurt. It didn't hurt too much, but she was afraid to touch it again. She went back to her room, but running this time.

Downstairs, the vacuum started up again, and so did Marissa's headache.

Sunday morning.

Jason had spoiled me here as well. He got up, marshaled the troops with amiable authority and had them quick-march into the kitchen for pancakes.

I snuggled down into the comforter, which needed a good Mairead-style wash, but which smelled of me and Jason and so gave me an excuse to wait until next weekend.

Then the doorbell rang.

I always expected bad news when the phone rang, and when there was someone at the door, it was all the more frightening. The Gestapo. A telegram with the news that someone had died.

Alex — returning with Marissa! *I knew the bastard would cave*. I jumped out of bed.

Our front door opened straight into the front room: a lack of privacy and elegance that I was ashamed to say bothered me. But there, by the front door and therefore right in the living room, was a Japanese-American man who looked very familiar. I suffered from a smaller degree of Jack's difficulty in recognizing faces.

"Hello!" the stranger said. "Nice to see you, Mrs. K."

So I was going to have to fake it.

Jason to the rescue yet again: "Coach. Good to see you."

Trevor's track coach.

Jason shook Coach Takanawa's hand in that man's man way some men have and other men aspire to.

The Coach was wearing a white polo shirt, suspiciously tight across the chest, so that his pectoral muscles and firm man-boobs were outlined. From out of the short sleeves emerged biceps and triceps rarely seen this side of a Chuck Norris exercise infomercial.

I'd managed to pull on jeans and a cerise V-neck sweater. I did not like to go barefoot in front of strangers so I had slipped into my Ann Taylor flats, the ones with the gold-tone heel. Quite affordable at one of A.T.'s frequent 40% off sales.

"What can I do you for?" Jason asked, slapping Coach on the upper arm.

"Would you like some coffee?" I asked. I hated it when people dropped by unannounced, but the first thing I did when I got out of bed was to make a big pot.

"No thanks. I was hoping to surprise The Flash."

There was a half beat during which I, and I believe Jason, did not know whom he was referring to. Before it became noticeable, Jason said, "Hey! He'll be pleased. *Trev!*"

Trevor slouched in. "What are you doing here?"

If we'd been listening to this exchange on the radio, Trevor would have sounded sullen, or even rude. But his face was alight.

"Your new personal best on Friday?" Coach prompted. "Six-thirteen-fifty?"

"What about it?"

Once again, Trevor sounded more hostile than happy; once again his smile said otherwise.

"I think we should celebrate, don't you?"

"Huh." Trevor shuffled his feet.

Coach Takanawa slapped Trevor on the back — a little forcefully, apparently, because Trevor lurched forward, though he quickly regained his balance.

"Brunch at Ella's," Coach announced. "Whatcha say, Flash?"

I knew Ella's; it wasn't far from where Alex lived. It was kitty-corner from the JCC and mysteriously popular. On a Sunday morning one could see a line stretching halfway down the block. I'd never eaten there, but I'd often wondered what pharmaceuticals they were slipping in the Mimosas to make it worth an hour's wait.

"Okay," Trevor said, as if agreeing to join the bomb squad, but Coach put his arm around Trevor's shoulders, and gave them a shake.

"Good man."

There was an awful lot of "manly" touching going on.

It was then that Jack appeared.

He didn't look any worse than Trevor, but that was saying about what you'd expect. The boys had been up until some ungodly hour. I didn't know what ungodly hour, because Jason and I had fallen asleep before they had, in spite of the racket they'd been making. Both had bloodshot eyes and uncombed hair. If cowlicks were a cash crop I'd buy futures in Jack's.

They could also both have used a shower.

"What's — what — what's going on?" Jack asked.

Coach jumped right in. "Jack, isn't it? I've heard about you from Trevor."

"You...." Jack clearly wanted to say more but couldn't.

We all waited a couple of beats, but then Coach said, "Whaddaya say, Flash?"

"He needs to 'freshen up' a bit," Jason said. "And why don't you take Jack along? He'd like to celebrate."

"Yes!" Jack cried, pumping his fists.

"Well...." Coach Takanawa hesitated. "Jack's always welcome of course, but I was hoping to have a little one-on-one time with — "

"Trevor wants him to come along." Jason slapped Trevor in the lumbar region. Trevor grunted. "They're brothers now."

I watched through the window as those brothers got into a red SUV. Trevor had called "Shotgun!" — three times, in fact, but Jack was pumping his fists in a way that told me that he was just happy to be included in this spontaneous outing.

Jason adopted a Pepe Le Pew accent when he whispered in my ear, "We haf zee house to ourselves, ma chere."

"*C'est vrai*, oh *ami de ma coeur*."

"You are such a damn show off." Jason pulled me toward him.

My thoughts flowed swiftly: *This is so awesome having the house to ourselves, we can make as much noise as we want and maybe do something kinky though I'm not sure what, but it sucks we didn't meet each other first and have time as a couple before we had three kids....*

Three kids.

"I need to talk to Marissa."

"Zen you must call her." He kissed me on the neck. "Although afterwards...."

Usually I had to wait for Marissa to call me; whether I phoned Alex's office, home or cell, he would dodge me with some excuse. I would not have expected to want my five-year-old to have her own cell phone (as did some of her classmates) but I was already planning to give her one for Hanukkah. I'd give it to her in private — then let Alex try to take it away.

This time, the voice on the other end said, "*Hola?*"

One of his nannies. He had two. I wanted to meet them, but so far Alex had evaded me on that front as well. When I did speak to Marissa, though, she boasted about the Spanish she was learning. Her Spanish teacher often held her up as an example to the rest of the class.

"This is Anna, Marissa's mother. May I speak to her please?"

"*Que?*"

"Mar-ee-sa. Madre." I hated how patronizing I sounded.

"Meester Kagen no home."

In movies she would have said "Senor Kagen," to authenticate herself as a Spanish-speaker, but of course the woman on the phone knew the word "Mister."

"*Mareesa*," I repeated.

"No home."

I motioned to Jason, covered the mouthpiece with my hand (which was completely unnecessary), and whispered, "Can you bring the laptop over?"

From the laptop I cued up Google Translate, but not quickly enough. The voice on the other end said, "No home," a final time and hung up.

"Either she doesn't speak English or Alex has told her not to let me talk to her."

"Then I'll call in a few hours. She won't recognize a man's voice and I'll ask to speak to Alex first."

Jason got no further than "no home," either, and what was more troubling, since we had the speaker on, was that I could tell that it was a different woman.

There were limitless possible explanations: Alex was having the house fogged; he was helping with the mortgage payments by letting the first floor out as a brothel on weekends. The simplest: "They're just out for the day, right?"

"Right," Jason agreed. "But I have an idea. Just to speed things up."

I didn't have a lot of favors in the bank with Rose Gonzales, but after I made a $200 contribution to the Mexican-American Legal Defense Fund, I asked if she'd help me get a hold of Marissa before school started one morning.

I knew that Alex would have left for Bryant Street before Marissa left for school, even though her school day began even earlier than Jack's, just as it lasted longer.

In Rose's office, I listened to her rattling off the niceties, such as *buenos dias* and *me llamo Rose*, while thinking that it *was* good for Marissa to learn Spanish, and wishing I hadn't studied French, though it wasn't as if I could have discussed the day's headlines with a French nanny either.

After that, Rose's manner became more forceful. That was an even better reason to choose her than for her language skills: even if the letters INS never came up (Alex would never hire an undocumented worker), she'd make Alex's personal Torquemada see the light.

"Marissa's on the line." Rose extended the phone. "I'll give you some privacy."

She stepped outside her office where I could watch her pace the floor, with frequent stops to look at her watch.

Marissa and I couldn't speak for long anyway, since she had to leave for school. She volunteered that Lakshmi Persons had left Sunshine Academy, apparently (and I praised God for it) without telling her successor that Alex had offered me up for the thankless job of room parent.

Since Lakshmi had taken a leave of absence before Thanksgiving, I was officially off the hook, but Alex would make sure that Marissa's academic life was in perfect order. It was the rest of her life I wanted to hear about. Was Emma still her best friend? Was Chad Yardley still mad that she hit him with the paper airplane during recess? Did Buchanan still do the trick where he stuck the spoon to his nose?

Through the glass door, I saw Rose pull back the sleeve of her gray suit and look at her watch.

"The babysitters?" I hissed to my daughter. "How do you talk to them?"

"I'm teaching them English."

"What about Daddy? Are you spending any time with him?"

"He's taking me shopping this weekend."

"What could you possibly need?" I blurted.

"I don't know."

Marissa had what we therapists called a "flat affect."

"Are you happy?" I demanded.

"You asked me that before." Pause. "I have to go, Mommy."

That night, with Jason, I used the F word frequently. "And I've tried talking to Alex, but he keeps dodging me."

Then I started to describe a rather inventive way in which a man could be castrated; Jason interrupted, "This isn't something a guy likes to talk about."

He'd only been home a few minutes. He was stretched out on the sofa, still in his uniform, but this time, I thought, not because he knew I loved him in it, but because he was too tired to change.

He was always exhausted when he came home. He had to make a thousand decisions each day, most in the space of half a heartbeat. Most of those decisions did not carry life-or-death consequences, but at any moment, a deadly encounter could be a traffic stop away.

Sometimes the tedium was worse than the danger: three hours for a scrap metal thief to be processed, when the same scrap metal thief would be back in business the following day.

Jason must be sick unto death of hearing me kvetch about Alex. He never spoke about *his* ex. True, she'd been out of the picture for a long time, but he must have been tempted to remind me of Alex's generosity, his finagling on behalf of Jack, and the very fact that he was still in the picture, while Jason had been a single dad with a single income for six years.

I brought him the remote. "Peace offering for a peace officer. It's not your problem. Bring you a beer?"

"I didn't say it wasn't my problem. I just need half an hour to myself. And yes to that beer."

When I came back with his Heineken the TV was on one of the sports channels.

"You had a good idea about asking Rose for help." I hoped that the praise would outweigh the negative of bringing up the subject of Marissa again.

He didn't answer right away as the bottle was tipped into his mouth. He chugged four times without a break. And then, inevitably, came the belch.

"Listen to me," he apologized.

"Music to my ears."

I started to leave but he called me back. "I have another good idea."

"H'm?"

"Let's make sure that Marissa comes home for winter break."

CHAPTER 15

The ride to the field trip was twisty and bumpy and Jack felt a little nauseous.

He hardly ever got to go over the Golden Gate Bridge. It was so tall and beautiful. The fog wafted through like cotton candy, only white. What would white cotton candy taste like? Why was it always pink anyway?

Ashleigh had said many times that she needed his help to make this trip a success. But she'd also said she wants to help him and his friends. So who was helping who?

Sometimes she let slip the words "autism" or "Asperger's" and then she put her hand on her mouth. But he figured out that the autism or Asperger's is part of why she's interested in him and he felt different about the words now. At first he thought it would work as a good excuse ("I hide food because I have Asperger's!" "I can't do homework because I have Asperger's!"), but that didn't work out. Still, the label didn't discourage him so much anymore. It was part of who he was. He saw no reason why he should change for the world. There were others like him. He was very lonely sometimes. But so were the people on TV, sometimes, and they always ended up happy in the end. He just had to be patient.

When Ashleigh stepped out of the bus she was hot and tired, but the moment she hit the cool air of the Marin Headlands she went from miserably hot to unbearably cold, from a sharp westerly wind. The bus, a district school bus that either Ms. Gonzales or Mr. Takanawa managed to swing, had no air conditioning.

The noise of the crowded bus had almost deafened her. She tried to take charge and lead them in singing but Ms. Gonzales said she would just overstimulate them, Aspies and NTs alike.

But there were twenty kids on the bus, including her, and the singing would have been so much nicer to listen to than the black noise of kids shouting and arguing. One boy kept repeating, "I don't like it when people don't think I know something I know!"

She'd wanted to make this trip even bigger, but now she was hella glad she wasn't able to.

She looked behind her and for a split second she caught the eye of the driver. He was a stout, mustachioed man who didn't say a single word during the drive. The very second their eyes met he looked straight ahead to his escape route and never again wavered, but she was sure that he was both feeling sorry for her and thinking that it was her own damn fault that she got herself into this.

The next moment someone jostled her, and jostled her hard. Then someone else did the same. The kids were pouring out of the bus and hardly noticing her. This had nothing to do with autism, she thought. People were just rude. In fact, in a group the Aspie kids disappeared: you couldn't tell who was on the spectrum and who was just being an asshole. Now *that* was what full-inclusion was about!

It made her feel, at least for a second, that all the work she did (which was most of it) was worth it. The biggest problem was money, and in the end they had to make the full-inclusion parents pay enough to cover the cost. The surprise was how ready they were to pay. She could have saved herself some grief by starting with them.

The other problem was chaperones. Ms. Gonzales and Mr. Takanawa were the only ones — but the parents signed the waivers, so now it was up to her....

"Hey!" she called out. Mr. Takanawa had praised her for her leadership skills but in such a way that she knew that he wanted her to improve them. When every single one in the group ignored her — except Jack who had frozen in a position of staring at her with that expectant look — she was irritated and turned to Ms. Gonzales, who was just stepping off the bus, with Mr. Takanawa behind her. They were the last two.

Ms. Gonzales read her mind. "This is your baby, *chica*. Get your kiddies in the guest house and settled in." Then she said more softly, but in a voice meant for Ashleigh to hear, "*et bonne chance.*" More loudly: "I have some work to do." Ms. Gonzales raised her left arm a few inches, drawing Ashleigh's attention to a case that looked like an old-fashioned doctor's bag.

"Wh — " Ashleigh looked to Mr. Takanawa for help. They didn't expect...?

Mr. Takanawa looked as though he were struggling very hard not to smile. It was an exaggerated version of the look he almost always gave her, in which he was very amused with her. "I think Ms. Gonzales is right," he said.

And just that fast, both the teachers vanished, as if their legs never moved.

Ashleigh looked up at the guest house. She had to blink; it was another magic trick. She'd seen the online pictures of the guest house when she was making the plans: It was a roomy stick Victorian, large and freshly painted white, with a blue roof and blue plantation shutters. But anything that might once have been blue was now the color of veins through pale skin. And the building was half the size she'd expected, with horribly peeling paint, and the remaining paint dirty. The boards of the steps sagged in the middle. It was like some pioneer's cabin that was abandoned after the gold rush.

What a rip-off! She wanted this to be nice for the kids. They must have Photoshopped the picture. Wasn't that against the law? She was hardly expecting a hotel like somewhere *Mother* would have stayed, like the Ritz Carlton. What had she been expecting, then? She must have had a picture in her mind, but she couldn't conjure it up. Was this something like the way it felt to be Jack, to have these weird blanks in your head?

She shook her head to rid herself of the image in front of her. She had to get this huge crowd of kids up into the guest house and settled — settled where? Why would they look to her as a leader?

You have to believe *you're the leader,* Mr. Takanawa had told her during one of their planning meetings.

So she forced herself to raise her voice, even though she didn't like to shout. "Everyone — everyone make sure you have all your stuff before the bus drives away! And wait for me by the steps!"

She jumped on the bus, bounding over the two stairs in one leap, glanced down the aisle, which was empty, and jumped off again, never hearing another word from the bus driver. The moment her hiking boots hit the ground she heard the engine start behind her. It wouldn't be back for two afternoons. She found herself looking around the guest house for signs of another motorized vehicle.

Nothing but a rusted bicycle, leaning against the side of the building. One tire was flat.

The kids were restless, milling around. Ashleigh raised her voice again. "We're all happy campers, aren't we?" she asked, arms now akimbo. The gambit was unsuccessful: she saw eyes rolling and a few snarkies came from the group, mostly unintelligible, though she made out, "Who died and made you Queen of Marin fucking County?"

Audrey, the only autistic girl, was scratching herself near her crotch. Nicholas — who was neuro-typical, so what was his excuse? — was trying to tickle Sarah, who was batting him away.

Then she heard Jack, loud and clear: "I'm a happy camper!"

That set off laughter from everyone. It was mocking laughter, but she decided to pretend it wasn't.

"Well, come on, let's get inside."

Suddenly it was Freddie to the rescue. "Didn't you hear the lady? C'mon, boys and girls, we're happy campers all!" He broke into a dreadfully off-key song, "You're in the army now ... you'll really hate the chow. Let's form a line, we'll all do fine, we're in the army now...."

Miraculously, they did. Ashleigh joined in, trudging up the steep, uneven wooden stairs.

Inside, the smell was nauseating. It came from the kitchen and it was some kind of cleaning product that made her seriously gag. More than that: something awful cooking. Maybe even liver. And a smell she remembered from St. Elizabeth's: the same scent that homeless people had.

The second thing she knew was that that building was very dark. But as her eyes adjusted the third thing was that it was deserted, or it was now. Mr. Takanawa and Ms. Gonzales must have been there, but they might as well not have been.

There was a window, like a cashier's window, to her right, but no one was sitting on the chair provided. To the side of the window was a large poster, printed with all the rules for visitors. The usual shit about quiet and clean up, but also, since it was a nature center, you weren't allowed to kill *bugs*.

They could have done with fewer posters and more staff.

"Upstairs!" she announced, and when Freddie echoed her command, everyone clambered up creaky, narrow stairs that needed sweeping badly.

Upstairs there were two dorm rooms: one for boys, and one for girls. Then there was another, narrower flight of stairs. The brochure had said that there were also two "chaperone" rooms up on a smaller third floor: She had seen the dormer windows from the outside, so that at least was probably true.

Mr. Takanawa and Ms. Gonzales found their way up there pretty darn quick. And maybe Mr. Takanawa wasn't gay after all. But then, she'd always thought that Ms. Gonzales might be. Why should she care anyway, if they got together or not?

Ashleigh went into the dorm room and immediately drew a ragged, painful breath. It looked more like something you'd find in a prison: bare gray walls, wooden bunk beds crowded together, with nothing but the thinnest, raggediest mattresses she'd ever seen.

Freddie, God bless him, led the boys across the landing to the other side. She asked him to keep an eye on Jack, though Jack was the best behaved on the way. A couple of times he got carried away with the shouting, but the troublemaker was Nicholas.

She took the top bunk nearest the door without thinking. When she threw the duvet that she'd brought from home she saw that there were crumbs and full-on dust bunnies under the thin mattresses. Dust *rabbits,* she thought, trying to cheer herself up.

Here in close quarters, the gap between Audrey and the NT girls was more obvious, and inevitably so, because not only was she the only Aspie (only 20-25% of those diagnosed with autistic spectrum disorders were female — she learned that from her research, too), but sadly, Audrey was the most affected of all. Although she wrote touching poetry and had even had some published (and not just in the school newspaper or something, but in real poetry magazines) she was barely verbal, a condition that had made Ashleigh wonder really hard about brains. But Audrey made other girls act very motherly. Those other girls were taking good care of her, so Ashleigh quickly slipped into the women's bathroom.

There was mold in the grout. The concrete floor was something Ashleigh wouldn't step on in hiking boots. The plain white — formerly white — shower curtains on the two stalls were a light gray and there was mold on them, too. The three toilet seats were fully exposed.

She couldn't imagine. She just couldn't imagine.

She thought how now the dorm wouldn't seem so bad, but she was wrong.

"It's like Camp Runamukka," someone said.

"How about Camp Wannafucka?"

The giggling was out of control.

Seriously? Can you guys reinforce the stereotype of teenage girls any more than this?

"Think we'll do ghost stories?"

The other girls didn't seem so bothered by the conditions. Ashleigh would have to hide her disgust.

But then she heard a scratching sound. It might have been something else, but … no, it was a scratching sound!

I'm gonna see a mouse tonight. She shuddered.

JACK FELT proud and even a little smug. None of the other boys went to his elementary school, Clarisse Heims, so they hadn't been here before. He came up for Outdoor Ed with his whole grade, 60 of them, when he was twelve. His mom did one of the volunteer shifts; he'd heard her laughter from inside the house when they were coming back from their hike, and then, when he saw her in the kitchen, as they all piled in and the sixth grade teachers were yelling at them, and shoving them on the shoulders — "Upstairs! Upstairs! Never mind the kitchen!" — he glimpsed her as he passed, and saw that she was watching for him, her big eyes on him and her pretty, clean clothes and her glossy black hair and her soft bosom that was always waiting for him.

When he came up in the line for more spaghetti she whispered that she was giving him the part with the most sauce.

Now he was glad she wasn't here. She'd be watching him too closely, picking out things that he was doing wrong. Not that she'd tell him what he was doing wrong. She'd make those faces over someone else's head, and tilt her own head, and draw her fingers across her neck in that motion that Ashleigh taught him means "to stop." But he wouldn't know what it was that she wanted him to stop.

No matter. She was off with Jason for the day, and the night, and the next day and the next night, and let them have fun.

It was hectic in the boys' dorm. Ashleigh's friend Freddie was helping the other boys unpack. Freddie was gay and Edward was his boyfriend. Jack was jealous, because even though Freddie and Edward were boyfriend and boyfriend, and that was the same as being boyfriend and girlfriend, they got to be in the same room together. It didn't seem fair that he couldn't be in the same room with Ashleigh, but they could be if they were both girls and they were gay.

At least tonight she'd sleep across the hall from him. This was as close as they'd ever been together at night.

He was disappointed that she didn't sit next to him on the bus. He saved a seat for her. He even told Trevor, who plunked down next to him, *you can't sit here, I'm saving it*. Saving it, huh? For a moment Jack thought that Trevor would take offense and that would be very bad — the rages that Trevor was capable of had disappeared, but nothing disappeared forever, did it? He learned that in science: the conservation of energy. Either Trevor's rages changed to something else, or they hadn't, and if they hadn't, then they were still there.

Trevor went to a different seat. There was plenty of room on the bus. But after they'd been driving for a while, Jack looked around and saw that Ashleigh was sitting in the front *by herself* and Trevor was sitting near the back the way that African-Americans used to have to, and he was sitting *by himself*, too, so Jack went and sat next to him, without any explanation and that was the rest of the ride, except that Jack got kind of sick to his stomach with all the bumps.

But why didn't Ashleigh sit next to *him?* He kept rolling the question around in his head, the way he used to like to roll his toy cars back and forth.

Jack unzipped his duffle bag. He told his mom he could pack for himself, but then she rummaged through the duffle bag and found all the half-unwrapped bags of HoHos and Goldfish. When she threw them away he yelled at her just like she deserved. She yelled back while she shook out his clothes, and then she said that she couldn't get rid of the crumbs, and then she packed different stuff in his bag. As if anyone cared what he wore! Ashleigh didn't care what she wore. She said that all the time, that what you wear didn't matter, so what difference did it make if there were crumbs in his clothes?

"Dude, you gonna unpack or you gonna stare at the mattress 'til it puts a sheet on itself?"

Freddie's voice snapped him out of thinking about Ashleigh.

"You need some help, Jack-o?"

"No!" He pulled everything out in a tangled ball: the pajamas, the Ziploc bag with his deodorant and toothbrush, the underwear, and the HoHos that he put back in when his mom wasn't looking.

Freddie was looking, though. "Dude, we are gonna get some big rats tonight if you have that crap in here."

"I'm not scared of rats!"

"Well, you should be. They eat your eyes out of your head."

That was kinda scary. He clung to the mix of crumbs and plastic wrapper and remaining hunks of HoHos in his cupped hands and waited to see what to do next.

Ashleigh finally forced herself into the kitchen although the odor made her even more nauseous once inside. *Get busy,* she told herself. *That will get your mind off it.*

So she hastily made a duty roster from a piece of binder paper and, using her pen as a conductor's baton, she assigned various duties. Setting the table, washing vegetables — oh, and first, clean off plates before anyone uses them. Turned out that making salad is a three person deal: scraping carrots, slicing avocados, washing lettuce....

And clean-as-you-go: put scraps in the compost bin, wipe down surfaces with that nauseating disinfectant....

Little quarrels broke out. "You're doing it wrong!" "I am not doing it wrong!" And then, three more times: "I am not doing it wrong!"

And then there were the knives. Ashleigh ran around checking to make sure that as few knives as possible were in use, and that those that *were* in use were in the hands of those least likely to maim themselves, or — *holy shit!* — one of their classmates.

Freddie and Edward helped a lot, but Ms. Gonzales and Mr. Takanawa were still totally invisible. Ashleigh tried super-hard not to think about them up on the third floor. Just because they were teachers ... well, they were human, too, and remember what happened last year with Gloria Leemis and Mr. Lyu....

Kindness begins with me, kindness begins with me.... She couldn't let herself be distracted, not even for affirmations. Everyone was getting hungry, and restless; she could almost hear stomachs rumbling.

Just get food on the table.

The table. Check to make sure they set the table.

She wiped her hands on a dish towel, then slapped the towel over her shoulder. As she was heading out the door three people called after her: "Ashleigh, what do I do with — "

"Ashleigh, Blair isn't — "

"Nicholas is — "

Ashleigh, Ashleigh, Ashleigh.

She turned off her hearing. She could step out of the kitchen, for God's sake, at least before she passed out from that awful smell. But the air in the dining room was almost as bad, in a different way, and she stopped, putting her hand on her forehead, actually afraid she *might* faint.... She sank onto the bench just in time, and froze there, staring.

Jack and Trevor were circling the two indoor picnic tables, laughing, while they put forks, knives, spoons and napkins down in no order at all. DeShawn followed them, mostly silent, sometimes grumbling, rearranging everything, but in a pattern of his own design: three spoons at one place, three forks in another....

Her head sank down to her folded arms. In her exhausted mind a question was circling, buzzard-like: *Who the hell doesn't know how to set a table?*

Another surge of the raucous laughter assaulted her and suddenly, with new energy, she leapt to her feet, on the verge of screaming to all the boys, *Go back in the kitchen! You're just making things harder for other people!* — but then she saw that Jack was looking right at her, waiting for praise, she could tell, while DeShawn stared out the nearest scummy window.

"How is it?" Jack asked, with such heart-breaking sincerity that tears came to her eyes and she said, "It's beautiful," and then turned to go back into the kitchen.

Jack was so confused, because Ashleigh said the table was beautiful, but he knew she didn't like it. Why couldn't people mean what they say? It was hard enough for him to understand English without people using the words wrong.

Usually with Ashleigh he could tell what she really meant. Over these past few months he'd become more in tune with her. He didn't know the word for it, but it was like ... well, he could just tell.

So he followed her into the kitchen.

He'd had — he still had — such high hopes for this weekend. A trip with Ashleigh! It would have been better if they were going together, just the two of them, but this was still good. Wouldn't there be some opportunity for the two of them to take a walk? Yes, they walked home from school often, but this would be different.

When he came here with his fourth grade class on Outdoor Ed, it was fun. They all had to make lunch together then, too. Maybe he could help now.

The kitchen was hard because everyone was doing different things at the same time.

"I want to help," he told Ashleigh.

She was putting her hair back in a ponytail. He loved her hair so much. "You don't need to, really."

"But I want to."

She shook her head, and had to start the ponytail over. "It's okay."

"But I *really* want to."

He heard the *snap* of the pony holder, and then the click of her tongue. Finally:

"Well ... you know we're having hamburgers."

"I love hamburgers!"

"Can you help make the hamburger meat into patties?"

He didn't know the word patty except that he heard it once as a girl's name.

"Here — oh hell, Freddie, can you show Jack how to make a patty?"

"Yo, dude, c'mere."

Jack knew who Freddie was, but he couldn't pick him out among all the faces. Then he saw that someone was gesturing toward him and he decided that must have been Freddie.

On the counter, there were raw hamburgers on a large metal tray. Freddie was slapping more hamburger between his hands.

"See, bro, what you do, it's easy, you roll up the meat like this — " Freddie made a rolling motion with his hands — "then you flatten it out. See? *Eee-zee.* Eh? You do it."

Jack put his hand in the giant bowl of hamburger. It sickened him to feel the gooey stuff against his palms and when he squeezed it and it moved through his fingers his stomach revolted. He dropped the blob back on the mound.

"Hey, bro, got an idea here. Why don't you wash your hands?"

"Okay." Jack made his way to the giant double sink. He'd never seen a sink like this. The way it smelled made him back away.

"Go into the bathroom!" one of the girls said. "Jesus!"

So he trekked out to the hall and wandered around. Finally he saw the bathroom marked "MEN." Inside there was a rusty sink and two faucets that were too stiff for him to twist.

So he decided that it didn't matter if he washed his hands after all, and he went back to the kitchen.

"All right, good job, li'l bro," Freddie said.

"I'm not little!" Jack protested.

"No, no, my bad. C'mon, we almost got these patties made. You wanna help or not?"

"Yes!"

"All right, let's see."

Freddie stepped back.

Jack grabbed a handful of meat again, still cringing at the sensation against his skin, but clenching his teeth tight to stand it, because he wanted to do it right.

"Good, good, you're doing it, bro!"

He felt Freddie slap his back. The approval kept Jack going, mashing the raw meat against his hands until it became a little easier to stand.

"Yeah, yeah, that's it … uh, let's see … tell you what, let me take that and show you again…."

Freddie had the meat back and he was making those circles again and — wow! It was a ball!

"Here." Freddie put the ball in Jack's hand. "Slap that sucker down now."

Jack imitated Freddie's motion, and — he was doing it! The ball was becoming a flat circle, like the other raw hamburgers on the tray.

The next one was even easier. Freddie kept pumping Jack on the back, and pretty soon he was singing a song to the rhythm of his own rolling and patting. "You like Kid Cudi, bro?" he asked, and Jack said yes, although he wasn't quite sure what Freddie just asked him.

Soon the tray was full. It looked like a giant sideways version of that game he used to play, Connect Four. He liked the pattern. And he helped.

"Dude, you did you a good job," Freddie said. "Why don't you take these over to the oven over there?" Freddie lifted the tray.

Jack swelled with a good feeling. He helped.

As he turned, the tray made a wide, wide circle. The next thing he heard was a squeal from one of the girls just as he felt the thump of metal against flesh.

It didn't happen in slow motion the way it did in the movies. It happened in so quick a time that Jack could never remember how it did happen.

There was the tray, upside down on the floor, and all the hamburger patties spread all around it, most of them crushed, some of them stepped on, and all of them, he knew, ruined.

"No fucking hamburgers," someone said. Jack didn't know his name.

Why do they care so much? Jack wondered. They had salad. They had potato chips. And they could put peanut butter on the hamburger buns. That was just as good. Even Mr. Takanawa said, "I like buttered buns." So why was it such a big deal? His mom dropped stuff all the time.

But he knew it was. He knew he messed up.

"We all know who did this," one of the girls said darkly.

"Now stop!"

It was Ashleigh. He'd never heard her yell like this before. He pulled back a little, so ashamed and so hurt....

"Do you guys know that millions of people all over the world don't have anything to eat today? And a lot of them are children!"

Then everything was totally, totally quiet, the kind of quiet like when the TV goes off but no one else in the house is awake.

Then finally she spoke again. "All right," she says. "Let's put this behind us. Let's move on."

ASHLEIGH WAS shocked. *How rude everyone was to poor Jack!* All this time she felt like she empathized with him, when she didn't have a clue until this afternoon what it must be like to be him. Maybe she still didn't know.

After being totally MIA all this time, Rose Gonzales came down after lunch and announced that it was time for the Social Skills Workshop.

When those words came out of Ms. Gonzales's mouth, Ashleigh never loved anyone so much. She was *so* exhausted.

Ms. Gonzales got a circle of chairs together by getting all the kids to pitch in, dragging folding chairs from all over the main floor. Now she was sitting at the head.

Ms. Gonzales started the group with, "I understand there were some challenges at lunch." Then she got everyone talking about being flexible and coping with change. She wasn't all goopy-woopy, as if going without hamburgers were a big deal, but she didn't criticize anyone for being upset, either, and if she knew that Ashleigh got upset, too, she wasn't letting on. And she never mentioned Jack, either.

When someone said, "He fucked up," she only said, "Let's use more helpful language."

After a short time Ms. Gonzales let Jack (on purpose?) sum up the findings of the group: "I don't like it when things change."

"Most people have trouble with that," Ms. Gonzales agreed. Then, "We're going to do some role-playing." She dipped into the doctor's bag and brought out a camcorder. "Ashleigh, I'd like you to record this session from here on. I can use it for … to train other teachers."

"I'd be glad to, Ms. Gonzales." Ashleigh stood, probably too fast, that way letting everyone know how relieved she was not to have to participate in the role-playing. She was *so* not ready.

Ms. Gonzales asked for volunteers, and, of course, Jack was the first one. Ashleigh was watching him only on the camcorder screen. He looked even smaller there. She'd always hated being an only child, and now he felt like a little brother to her.

No one else volunteered and Jack looked hurt and now Ashleigh wished she *weren't* behind the camera because she would volunteer. She was just starting to lower the equipment when Trevor said, "I'll do it."

Rose put Jack and Trevor in the center of the circle. "You're going to practice introducing yourselves."

Trevor had a little trouble understanding how they were going to introduce themselves when they already knew each other. He got it pretty quickly, but they weren't a good twosome: They each made the other laugh until Ms. Gonzales had to start again with a different pair.

The next role-playing went better: Grace and a boy named Leo pretended to be waitress and customer, with Leo ordering in the restaurant. Then Ms. Gonzales had another pair of kids pretend to be returning a broken iPod to a store.

And Ashleigh was having a big "duh" moment. It was like that story of Helen Keller with Anne Sullivan at the water-pump. She'd seen how Jack had trouble with simple, basic interactions that she'd always taken for granted, like that day at the One World Club when she tried to introduce him to her friends and to the other members and he — well, he embarrassed himself. Somehow — somehow for some reason that apparently no one understood — the kids on the spectrum didn't learn how to do these everyday things that people did, things that NTs learned without thinking, the same way ... *the same way they learn to talk!*

She remembered a time when she showed Jack how he could open a binder by pressing the two tabs on the end. Until then he'd always opened his binder by yanking on the middle ring, and he could only do it with a lot of really unattractive grunting. But once she showed him the easier way, he got it, and never had a problem again.

So could it *all* be taught — ?

They were role-playing ordering at a restaurant now. Most of the kids got with the program and were having fun.

Then Ms. Gonzales called on Audrey to come to the center of the circle.

Ms. Gonzales would obviously know Audrey from school and Ashleigh understood why she waited 'til the end for her. Ashleigh didn't think she'd even give it a try. But there she was.

Then Ms. Gonzales called on Nicholas to be her partner.

Ashleigh saw why Ms. Gonzales chose Nicholas, too: He was the only one of the group who hadn't taken a turn. But Ms. Gonzales didn't know Nicholas the way she knew Audrey. Ashleigh did. When Nicholas asked Ashleigh out last year, she had said that her mother wouldn't let her go out, which was true, but that wasn't why she said it. Ashleigh was pretty sure that he expected this weekend to be way different than it was: that there'd be long walks in the woods, so that they could wander off and pretend to have gotten lost, and extra rooms for the kids to hide in, and someone would definitely bring beer, or even margarita mix, plus the other stuff for making margaritas. And oh yeah, that he'd finally get laid.

Nicholas had been getting anstier and anstier since they got off the bus and he took his own first look at the guest house.

"Audrey, I want you to pretend that you are in class." Ms. Gonzales spoke slowly and firmly. "That you are in class and that you have to go to the bathroom."

Ashleigh could guess immediately that this had been a problem. Audrey was 15 but looked 12: She was six inches shorter than anyone else and had a round face and a round body. Unfortunately, her chest looked about a triple D, and the pink tent she was wearing didn't do anything to hide it. Sometimes she'd burst into screams: like, while they were making lunch she'd run screaming through the kitchen and Ashleigh sent her upstairs to chill out with the Raggedy Ann that her mother said she should bring. It worked, and Audrey joined them in time to eat potato chips.

Audrey didn't look like she was paying any attention to Ms. Gonzales. She kept plucking at the hem of her dress. Ashleigh was afraid she'd stick her hand between her legs next.

"And — Nicholas, right? — you'll act out the role of the teacher."

"What subject?" Nicholas challenged.

"Doesn't matter," Ms. Gonzales said lightly. "Audrey?" she prompted. "Can you pretend that you need to go to the bathroom? To go pee-pee? This is very serious," she added without a pause, which was smart, because at the sound of the first "pee" the snickers started up.

Nicholas kept snickering. Ms. Gonzales ignored him.

Audrey was flapping the hem of her dress so that the camera was picking up flashes of her underwear, with a narrow rim of pubic hair sticking out from the crotch.

Nicholas elaborately fanned himself with one hand, and some of the kids couldn't help breaking up: girls in giggles, boys in suppressed guffaws. Ashleigh forgave them; they didn't mean to humiliate Audrey, they were just so very embarrassed.

"Audrey," Ms. Gonzales said firmly, "You have to go pee."

"No, I don't."

"*Pretend.*"

"You'd better not encourage her too much, Ms. G.," Nicholas says. "Have you ever read *The Yellow River* by I.P. Freely?"

Waves and waves of laughter, to which Jack joined in. His laugh *could* be hard to take.

Ms. Gonzales stood and shooed Nicholas away. She actually said, "Shoo," in a voice even he wouldn't argue with. He crawled away, still acting the class clown, miming exaggerated fear from poor, freaky Audrey.

Ms. Gonzales took his place. She reached out and put her hand on top of Audrey's, the hand that was flicking the hem of her dress. "You have to go pee. Okay?"

"Okay," Audrey echoed.

"So what do you say?"

"You have to go pee."

"No, say '*I* have to go pee.' "

"*I* have to go pee."

Ashleigh knew that it was just parroting, but it was a big step, and she knew it was a big step because all the laughter had stopped.

But Ashleigh turned her attention to Ms. Gonzales. Her face was … was *aglow*, like the pictures of saints that hung on the walls of her old Catholic school.

Ashleigh was alone in the dark, leaning against the fence in the back of the guest house that separated it from a service road behind. It was cold, and she was cold, but she didn't want to go back inside until it was time to go to bed.

Darkness came early this time of year; tonight it fell when they were still making their way through another cray-cray dinner and an even crazier clean up.

But it was nothing like lunchtime. Everyone was relaxed now. The role-playing was genius: all the barriers were down. The NTs and the Aspies were getting along like the Porcupines and the Cardinals (the football team of Takei's rival high school) would if they all came to a Christmas party without their jerseys. See, this trip wasn't just helping the kids with spectrum disorders, it was helping the kids *without*: to be more compassionate, more patient, more understanding.

Ever since her afternoon at St. Elizabeth's, Ashleigh had been battling a disagreeable thought. Today, facing dust bunnies and the stink of disinfectant, she surrendered. She wasn't cut out to live in a hut in Zambia. She would love the people, but she couldn't live on nshima or go without toilet paper.

But now she knew her true path. Did the Universe show her the way? Did God? Was it random, or fate?

It was Jack.

Since they became friends she'd wanted to help improve the lives of the Autistic Nation. She started it when she took Jack to the One World Club, and look where they were now. She thought working with her autistic brothers and sisters was a stop-gap measure, but it turns out that it was an on-ramp to her life.

She took a deep breath of the chilly air. She just had to tough out another 40 hours here, with the grimy floors and threat of rodents.

"Hel*lo*, Beautiful."

She shivered at the sound. The temperature just plummeted another ten degrees.

It was Nicholas.

"I was checking you out all afternoon during that stupid group."

Nicholas already needed to shave. She could see the sleaze ball old man he was going to be at 25: unshaven, reeking....

For now, Nicholas smelled of the kitchen. He was no help at dinner and he even baited Leo, tossing vegetables at him that he couldn't catch and making comments about Audrey's tits. *He* sure hadn't been improved by this trip.

"Aren't you ready for a little relaxation?" Nicholas scooted toward her, not even trying to make it subtle.

"I am." Her voice was as cold as the air around them. "But alone, please."

That's the kind of thing her mother taught her to say. *Don't let them see one crack in your armor. Smile at them once and they'll come after you like a hunter on the first day of deer season, and they won't give up until they can drive you home strapped to the trunk of their car.*

Mother came from a hunting family, apparently.

It was good advice, Ashleigh admitted. *Even a stopped clock is right twice a day.*

"Now, why would you want to be alone on a beautiful evening like this?"

Ashleigh stood as straight as she could. "I want some time to think."

Nicholas made a laughing sound in the back of his throat. "You think too much."

"Not hardly."

"C'mon, cutie."

Nicholas reached for her arm. Memories of Dylan Whitfield flooded her; the water rose so high she might drown. Who was here? Who would hear her scream over the sounds of the music and arguments in the guest house?

Then:

"Nick, my boy."

Mr. Takanawa. He shot up right behind Nicholas, just like Jack's beanstalk.

"Hi, Mr. T.," Nicholas said. He was trying to sound cool, but his voice cracked on the last syllable and he scraped his hand against his face, brushing something invisible away.

"I bet you were just heading back to the guest house. You play the guitar, don't you?"

"I'm in a band, but — "

"I know, and you don't play some pussy guitar like the one Grace has. *Up.*" Mr. Takanawa threw a hitch-hikers thumb over his shoulder.

Ashleigh had to peer around Mr. Takanawa to see Nicholas slinking off, muttering words like "lame" and "skank."

"He's harmless." Mr. Takanawa answered the question that Ashleigh hadn't asked. "When you see that no one's watching the cookie jar, it's hard not to put your hand in. Aren't you cold, Miss Allen?"

"Not really." She turned away, to the fence, to the sky, anywhere. She didn't want him to notice how excited she was to see him. She didn't realize how much she wanted to talk to someone. Not sleazy Nicholas: someone with an IQ in triple digits.

He laughed. "You *are* shivering, Miss Allen. Here."

She saw the corduroy sleeve in her peripheral vision just before she feels the smooth satin lining of the jacket go around her shoulders. She closed her eyes tightly. Was he straight after all, and therefore like all the other guys? If so, she knew what came next: a fatherly pat on the back, and then maybe the reassuring stroking of her hair, or maybe he'd skip that and go straight to the supportive hug....

But nothing happened, and when she opened her eyes Mr. Takanawa was resting his forearms on the fence and looking at the sky. "You've worked very hard today, Miss Allen."

"Thank you." She was still shivering, in spite of the coat. Her mother taught her one other valuable thing: Don't fuss over a compliment. Just say a sincere "thank you" and shut up.

"The sky is beautiful tonight, isn't it?" he says.

She looked up. It is beautiful: so many stars. She'd forgotten that you couldn't see stars in the city. They were diamonds embroidered into black velvet.

"Such a clear night. Remember I warned you it might rain?" He chuckled softly. "That was the first time you told me about this idea. I liked it from the beginning, but I gave you a hard time, didn't I?"

"You did."

"Well, I wanted to make sure you were serious. But you were, and you worked very hard to put this together."

She never meant these two words more sincerely: "Thank you."

"And listen to those crickets."

It was a steady chirping sound, as loud as a car alarm.

But there was silence between them and it was partly out of nervousness when she continued, "What Ms. Gonzales did this afternoon … I mean, she has such a gift for drawing out these kids."

He clucked his tongue. "Perhaps I shouldn't tell you this. But Ms. Gonzales has her own agenda."

"Her own…. What do you mean?"

"Damn, I shouldn't have started this." He drummed his fingers on the edge of the fence. "But I guess it's too late now." He sighed. "Ms. Gonzales had someone put her name out for the Special Ed teacher award for SFUSD this year. The voting is coming up in March and with a little of the video she took today — "

"But she said she was going to use the video to train other teachers."

"Train teachers? She wants to go to law school next year. Boalt, if she can get in. Hastings, more like it. A Special Ed teach award would help with either one."

"No!" She sounded really girlie and pathetic.

"I've hurt you," he said, and in the light from the house above, for the half-moon was low in the sky, she could see that he truly was upset. "But I supposed it would hurt more if you found out later that she got the award — " he made a dismissive gesture — "and then just left us."

So Ms. Gonzales was like the rest of them: out for what she could get, not for what she could do.

Mr. Takanawa gave her shoulder one quick "sack up" squeeze. "Move on."

"Right," Ashleigh said, but she needed time to take all this in. To process the disappointment. She had still been hoping to talk to Ms. Gonzales before the weekend was over. She had questions she wanted to ask, and maybe, just maybe, her own suggestions to make. Like, Ashleigh thought that Audrey might be better off in a special day class instead of full-inclusion. She thought Ms. Gonzales would be impressed by her idea. And then they could talk about Ashleigh's new plans.

The shouting from the guest house was a little louder. She could go inside, but…. "I've told you about wanting to join the Peace Corps."

"I think you have mentioned the Peace Corps once or twice." He was being facetious. "In fact, the last time you mentioned it was…."

He looked at his watch.

She couldn't tell if he was making fun of her or trying to be nice. "Well … to tell you the truth, I never thought you took me seriously."

"And perhaps that's you doubting yourself, and projecting that doubt onto me."

"Oh, wow." Shit, she sounded like a brain-dead cheerleader. Her cheeks got warm even in this chill air. But he was right! Exploring the guest house that morning wasn't the first time she'd doubted herself, it was just the first time she'd admitted the doubt to herself. "Well, now I'm wondering if it really is my calling."

"At your age — "

"No!" She slashed the air with her hand, because she knew he was about to start that condescending, patronizing *bullshit* that twentysomethings hit you with, as if just because your age starts with a "1" you can't make any plans that don't involve crayons. "My calling is to work with kids on the autistic spectrum." She stated this as a fact. She wasn't going to let him patronize her.

"And I was going to say," Mr. Takanawa said calmly, "that at your age, most people don't have the maturity to recognize their calling." He let her be embarrassed for a moment before he continued, "Miss Allen, I believe you would be a phenomenal addition to the Peace Corps, or any corps for that matter, but I think I've gotten to know you a little bit these past weeks, especially as we've talked about this weekend, and you would be wonderful with autistic kids."

"Thank you."

"Imagine," he began, but then, "No, let me start again. No one knows for sure why the ASD population is growing. But what if nature — or nurture — is creating people to help them at the same time?"

"I never thought of that."

"You are a young lady with a very strong sense of self."

"What do you mean?"

"I've seen the pressure you're under. The boys who harass you, like our young friend Nicholas there."

Before the night with Dylan she was flattered when guys hit on her, even if she wasn't interested. Now they scared her.

"Evolution still rules," he said. "No matter how far we've come as a culture, men will still pursue a beautiful woman."

Well. There was no point in pretending to him that she didn't know that she was beautiful, because that would just sound as though she were fishing for more compliments.

"And with years of that kind of pressure, most beautiful women will follow the obvious routes."

"What's the obvious route?"

"Miss Allen, please. Acting. Modeling."

"Oh!" But, "Victoria's Secret probably does more to cause bulimia than Ipecac."

"Wise beyond your years."

She wanted to believe that he meant it, but he had that teasing, laughing-at-her-behind-his-eyes look.

And she feared that he was really mocking her when he said, "On the other hand, there are young women who have used their beauty for the good of the world."

"How?"

He sighed. "You're too young to know about Brigitte Bardot."

"Without the Internet I am," she said, trying to make it a joke.

"Before my time, too. But she was a famous actress in her day, and a famous beauty. A sex symbol, I'm afraid. But she became an outspoken advocate against killing animals for their fur."

She could only make a choking sound of disgust. Killing animals for their fur is so cruel, so abominable, that if there is a Hell, then it's full of people who wore their minks to the symphony.

"Look at Angelina Jolie. She's done incredible humanitarian work that she never could do without her fame — or her money. Look at Jenny McCarthy, if you want an example of an advocate for autistic spectrum disorders."

"I don't follow celebrities much." She's proud of that. "So ... I guess I need Google again." It felt like a private joke already.

"You know, I'm just thinking out loud here." He looked up at the sky again, but this time bending his head back so far that the rest of his body followed, and he bent his knees, as if to see all the heavens. "But I can envision how you could start with Hollywood and grow that into a base that could rock the world. Otherwise ... I hate to say it, but society still doesn't take a very beautiful woman seriously."

The crickets, the shouting from the guest house ... everything went silent for a moment.

"After all," Mr. Takanawa says, "Sometimes the shortest distance between two points isn't a straight line."

JACK WAS alone outside the big house. He'd been wandering here for forty-six minutes. It was cold, even with his Takei Porcupines sweatshirt on.

At first he could see his way clearly enough, with the light from the house, but when he couldn't find Ashleigh, he crossed the road in back and went into the trees, and it was very dark. He might even be lost.

Then he saw the shiny figure that looked just like a ghost. He was scared, but only for a moment. It was Ashleigh! She only looked like a ghost because of her white shirt.

"Jack!" She'd finally come close enough to see him. "What are you doing out here? You're supposed to be hanging out with the other kids."

"So are you."

"Touché."

He didn't know what that meant. He only knew how glad he was to see her. "Why — why didn't you stay in, in the house? I wanted to play 'Sorry' with you."

"Oh, Jack." She put her hand on his shoulder and gave it a quick squeeze. Did she know that just touching him made him get hard? But she still treated him like a kid.

"Tell you what. Let's take a walk."

That was just what he'd been hoping for this whole time! Forget "Sorry"!

They were already far away from the house, but they walked farther away, into the trees. There was a dirt path they could follow.

Looking up at the sky Ashleigh said, "Do you see how many stars there are?"

She was right. Why were there more stars here than at home? The only stars he saw in the city were the moving ones that made his dad chuckle and say, "That's an airplane, Jack."

He couldn't hear the girl's guitar any more, or the wallops of the pillow fight that started just before he left. They were totally alone. Except: "What's — what's that noise?"

"What noise?"

"It goes … *eeeeeeeh.*"

"Oh! Crickets. They're loud, aren't they?"

"They're *really* loud."

She laughed a little. "You're so funny."

It still came as such a pleasant surprise when she said that. "I am funny," he agreed, then almost panicked. That was a stupid thing to say.

There were so many things in his heart, and in his head, too. Just not in his brain.

Help! he thought. *Help*! He almost said it aloud before he stopped himself.

"Oh, Jack," Ashleigh said, and her voice calmed him the way flipping a pencil in front of his eyes did. Calmed him enough to think that he didn't have to do anything to keep her here, at least not for now. "There are so many different sounds out in the wild. This isn't even the wild. This is just the 'burbs."

He had no idea what "burbs" meant but he didn't want to ask.

"That's why I wanted to get all of you out here...."

She must have thought he was stupid. He knew that he wasn't, but he also knew that many people thought he was, and that it was easy to confirm that for them when he revealed his lack of understanding of the English language.

But no, Ashleigh didn't think he was stupid. She understood him better than his parents. He used to think they understood him, but they'd changed now.

"I think you enjoy nature more than most people," Ashleigh said.

"Yes, I do." He didn't.

"It's like — it's like — " She sounded like people do when they were talking to themselves. "It's like you're an old soul," she finally concluded.

He *really* didn't know what that meant, but he could tell that it was a compliment. He wasn't cold any longer; the sweatshirt was keeping him warm after all. No, Ashleigh kept him warm. Why should this time ever end?

"...*enjoy* a trip like this, but especially you." She paused and looked at him. "I did this for you, you know."

Jack's hand moved of its own accord. His fingers searched the darkness. They found Ashleigh's fingers. And then, together, yes, at the same time, his fingers and her fingers slipped together, each between the other until their two hands were clasped. He didn't dare look at her. His heart thumped so hard he thought he might fall over.

Ashleigh let out a satisfied sigh, but it felt as though it came from him the way you talk into a phone and your voice comes out another phone.

They walked farther into the trees. Jack had never known that "outside" could be this dark. He couldn't see the stars or the half-moon anymore because the tops of the trees blocked them out.

He walked into a tree.

"Oh, God, Jack! Are you okay?"

"Yeah."

"Let's sit down."

After groping for the circumference of the tree they sat with their backs against it. He didn't like the feel of damp dirt under his ass, not to mention the leaves and the pebbles, but he quickly forgot that, as all thoughts and sensations were absorbed into Ashleigh. This was why he loved her and why he knew that they'd be together some day: they didn't need language, that wall that separated him from the rest of the world.

She sighed again, but in a different way. "I can really talk to you, Jack," she said, as she had before. Why would she say that if she didn't like him? He was sure she liked him – but then, she had never said, "I love you," or even "I like you," and they did that all the time on TV.

But wait — how did he forget? That episode of *Drake and Josh,* when Josh was afraid to tell the girl in his English class that he liked her, and he and his friend agreed that boys didn't do that, they waited for girls to do it first. So he should be waiting for her....

"I can talk to you, too," he said. He said it without thinking! Without planning! He just *said* it and she was squeezing his hand, oh, she was squeezing his hand, but damn it, his penis was getting hard and that was bad, right? Or was it? His mom was right, he shouldn't watch *Family Guy* because there was never anything to learn from that show. Lois liked sex, Peter liked sex, and Quagmire liked sex, but no one wanted to have sex with Meg. Why not? He wished he knew what Meg did wrong so he could not do it.

She scooted down so that he could hear her t-shirt scratching against the tree bark. She hadn't let go of his hand. So he scooted down along with her though somehow it didn't work and he ended up entirely on his back. Ashleigh laughed softly, the good kind again. No, a better kind. Then she giggled, that giggly way that the girls at school had that usually annoyed the hell out of him but when she did it, it tasted wholly different, ice cream melting on his tongue, and she lay down next to him.

Now that he was lying down, he could see bits of the sky through the branches of the trees, and some of the stars. He was staring, almost hypnotized by those stars, when his entire view was blocked out. He was frightened for a second — was he going blind? — before he realized that it was Ashleigh's face, though he only knew that from the shape of her head, because she was completely black. He couldn't see her eyes or her nose or mouth at all. He could smell her fresh girl smell, separate from the rotten leaves and wet dirt around him.

Her mouth pressed on his.

His whole body seized up; his mind seized up more. He couldn't move. He couldn't think. He was hard, hard, hard so that it throbbed, throbbed, throbbed, but he was used to that ... *think!* What did this mean? He knew what it meant! On TV... on TV it always meant....

"Does this mean — " he choked. "Does this mean — "

It was too dark but he thought she was smiling.

"That I'm, that I'm your boyfriend?"

She laughed, but it sounded different from the usual way. "I guess you could say that."

CHAPTER 16

Jason was right about getting Marissa home for winter break.

I had to fight: Alex had found a program that spanned the entire two weeks, called Hit the Playground Running. It even met on Christmas Day (granted, on Christmas the program didn't start until noon). It was only after I convinced him that it was aimed at kids younger than Marissa that he relented.

Jack and Trevor were at Marin Headlands for the field trip that Ashleigh had arranged. I was proud of Jack, who had apparently helped with the planning; as far as I could tell Ashleigh really had become a friend to him.

When one of the nannies — Marissa said it was Leonora — dropped her off, I couldn't wait to show her the Christmas tree. Jason had brought it home the day before, lashed to the top of my van.

"You said we could never have one!" she protested.

"Because we're Jewish. But Jason and Trevor aren't. They'll celebrate Hanukkah with us and we'll celebrate Christmas with them."

"Christmas is better."

I squired her off to her room. "Look — it's just the same as when you left!" Then I fussed around her as if she were a celebrity I'd always wanted to meet, tossing childhood clichés at her: hot cocoa and a blanket around her shoulders, although it was 56 degrees outside.

When she was sitting on her bed with the cocoa in one hand and HannahSophia in the other, I knelt beside her. "So!" I began cheerfully. "How's life at your father's house?"

She performed a juggling act with the cocoa and the stuffed leopard, transferring first one then the other to the floor and then to the opposite hands.

But then it came spilling out: homework alone; dinners alone; Mrs. Persons and her beautiful saris — gone.

She spoke faster and faster and her confession was spackled with Spanish, when she talked about the nannies. I didn't understand Spanish, but when she cried, "*las odio!*" I got the message.

The worst was yet to come:

"And I have to see stupid Linda and I can't get the dirt out of my fingernails even though Leonora scrubs really hard…."

"I knew it, I knew it!" Although I had only suspected. I pulled myself up by holding onto her knees. "You are not going back there and that's final."

"But Daddy — "

But "Daddy" can kiss my ass. I restrained myself from unleashing the stream of invective that Alex deserved. I struggled to find a diplomatic way to describe how we needed to weigh the pros and cons of each setting, but the only words that came to me belonged in that stream of invective.

I settled for, "Your father can take care of himself."

I postponed the showdown with The Enforcer so that it wouldn't spoil our family time together.

Marissa had returned home on the last night of Hanukkah, which holiday messed with Jewish parents' heads each year as they tried to make it stand in for Christmas. When it was late and overlapped Christmas it was doable, but it usually came and went well before December 25th.

The day Marissa came home we had one more night to celebrate.

And I made the most of it. I lit all nine candles on the menorah (one for each night and the Shamash), recited the blessing (one of the few I knew by heart), while Jason shifted his weight from foot to foot, moving his lips silently.

Then I gave her eight presents to unwrap: little girlie outfits with smaller, matching ones for HannahSophia. DVDs. Craft kids. A toy piano that had all 88 keys.

It was a frenzy of capitalist excess, and I was foolish to compete with Alex on that level. I didn't even try telling myself that it was an attempt to reinforce her Jewish identity.

In the absence of the boys I let the candle burn all the way down instead of blowing them out right away.

When Jack and Trevor returned from Marin Headlands — in good spirits, I saw — we decorated the tree. I'd decorated a few trees in my life at friends' houses, but I'd never had a tree of my own.

I'd always thought, if you want to see your family so badly, go visit in January! In April, when the weather's better! Why such an obsession with that one day?

But the night we decorated the tree, I got it.

Christmas.

This was what all the fuss was about: why people talked about being home for Christmas; about getting their gifts in time for Christmas; about the unparalleled excitement of Christmas morning.

My own excitement was blurred with the fact that this was not only my first Christmas, but my first Christmas as a family-to-be: the Kagen-Armstrongs.

It wouldn't be easy, but we'd make it work.

But the first Kagen-Armstrong Christmas was a happy day for me, all the more so because of the novelty. After all, I had no "good" or "bad" Christmases to compare it to.

Jason had brought an enormous box of ornaments from his apartment. There were the standard-issue colored balls, but the rest had been lovingly collected over the years: stuffed reindeer and Santa Clauses; two Nutcrackers; a Giants cap; angels blowing horns, a plastic snowflake. Commemorative ornaments issued by the police department, with stuffed bears in blue t-shirts wearing blue hats with badges.

Marissa could only reach the lower branches of the Christmas tree, so Jason put her on his shoulders: after that, she boasted nonstop that she could reach higher than everyone.

We had eggnog.

The inevitable crisis, the moment that made me believe that this wasn't all a delayed reaction to the psilocybin mushrooms I'd eaten in college, came when Trevor dropped a clay ornament that resembled a starfish. It shattered.

Trevor cried.

Jason took him into Jack-and-Trevor's room. He returned alone.

"He's being a baby!" Marissa declared.

"He made that star for his mom," Jason said, and that silenced her.

Christmas morning: I stayed in my bathrobe, the kids in their pajamas, Jason in the sweatpants and undershirt he slept in.

Jason and I had skipped ahead five, ten, years to the part where you don't bother to put on mascara. We'd missed the romantic stage, when you wonder, will-he-call, should-I-call?

It would be texting now. Either way, I didn't miss it.

Jack and Trevor yelled loudly enough at the sight of their presents that Marissa covered her ears and formed the mighty V of disapproval with her eyebrows. Jack spilled eggnog on the carpet.

I gave Jason a navy blue coat. Cashmere.

He gave me a photo album with pictures he'd taken on our trip to Stinson Beach. We'd fill the rest of the album together.

And then, of course, it all collapsed.

Alex called.

You know those movies where someone wakes up from a coma and doesn't remember who he is? People tell him, we're your family, and this is your job, and here's your pet parakeet who knows how to whistle the Marseillaise....

That was how I felt after I talked to Alex: The question kept circling in my head, *How did I get here?*

When the conversation began, I was holding good cards.

"She's told me everything," I said. "You took her to that stupid garden when we agreed you wouldn't."

"I don't remember that," Alex said. He sounded surprised, and a little hurt. "I thought we were going to try it for a few weeks."

"We were *not!*" I yelled.

My words echoed through the phone line. I was "hysterical and overreacting."

Calm down, I told myself. *Calm down....*

I took a deep breath — and resumed shouting. "You never eat dinner with her, and you leave her practically alone on Saturdays — "

"Now, now." This was Avuncular Alex. "You forget she's only five."

"No, *you* forget she's only five."

"What I mean...." Alex was cheerfully dismissive. "Is that she exaggerates. That's normal at her age."

A pinprick of doubt.

"If you want us to stop The Garden...." Alex spoke slowly. Patiently. "We'll stop it."

I fumed. How was it that he took my *perfectly reasonable* request and made it sound childish?

"Tell you what," he offered, "if you don't think we've been having enough 'fun,' I'll take her to Hawaii. Tomorrow. How about that?"

Tomorrow? Tomorrow was the 26th of December. "How can you do that?"

"I'm glad you asked that question!" He was joking now, imitating a used car salesman on TV. "I've been planning it for a while as a surprise."

There was only one way I could make sense of this. "Are you taking a woman with you?"

"No, I'm not." He sounded amused. "It will be just the two of us. You can ask Marissa when we get back."

What could I say? "No, you can't take Marissa to Hawaii"?

I did almost say, "when you get back she's moving back home!"

But I did not. The lion was awake. I'd better not piss him off.

Marissa was changing HannahSophia into her new red velvet dress with the white trim that was going to be her Christmas outfit forever. Because they would always have Christmas now.

Then Mommy came in. She said, "I have a surprise for you," but she said it in a way that Marissa didn't like.

"It's a good surprise. Daddy's going to take you to Hawaii for a week."

Marissa knew a lot about Hawaii from other girls at school who had their own houses there. Olivia was the one who was really braggy about it. Olivia said that everyone had their own swimming pools and that the weather was always perfect for the beach and that the fish wasn't gross like in San Francisco and that you never had to do anything besides play video games and watch Netflix.

"Your father's coming over very early to get you so we'd better start getting your things together."

Marissa felt like she did on the Peter Pan ride at Disneyland, when you go up really high and it's exciting but it's scary, too. "How do we get to Hawaii?"

Mommy thought this was funny, which made Marissa mad. "On a plane. But it takes about five hours."

That was a really long time to be on a plane.

"I've never been to Hawaii," Mommy said. She was playing with the floaty white trim on HannahSophia's dress. "You can tell me all about it."

"Can HannahSophia come?"

"You wouldn't go without her, would you?" Mommy pushed herself up by pressing on Marissa's knee. "Right now we'd better get your things together."

"O-kay."

"Daddy says that this is his chance to have some real fun with you. Do you know that he's never taken a week off from work?"

"Never ever?"

"Never ever. And you almost never get a chance to swim outdoors around here and — "

"And I'm a good swimmer."

"Yes, you are." Mommy opened one of Marissa's dresser drawers.

Jack and Trevor came in right then, and now Marissa was mad because they were interrupting her alone time with Mommy. Also they were making a lot of noise, and Marissa was about to put her hands over her ears, but then Jack said that they forgot to give Marissa the Christmas cards they made her.

"Mom said we shouldn't spend — shouldn't spend ... more money on gifts," Jack said.

"So these are our gifts," Trevor said. "*Gifts.*"

"We made cards."

"*Cards.*"

Trevor's lower teeth always showed, but now she knew that he did that to be friendly. They were both like big slobbery dogs that always jumped on things and sometimes pooped on the sidewalk, but you got used to them.

"Mine first," Trevor said. "*Mine.*"

Trevor's card was on purple paper and he used red marker to draw a picture of a boy but it was just a stick figure. She could hardly read what he wrote because the letters were so sloppy. Mrs. Persons would have made him do it over. NOW I HAVE A NEW SISTER.

"Here's mine!"

Jack couldn't even draw a stick figure. He did a circle for a head, and then just two long lines for the rest of the body. His printing was worser than Trevor's. They weren't even real words: WELCOM HOM.

Another aspect of Christmas that was new to me was that it was a letdown when it was over.

Marissa was gone; the floor was covered in pine needles; the hampers overflowed, and there were lunches to pack again.

Yet there was reason for hope as well.

As I stood in the basement, watching Jason and his friend Luther conjure a bedroom, I felt as though I had just traded a wizened cow for magic beans.

The room would be small, and I would have to turn sideways when I squeezed out of my Town and Country, *and* it still wouldn't be finished until after the New Year, but there were four wooden posts where yesterday there had been none. That and the smell of fresh-cut wood, reminiscent of the Christmas tree that now lay on the sidewalk, were reassuring.

"This is so freaking amazing." I was holding a plate of sandwiches. "Lunchtime?"

"It ain't rocket science," Luther said. I never failed to amaze and amuse him with my ignorance of sports, automobile engines, and household repairs.

"The lady is giving you a compliment, Fathead." Jason grabbed a sandwich. "Extra mayo. Just the way I like it."

I had never been more in love with Jason than I was at that moment. Perhaps I *would* always be a little sorry that we'd missed the intoxicating first phase: For in all the world there is no drug, no music, no art or architecture, no breathtaking view, no food, no amusement park ride, no award, no recognition of your accomplishments by your peers, no appointment by the governor, no new Valentino suit, that compares to falling in love with someone who is falling in love with you.

But then, my first attraction had not been to him, but to Trevor, and not Trevor himself, but as a friend for Jack. Had it not been for Jack's difficulty making friends, I doubted that Jason and I would have gone on one date, let alone….

I spread out the fingers of my right hand, so that I could admire my engagement ring.

And soon, I was certain, Marissa would be moving back. She'd broken her promise to Alex by telling me about Linda and The Garden, and that was her way of letting me know what life was like for her *chez* Headmistress Trunchbull.

But if I confronted Alex, I'd put him on the defensive and at the very least prolong the fight; quite possibly, if only for the sake of his pride he'd take me to court for custody. He'd threatened it the morning he found Jason in my bed. And even when Jason and I did get married, I could all-too-easily imagine Alex painting my own household as dangerous, to the point of convincing a judge that Trevor and/or Jason were pedophiles. I had to let it play out for a little while.

"I'll leave you gentlemen to it," I said. "If you need me, you'll know where I'll be."

A FEW hours later Jason and Luther came upstairs. I left them alone to watch sports, to talk about sports and, when they were silent, to think about sports. Before Jason, I could never have imagined that there were so many games being played on so many channels every hour of the day.

Jack and Trevor returned from a bike ride. Jack was only just now learning to ride a bike after some aborted attempts when he was much younger. Trevor could quite literally ride in circles around him, but Trevor was patient and Jack was improving.

"Did you boys have fun?" I had just opened the garage door and they were walking the bikes in.

"Look! It's going to be my room! My *room*."

"It was the best bike ride ever!"

It was because Jack pronounced the afternoon's bike ride as "the best ever," that I thought, *his motor skills aren't so bad. And he keeps getting better.*

Jack's declaration at the grocery store that he wanted a driver's license was not the end of the topic. That I'd hoped it might be was as good an example of "the triumph of optimism over experience" as I'd ever come across.

When I brought it up that night Jason said, "Don't even *think* about it."

"But he wants it so badly,"

"And I would like a Porsche," Jason countered. "No, I'm putting my foot down on this one."

"Excuse me?"

I was not re-marrying to get bossed around by yet another man who thought he was Alex Trebek: the man with all the answers. Alex Kagen's recent lack of interest in Jack had given me not just unwanted responsibility but *wanted* responsibility: There was no one to interfere with my decisions. In olden days, Alex might have given me a hard time about that field trip that Ashleigh had organized, but Jack went, and it had been a success.

Jack didn't want my opinion anyway. What he wanted was a driver's license, because, "If you want to have a girlfriend you have to have a license."

Jack did have his learner's permit now. We'd downloaded the manual from the Internet, and he studied for the written exam, which he then failed fourteen times. By the time of his fifteenth try he'd memorized all the questions and answers, and passed. Had the DMV reworded the questions in between his test-taking times, he probably would have failed yet again.

One by one, I heard from Jack just who was driving. "Taylor has a car!" "Parker has a car!" "Sue has a car!" When the driver was male he always added, "And he has a girlfriend!"

One afternoon he came home and named all forty-two.

Maybe the kids weren't showing up at the DMV the day they turned 15½ in the same numbers, but they were still showing up.

Why couldn't Jack get behind the wheel? He'd become so much more … *tuned in.* And his video game skills had improved from competing against Trevor.

When Jack was little I'd been proud of my honesty with myself about his abilities. I didn't need to pretend that he was part of God's plan to bring out the good in others.

But that had been when he was little and I could take care of him, and be a martyr — all the while planning that in adulthood he would become exactly like everyone else.

"*I* wouldn't teach him," I said. "I wouldn't ask you to teach him. I just think…." I traced the lines of the comforter's checkerboard pattern. "He wants it so badly," was all I could think of to say.

Jason stood up. We'd been sitting on what I loved thinking of as "our" bed. "If you saw what I saw at accident scenes — " he began, but I cut him off.

"I don't want to hear gory details," I snapped.

"Well, you should, unless you want the first time to be when Jack is involved in one."

"Trevor's learning to drive." Trevor had his learner's permit now, too, after taking the written test even more times than Jack.

Jason sighed and sat down again. "Annie."

"Yes?"

"Trevor is better at some things than Jack."

I folded my arms across my chest. He was right. Of course he was right. And sometimes I found myself going down a checklist of these future stepbrothers, comparing their strengths and weaknesses: Trevor the more volatile, Jack the more polite. Trevor was less responsible: He was the one who engineered their escape on their first sleepover, and the last time Denise had left him alone he'd started a fire in the microwave.

Now that Trevor did have his permit, he'd probably have a license before too long.

I was ashamed of my tendency to compare them. We would never be a family unless I unplugged myself from the habit.

"So you mean it's not even worth trying."

"I just said … no, look, really." He took one of my hands in his. "I don't want to hurt your feelings but the stakes are pretty damn high here. I *won't* give you gory details, but once a week I'm at the site of a fatal crash — "

"But aren't those usually caused by drunk drivers, or on the freeway? He doesn't have to drive on the — "

He stood up again and started pacing. I knew he'd seen ugly things. Severed limbs. Pools of brain matter.

"They're caused by a split-second of inattention. People are *dead,* Annie .... or paralyzed from the neck down. Or.... He doesn't have enough focus, and that's the end of it."

For a split-second of my own I knew he was right, and then an old dragon reared its head inside me. A dragon of protest, the very final words I'd spoken to Jack's last therapist after I'd fired him: "He may not be a person of unlimited potential, but he is a person of unknown potential."

"Jack has his own strengths," Jason said. "Besides, this isn't a competition. It's sad if we're going to pit the two of them against each other. Jack is a — "

"If you say that Jack is a sweet boy I may become violent," I said. "I have butter knives and I know how to use them."

He laughed, and although it was more than a little forced, I was glad to hear him say, "I don't like to fight, Annie."

Jason had been gradually bringing in various items of his own, starting with his non-uniform clothes (which I now chose for him). I cleaned out a drawer and he filled it with his own socks and underwear.

Then one evening he took out from his man-bag his two medals of valor (one bronze, one silver) and hung them above the gallery of photos that were already atop "my" (now "our") bureau. My heart beat to the rhythm of the blows of his hammer — three each — as he nailed them to the wall.

And yet … as Marissa might have put it, he was not going to be the boss of me.

So as Alex might have said, it was time to make a few calls.

I had never fit into the community of autism spectrum parents, any more than I fit into any community, but I kept my name on various listserves, and so received updates from other parents: the Asperger's version of the annual Christmas letter. "Sean is majoring in chemistry at UCLA!!!" "Philip has a new girlfriend and we adore her!!!"

And, "Cambridge has his learner's permit and he's taking to driving like a duck to water!!!"

The very name "Cambridge" bespoke the ambition and confidence of the delivery room after a healthy birth.

Cambridge's mother seemed no humbler a version of the woman who I imagined in that delivery room. From her I learned the name of Cambridge's instructor, "Mr. Hu. The six-A AAuto School. That's 'AAUTO' with 2 As."

I looked it up and found that AAAAAA AAUTO was located conveniently close by, on 19th Ave.

Love may not be stronger than death, but rationalization is stronger than reality.

There was no harm in letting Jack have one lesson. It was the only way to know whether — for now, at least — learning to drive was even possible.

So I called.

Mr. Hu, the sole owner and instructor, spoke heavily accented but lucid English. After he quoted the price and I'd given him my address and we'd agreed on a time, I said, "One more thing."

"Yes, yes one more thing."

"If you remember Cambridge Fuller…."

"Yes, yes, Cambridge Fuller."

"Well, my son is like him."

"Like Cambridge Fuller?"

"Yes, I mean, he, uh … his reflexes are … slow and sometimes he doesn't … respond quickly to commands," I finished quickly.

"Cambridge Fuller learn to drive."

"Yes. Yes. Umm … your cars have two brake pedals, right?"

"Yes. Very safe."

There was no need to mention it to Jason. It was only one lesson and I did not owe him an explanation. I never promised him that I wouldn't let Jack take a lesson, after all.

Any more than Alex had promised me that he wouldn't send Marissa to Linda-Violetta-Bartlett's Garden.

Mr. Hu arrived exactly on time. He was a middle-aged man with a few gray hairs to comb back over a liver-spotted scalp. He waited unsmilingly on the doorstep for Jack, but when he spoke I saw the yellowed and silver-capped teeth he was hiding. But he did say, in a tone that tolerated no disagreement, "Your son will be a good driver. Very safe."

"I'm going to be driving!" Jack shouted. "Driving, driving, driving!"

If Mr. Hu saw this as different from his usual, too-cool-for-the-room teen student, he didn't appear to notice.

I went to the window and was relieved to see that Mr. Hu was behind the wheel of a Taurus, backing the car out. Jack was in the passenger seat, looking down — at the second brake pedal? I clasped my hands together tightly and watched them until they were too far down the street for me to see any longer.

For a while I paced in front of the window. He was safe, he was safe. Or not. But who was safe, and when? Every time Jack left the house he might get hit by a negligent Muni driver or even one of the arrogant young cyclists who ran stop signs just to show they were hip. Anyone could stick a gun in your face in the middle of the day. This was San Francisco. That was life.

But I knew it was different.

When Jack started taking the bus on his own the year before, I'd been nearly paralyzed with fear on a daily basis. I learned that the only way to deal with it was capital-D-Denial. Don't think of him out there. Don't picture him at the bus stop, in the cold, waiting for the lumbering, smoke-spouting beast. Don't hear the bus driver's impatient remark when Jack can't find his fare. Don't hear the other teens shout "fuck you," when he steps on their feet.

Don't let him leave the house.

I distinguished the engine of Mr. Hu's Taurus from all other sounds in the world. I heard the engine shut off. Only half an hour had gone by.

The honking began before I got to the window, where I saw that Mr. Hu was again in the driver's seat. Though his face was screened in part by the windshield I could see that he was not happy.

Jack was grinning broadly — and no, that is not the same as a smile. Satan doesn't smile; he grins broadly.

When Mr. Hu got out of the car he was shaking. It got worse as he headed toward my front door: He was as unsteady on his feet as a drunk.

Jack got out of the car as an afterthought, after he punched a few buttons on the dashboard. I watched him veer to the house with the same drunken gait, the way toddlers do when they're first learning to walk.

Now it was time for me to rush to the door. When I opened it Mr. Hu was standing there with his fist raised. To knock — I think.

We stared at each other for a moment. He was having trouble drawing a deep enough breath to speak. "Ms. Kagen," he finally managed to say. "Your son should not drive a car."

He turned and walked back toward his old Taurus. I hadn't paid him yet and I wanted to call after him, but I didn't. As he headed toward his car, Jack passed him on the way in. Jack said, "See you next week, Mr. Hu!" but Mr. Hu didn't answer.

A week later, driving down 19th Avenue, I saw that the sign for AAAAAA AAUTO was gone. But Mr. Hu was near or past retirement age, so it must have been a coincidence.

CHAPTER 17

It was Marissa's first time on a plane going anywhere but Disneyland. They flew first class because Daddy said she was first class and there were seats that turned into beds and when the plane rocked Daddy explained about how there were bumps in the air the same way there are bumps on the street and she wasn't scared.

In Hawaii they stayed in a big hotel with a name that was practically all vowels, and it was even bigger and newer than the one in Disneyland, and there was a day camp with other kids her age, and she won most of the games, like Duck, Duck, Goose and Red Light, Green Light, and she bragged that she was in first grade even though she was still only five, and they all had yellow t-shirts with the name of the hotel. One of the boys reminded her of Jack because he flapped his hands a lot.

The air smelled like flowers and suntan lotion. Sometimes it was windy — and sometimes it would rain in a strange way: really heavy, but for a short time.

The camp was all day but she and Daddy were together the rest of the time. They went out to dinner every night and then in the hotel room he could work on his laptop and make phone calls. She overheard him use bad words a couple of times. Once he said, "This time change is a bitch."

On the last day Daddy took her to the pool after camp. There were three pools, and one of them was shaped like a river, and one had a waterfall, but this was the one for kids and their parents.

There were cocktail waitresses wandering around everywhere with little trays.

"I hope you're okay with not going to see Linda Bartlett anymore."

When Marissa heard the name "Linda Bartlett" she got a stab in her stomach.

Daddy picked up his Lava Flow. The Lava Flow was a special drink they had only in Hawaii, with strawberries and a fruity creamy sauce. He got her one, too, but she'd finished hers already.

"She had me quite taken in, our Ms. Bartlett. When you want to believe something badly enough, you believe it." He slurped up the last of his drink. "What do they say now? 'My bad.' You know, I double-checked her resume, called every one of her references." He set the glass down again. "There's a case for fraud there. I just don't know if I want to pursue it or not."

Marissa didn't know what he was talking about. She was only scared. "Mommy said I don't have to go anymore!"

"And you don't. She was just wasting our time." Daddy scooted up on the lounge chair and folded his hands over his stomach. He was wearing his regular clothes, only without the jacket and tie. His shirt was light blue and had short sleeves. At first Marissa thought he looked funny that way, because all the other dads were in swimsuits, but then she decided that he looked more important.

But now she was confused. "Mommy said I wasn't going back to your house."

"And you aren't. Unless you want to."

Mommy and Daddy were always telling her that she should say what she wanted. But Daddy meant she should say what she wanted to Mommy, and Mommy meant she should say what she wanted to Daddy.

So she looked at the ocean while she tried to think.

The ocean was really pretty in Hawaii. Daddy said it was the same ocean they had in San Francisco, but she wasn't sure she believed him. This ocean was a real blue, not like their ocean. And it was safe for people to go in.

"I haven't had the kind of time with you I want," Daddy said and he sounded very sad. "Your mother and Jason make it hard for me to visit."

Did they? Marissa frowned.

"Can I put my feet in the water? In the ocean water?"

"Heh-heh-heh. I want to talk to my big girl for a few minutes."

The sun had just reached that point where it was a yellow half-circle and safe to look at. You could go blind if you looked at it when it was high up.

"Okay."

"I didn't get to see you much when you were a baby."

I know that. Marissa squirmed. She didn't remember being a baby.

It was getting windy, and there weren't as many people in the pool as there were when they first got there. There was a girl who looked like she went to kindergarten floating on an air mattress. Her dad was pulling her along while she kicked. She splashed water on him and he laughed.

"And now … I'm missing so much of your growing up." Daddy chomped on the ice from his Lava Flow. Marissa cringed.

The girl's dad brought the air mattress to the side of the pool and the mom came to help her out. Maybe she was the nanny. But probably she was the mom and the parents were married.

"Your granddaughter is so cute!"

One of the cocktail waitresses had come over to them. She was wearing short-shorts and white sneakers and her hair was in a ponytail.

"Heh-heh-heh. She's my daughter, actually."

"Oh!" The waitress looked down at her tray and thumbed through the pile of little square napkins. "Can I get you anything else, sir?"

"Another of these Lava Flows," Daddy said, raising his empty glass. "Virgin. And a virgin for my daughter." He ruffled Marissa's hair. Then he asked the waitress, "What's your name, hon?"

The way Daddy was talking made Marissa feel squishy.

"Ginger."

"Looks like you might be a haole."

Marissa learned that week that a haole was someone from the regular part of the United States. Almost everyone was a haole.

The waitress switched the towel on her shoulder to the other shoulder, looking at the towel the whole time. "What was your first clue?"

"Blonde hair, blue eyes … I'm a criminal lawyer, so I've learned to notice these things." He touched his temple. "Sharp eyes."

"I guess so." Ginger smiled at Marissa. "Are you having fun on Maui?"

"Yeah."

"In fact — " Daddy twisted his glass — "I'm the District Attorney back home. San Francisco."

"Really."

"Where are you from, Ginger?"

"Minnesota. A town you've never heard of."

"Heh-heh-heh. Try me."

Ginger said the name of a town and Daddy said, "You got me."

"I'll be right back, sir," Ginger said and she hurried away so fast that she forgot to take Daddy's empty glass away.

Daddy chomped on the last of the ice and Marissa gripped the metal bars on the side of her lounge chair.

Then Daddy said, "I hope you'll never feel the need to drink."

"What if I'm thirsty?"

"Heh-heh-heh. I mean, drink alcohol. Does Jason drink a lot of beer?"

Marissa could tell that drinking beer was bad from the way Daddy asked, and Jason drank beer every day.

"No," she said.

"Have they said when they're getting married?"

"No." Mommy said that she could be a flower girl, but she didn't want to tell Daddy that.

"H'm."

The girl on the air mattress was getting out of the pool. The lady who must have been her mom was holding out a big towel for her and even though it was backward Marissa could see that it had a picture of Mulan. The mom dried her hair with one corner and Marissa heard her say something about not catching a cold.

Daddy raised his butt from the lounge chair. "I wonder where our drinks are," he said. "I'm ready for dinner. How about you?"

Pop! The yellow half circle disappeared at the end of the ocean.

Jason followed me into my — our — room.

I flopped backward on the bed.

"Why are you letting her go back?"

I heard The Policeman in his voice. It made me shudder.

I turned sideways and pulled my knees up into the fetal position.

"I don't like the way you let him run your life." He paced to the dresser and fingered one of the medals hanging from the wall. "*Our* lives. If we could disconnect from him financially…."

That was going to be hella difficult. I had to maneuver Jason past any manly pride he had concerning money we got from Alex — and quickly. There was no shame in letting a man support his own children; it was what God and nature intended.

"You stand up to him about so many things — why would you cave on this?"

I stared at the ceiling. I could hear Jason breathing through his nose. "Because I owe it to him."

This hit a nerve.

"Are you kidding? You don't owe him jack shit! I hate myself for putting up with all his bullshit for so long. I kept saying to myself, it's none of my business, but if you're going to — well, it *is* my business now, okay?"

He went on in this vein, whipping his rage into a froth, until I sat up. "You don't know the whole story."

"Then tell me."

"I don't want to."

"Oh, yes, you do."

I raked hair back from my face. "I told you that I had an affair at the end," I began.

"Uh huh."

"Well ... It was at the end but we didn't know it was at the end."

"Just. Tell. Me."

I took a deep breath. I should have told him the morning he told me about how *his* marriage fell apart, but he would have thought so much less of me, and it hadn't seemed necessary — then. Then when it was necessary, I put it off. This sin of omission became a gaping hole, yet one I continued to successfully step around.

Alex and I were unhappy. At least, *I* was unhappy. Very unhappy, and I had been for a long time.

But when you're unhappy, you talk to your husband about it, right? Then you go for counseling.

Alex would have said no to counseling.

Yes, but I should have tried.

Instead of talking to Alex, I cheated on him.

But we would have divorced anyway, wouldn't we?

We would probably have divorced down the line, likely even soon, but....

This was just the plastic wrapping on my obsessive thoughts. Sometimes I plucked at a daisy in my head:

It was my fault. It wasn't my fault. It was my fault. It wasn't my fault.

It was my fault.

The obsessive thoughts were starting up again. I shook my head violently, as if I could shake them out through my ears.

I gave Jason details on which I'd been vague up until now: It wasn't long after I started "seeing" Val that I found out that I was pregnant. I'd been trying to get pregnant with Alex for a good two years by then, with no results. They called it secondary infertility.

What it really was, was a defense mechanism. Rationalization? Denial? Reaction-formation? Did Freud have a clinical term for hypocrisy?

I wanted another baby, so I hadn't used birth control with Val, either.

Alex had been willing to raise Val's child, but by that time there were too many other problems between us.

"Are you saying…." Jason didn't finish.

"I'll tell you the rest."

Alex and I divorced; Jason knew that part. But I wanted to tell him about the months of being a single mom. On a budget for the first time since college. Sleep-deprived with a new baby. If things had been hard when I met Jason they'd been nightmarish during that first year.

But then "the baby" became Marissa. She wasn't an easy kid. She was high-strung, demanding, stubborn. But she was so *entertaining*. She sat with Berenstain Bear books, turning the pages and pretending to read. She talked to her stuffed animals in a firm, motherly voice. She refused every item of clothing that wasn't pink.

And Alex fell in love.

It was the best part of him, a part I hadn't seen in years. He read to her; he played Hi Ho Cherry-o with her.

When she called him "Daddy" he didn't stop her.

Coincidence? You be the judge. It was right about that time that he saw the resemblance between them and claimed her as his own.

"So you still don't know?" Jason interrupted with strange eagerness. "I mean, you don't know for *sure*."

"C'mon, just look at them," I sighed. "Their foreheads." And their eyebrows dipped between their eyes in exactly the same way.

Now it was Jason who sighed.

"She's his," I said. "But we didn't know that for a long time."

"Maybe — "

"She's his."

I was so happy that she was his. I was still happy, it was just….

When Marissa turned three, she started really reading, not pretend reading, simple books, and doing arithmetic in her head. She drew faces. Thanks to Jack and the unfeeling experts who had evaluated him, I knew about a lot of milestones that kids were supposed to hit, so I knew that she was advanced.

Alex had graciously relinquished the fantasies that every man has for his newborn son. When it appeared that Marissa — little Marissa who called herself "Mawitha" until she was four — might step into those fantasies the way she stepped into her ballet flats, the fantasies returned in vengeful force.

"She's very smart," I said. "But she's not 'gifted' in the way they mean that and she's certainly not a genius. And you know what? That's fine with me!"

Jason slipped his arms around me. "It's fine with me, too." He nibbled at my ear. I had hardly been in the mood for sex but the body has a mind of its own.

But Jason had other things on his mind, at least for the moment. "Let him have his little bit of time, then. *Little bit of time.* She belongs with *us.*"

"You can't know how much I love hearing you say that."

"Of course! I mean — "

He stopped himself. What was it? Was he going to say, *since we don't have to pay for her upkeep*? Or, *I don't want Alex to get his way?*

Apparently my generally low opinion of men was always ready to peck its way out of the egg.

"I mean ... she's a great kid. She's adorable. And...."

"And...."

"And don't you think I want to raise an NT child, too?"

Monday, Jack walked Ashleigh home. They held hands.

She invited him inside her house for the first time.

His first thought was that they'd watch TV, but he was so nervous walking into her house that he couldn't even say anything. She said she'd make him a snack, so they went into the kitchen. She made them peanut butter on crackers.

Jack had never understood why people cared about table manners. It was just eating. It was so much more fun when you didn't have to worry about crumbs on the floor or making smacking noises.

But when Ashleigh put out the peanut butter and crackers, he thought about table manners. He tried to eat with his mouth closed and when he saw crumbs all over his shirt and pants, he tried to brush them off. He could still hear his own chewing and still see the crumbs, but he thought he was doing better.

After that she asked him if he wanted help with his homework. He didn't want to do homework, but he said yes.

They worked on his math homework for a while. She kept pushing her hair back, because she was bent over the paper, and it kept falling over her face. He really wanted to kiss her again then, but he didn't know if she wanted to. Boys were supposed to start the kissing, right? But she was the one who kissed him first the first time....

He was so confused, but it was nice just to know that they were boyfriend and girlfriend. That was plenty for that day.

After homework they did watch TV. She said that she wanted to teach him to play Scrabble the next time he came over.

When he walked home he kept thinking how she said, "the next time you come over," and the sidewalk floated.

Ms. Gonzales did Lunch Bunch with some of the same kids who came on the field trip, and some other kids, too. She gave them a topic and they would talk. It was a lot like what she did with them on the field trip.

Jack had always liked Lunch Bunch because then he had someone to eat with. Since he and Trevor became friends they'd been eating lunch together but before Trevor, which was all freshman year and a little of sophomore year, he ate by himself. Sometimes in the cafeteria he would see someone from far away that he thought he knew, but when he got closer he couldn't tell if he knew that person or not. Once a really big guy stopped his conversation with his friends and said, "Is there a problem, Dude?" Jack said no.

Now he could eat lunch with Ashleigh on Monday, Wednesday, Thursday and Friday. But he invited Trevor to join them, because he didn't want Trevor to feel left out.

Half of the Lunch Bunch kids had gathered. They sat at the round table in Ms. Gonzales's office, and they'd be there until the next bell rang. Ms. Gonzales was often late. A lot of the kids were late. Zack showed up really late. Last time he was 34 minutes late, so he was only there for 11 minutes.

Jack wasn't going to say anything, but it came out of his mouth without his trying, the way so many more things did now.

"I have a girlfriend now."

"You do not," scoffed Logan.

"I do!" Should he tell them about the day before? About being at her house and how they ate peanut butter crackers together? No, it was too precious. "And I'm learning to drive!"

"Prove it," said Mario.

"I went to her house," he said.

"Yeah? And what does her house look like?" Blair was taking his Goldfish out of a Ziploc bag and lining them up in rows of five.

Jack didn't know what her house looked like. All he could see was Ashleigh, her face blissfully clear to him now, her voice a comforter that surrounded him. He was so, so sorry he ever told them. He wanted them to be impressed. Hearing them talk about her hurt his skin. At least they hadn't said her name.

"Well?" asked Logan.

"Well *what*?" It wasn't an answer but he didn't know what else to say.

"Prove it," Mario said again.

"Ask...." What could he say? "Ask her."

Then his heart beat hard. What if they asked her and she said no?

"You've got to prove it."

"I will!"

But he had to stop there because the door opened and Ms. Gonzales came in. She had one hand digging around in her big bag. "I heard you boys having a lively conversation. That's good."

She smiled. Jack could tell, because he'd learned to recognize smiles.

It was Wednesday of the first week after winter break and Leonora was vacuuming downstairs. Marissa was watching the ginormous TV in Daddy's room. She'd already had her hour of TV, but the vacuum was running so no one would know. She wasn't supposed to watch TV in Daddy's room anyway, because Leonora'd already vacuumed there that day. That was Leonora's rule, not Daddy's, so Marissa didn't feel so guilty breaking it, and she'd figured out that if she rubbed out the scoopy shape her bottom made on the carpet and made sure she left the TV on the same channel that no one knew.

She understood a lot of what Leonora and Dania said when they talked while she ate. She figured out that a man named Fernando was Dania's boyfriend and so once she asked, "*Como esta Fernando?*"

Leonora was impressed and Marissa thought that she'd forgiven her for the time she tricked her into going to Emma's house. But Marissa didn't like Leonora today, because Marissa wanted to go to Emma's house that afternoon, too, but it was raining and Leonora was scared of driving up and down all the hills in the rain.

Marissa had forgotten how boring TV was. All the kid channels were showing re-runs. And the grown-up channels were gross. The first time she snuck into Daddy's room she went straight to the channels that Mommy said not to watch, 43 and 44. There was a show called *16 and Pregnant*. There was a girl with spiked pink hair and an earring that looked like a little tire, and her boyfriend had a beard that made him look like a goat.

Marissa used to think that you had to be married to have a baby, and then one of her friends at school got a baby brother but her mom wasn't married. The girl was a super know-it-all and she told Marissa that you don't have to be married, but you couldn't get pregnant without a boyfriend who lived with you. So the high school boy on TV who looked like a goat must have been the boyfriend. Then they started showing the girl having the baby and Marissa got really grossed out and decided that she would never, ever have a baby.

Marissa switched the channel back to 26, which Daddy always watched, with people in a courtroom, that was the most boring TV channel in the whole wide world. But when she got up she purposely didn't brush the carpet the right way. She hoped Daddy *would* see! She wanted to mess it up some more. She wanted to pull down the blanket on top of his bed and throw the pillows on the floor.

She wanted to kick the TV.

She was so bored.

And the vacuum was so loud.

She could call Emma, but Emma's mom took her cell phone away because Emma didn't practice her clarinet two days in a row.

She could call Mommy, but if Mommy found out that she was alone in the house for the afternoon again, she might call Daddy and they'd get into a fight.

She could go try to read *Charlie and the Chocolate Factory*, but even though she liked to read, she was so bored of reading right now she could puke, yes, puke and she didn't care if that was a bad word.

Suddenly, Marissa was standing at the door of Daddy's study and she didn't even know how she got there. She put her hand on the doorknob. Fingerprints! She knew about fingerprints from Daddy.

She lifted up the bottom of her dress and wiped the doorknob, then used the same part of her dress to open the door.

Daddy's study was different from other rooms. It was more crowded, with big furniture and a zillion books. The strongest smell came from the polish that the nannies used on Daddy's special chess table. He got it from his Daddy and the table was all marble and had pictures of Rome around the edge.

She sat in Daddy's leather chair which was so big she could curl up like a kitten and go to sleep. But Leonora or Dania might come in and find her. She should just leave.

Except she still thought this must be where he hid the good stuff.

Since Daddy wasn't very good at hiding things, he probably put all his junk food somewhere easy, like right here at his desk. But opening his desk drawers felt like a bigger deal than coming into his study.

She ran her finger over the silky dark wood. Only a small area right in front of her was clear, covered by a green pad. The rest was crowded with big gold statues. She could read Daddy's name, "Alexander M. Kagen," at the bottom of them.

Then she sucked in her breath, grabbed the handle of the drawer right in front of her and yanked.

*Bor*ing. Just pens and pads, like the ones he has at his office South of Market, with that picture that he told her was "the seal of the city and county of San Francisco."

She stuck her hand in until she could feel the back of the drawer to make sure there wasn't something like a Hershey bar back there.

There wasn't. But she didn't even stop to think before she opened the drawer on her right, the top one of three drawers on her side.

Mostly the same boring stuff. Also a box with a word she couldn't read: PRILOSEC. But when she stuck her hand all the way back she found something crinkly and she yanked it out.

It was a bag of Cheetos.

She pulled on the sides and after a while it gave. *R-i-i-i-p.*

She munched on two at a time. Her fingers got covered with orange sticky stuff, and she wiped her hand on her dress, on the same place she used to wipe off her fingerprints.

The next drawer was harder to open, partly because her fingers were still a little sticky. But she got it open finally. It was a deeper drawer and this one had a lot of notes in it on pink paper. The top said WHILE YOU WERE OUT, but the rest was written in cursive, which she couldn't read yet.

There were magazines called *American Criminal Law Review.* There was a picture of an old lady in a picture frame and more boxes: TROJAN, and PREPARATION H, and EX-LAX. There was one that said BEN-GAY and she wondered if that was a boy who was gay.

Wait — did the vacuum go off? Marissa sat very quietly. All she could hear was the hum of the computer. But then, *whew,* the vacuum went back on.

He must have more than Cheetos here. She stuck her hand back and yes, she found a package of red licorice and a bag of Jelly Bellys. She hated licorice but jelly beans were good. Maybe Daddy would forget it was there.

For a while she ate jelly beans, until she began to feel sick to her stomach. She'd never be able to eat whatever gross stuff the nannies make for dinner, like broccoli and chicken without even any skin.

There was just that one more drawer, the biggest one in the desk. It was so big that it could hold a whole cake, like the one he surprised her with one time. What if there *were* a cake in there? Or … what if it were a door to a magic world? When she was little she would think of a lot of ways magic could be real. She really wanted to be able to disappear, and even more than that she wanted to be able to fly. Most of all, though, she wanted HannahSophia to be real and to talk for real.

She tried to open the last big drawer but it was stuck. So she used both hands and had to pull really hard but finally it gave and there was a burst of dust.

Inside it was just a bunch of pukey green cardboard files hanging from metal rods, with little white tabs on top. FINANCES. CORRESPONDENCE. NEWS CLIPPINGS. There was a tab she read right away: ELECTION.

Daddy talked about elections all the time. Maybe if she did get in trouble for what she was doing she could get out of it by telling him that she'd decided she wants to be like him and to run for office, like to be the first woman President.

She pulled on the tab and up came more dust.

Uh-oh. The green cardboard ripped a little. But now she could see inside. It was a bunch of newspaper articles. She pulled one out. It felt like dead leaves.

There was a headline:

AROUND TOWN WITH RACHEL LAPORTE

The article looked hard to read so she picked out the easy words and sounded out some others.

Then she saw Daddy's name — and her own name! So she stopped and looked at that paragraph very carefully.

"So now I've earned my heart attack sandwich." We wish him luck.....

SPOTTED AT CITY HALL HAUNT The Recount, Alex Kagen said that no, he is not a new father even though his ex-wife has a new baby (a girl, Marissa Rose). Our venerable District Attorney is always reluctant to discuss his private life, but we can be persistent. We quote, "The former Mrs. Kagen is now officially a single woman."

It's our business not to mind our own business, so we didn't stop there. Before the DA walked out on us, we confirmed that Mrs. Kagen is living alone....

WHAT RECENTLY MARRIED woman was seen holding hands with a woman-not-her wife in Sappho's Balcony last....

Marissa had a Jelly Belly in her mouth, but she didn't taste it.

She knew that she'd found something out that she wasn't supposed to. She just couldn't figure out what it was. Mommy was "Mrs. Kagen." Does being "a single woman" mean you have a boyfriend or not?

Two more tasteless Jelly Bellys.

The newspaper said that Mommy was living alone.

Daddy's study had gotten very messy.

Marissa could hide the Cheetos bag in her room until dinner and then put it in the kitchen *basura* when Leonora and Dania weren't looking. She crumpled up the bag really, really small.

A single woman couldn't have a baby. She needed a husband or a boyfriend.

Jason had taken to keeping a uniform in my closet, and when he spent the night on a weekday, I got to watch him put it on before work. I loved him in it as much as ever, with all his weapons and police *tchotchkes* swinging from his belt.

That morning it was still dark when he rose to take an earlier-than-usual shift. I woke to watch him dress, thus changing from Joe Six Pack into Dirty Harry.

"Ready to protect and serve?" I asked.

"Protecting the citizens of the City by the Bay from beautiful women who think that just because they're beautiful and smart that they can make left turns wherever they damn well feel like it, even between the hours of three and seven p.m., except on Sundays."

I giggled like an idiot teenager in love, which I was, except for the teenager part (although, aren't we all teenagers when we're in love?) while he leaned over and kissed me good-bye.

I slipped immediately back toward blessed unconsciousness, but when I heard the front door creaking open I jumped out of bed. "Wait!" I called. "Don't leave!"

I dashed to the kitchen and then out the front door, where I caught up with him in the driveway. "Surprise!" I handed him an old-fashioned metal lunch box, the kind with two clasps. "I got it from a website called lifewithoutplastic.com. It's even called the 'Big Daddy.' "

"Aw." He started to snap it open.

"No! Wait until lunchtime. And open it in *private*."

He bent over me, as he always needed to in order for us to kiss, and because it was still dark, we had a right old make-out session right there in the driveway.

I went back to bed and back to sleep.

Trevor walked in a short time later.

"Anna, I can't find my Five Finger Death Punch t-shirt."

Waking up this second time was more difficult. "Remember what we said about knocking?

"I forgot. I *forgot.*"

I was growing used to having a strange teenage boy more or less living with us, but this difference at least, remained: I didn't mind having Jack walk into my bedroom while I was in bed or wearing my nightgown, while with Trevor it felt inappropriate.

"I'll help you look for it later," I mumbled. *Another fifteen minutes,* I thought. *It's still early.* And even, *I deserve another hour,* in spite of my tightly-held philosophy that since there was absolutely no connection between what people deserved and what people got, it wasn't even worth using as a verb.

"I want fried eggs," he announced.

I turned my face into the pillow. Maybe I could smother myself.

Jack shouted from the kitchen, "I'll make eggs!"

That got me out of bed very quickly.

When I walked out the door I felt the pleasure of recognition at the sight of my Town and Country. Once upon a time it was brand new, with all the latest 'n' greatest features. Now the van's chassis had a number of pings, dings, and minor scratches not worth fixing at the price.

But we were longtime friends who had grown old together, surviving a divorce and pregnancy and the birth of my daughter, hundreds of rides with Marissa to Gymboree and MusicTime, and thousands to speech and occupational and psychotherapy for Jack.

While I was digging around for the keys, I saw the flat tire. *Shit.* Too bad Jason had left. He could fix it. It was thanks to him that there was a spare in the cargo hold. I couldn't call him on duty; not for something like this. I had to wait until he got off.

I quickly reviewed my other options: Call Triple A? Take Muni or a taxi? I looked at my watch. How much time....

Then I saw that the rear tire was flat, too.

My legs felt heavy but I managed to lift them and to walk, though very slowly, around the rear of the car. Yes. As I suspected. The other two tires were flat as well.

I squatted next to the passenger side front tire and looked for signs of vandalism. I didn't see anything at first, and the little cap on the thingie where you put in air remained in place. But when I ran my hand over the top of the tire – it was gritty and set my teeth on edge – I felt something very tiny but flat and cold, and when I looked more closely I could see it was the head of a nail. Someone had hammered it through the treads.

No, I decided, I'd probably picked it up on the road. People were always picking up nails in the road. Whenever anyone had a flat tire, the mechanic or the guy in the tow truck would say it was a nail.

I'd always wondered where all these nails came from, since I never, and I mean never ever, saw one on the road.

I stayed squatting until my hamstrings couldn't take it anymore. Only then did I rise and move on to the next tire. The nail was in the same place.

I didn't feel the need to examine the remaining two. But I couldn't keep squatting, either, so I plunked down on my derriere, clean black cotton-and-spandex pencil skirt right on concrete, and rested my head on my knees.

I thought about Kimberly in the kitchen of the house in St. Francis Woods. I thought about how determined she was that the field trip not take place. That she was willing to tear down the school....

But the field trip had taken place.

Jack hadn't told me much about it, but I'd gotten the impression that he and Ashleigh had spent time together. Had more happened than I knew? But what could happen? My life rested on my faith that a woman would love him. A woman who didn't need witty repartee. A woman who was a caregiver at heart.

I didn't think that Ashleigh was that woman. She wasn't even a woman yet.

Kimberly was, though. Was she cruder than her jumpsuit and brand-new Dombey and Whitfield mailers made her look? Had she hired someone? Once you were rich enough you could hire someone to be crude *for* you.

I looked at my watch. My palms were filthy. I put my hands on the pavement to boost myself up and saw that a run had started in my pantyhose, just below the knee.

This looked like a job for Officer Armstrong.

JASON SQUATTED in the same place where I had, running gloved hands around the edge of one of the tires.

"Can we get, like, one of those CSI teams out?" I had changed into fresh pantyhose and a clean skirt and so was reluctant to get down on the pavement again.

"Maybe not for this, Annie." He tried to joke: "There was a lot of tagging on the freeway overpasses last night."

"Ha, ha." I didn't think I was being narcissistic by considering myself more important than other "vics," but a narcissist, by definition, can't think of herself as narcissistic.

"We'll figure this out." He got to his feet and in a single motion that was graceful for a big man.

"You're not telling me something."

He looked down at the tire he'd been examining. "Well," he began finally, "they weren't flat this morning. We would have noticed."

"Right." I wasn't sure that I would have noticed — but he would have.

There was another pause before he added, "And someone used a nail gun."

Two officers did come out that night and took my statement. But as Jason had indirectly pointed out, women were being sexually assaulted every night. Houses were burglarized on the hour. Gunfire went off regularly in some neighborhoods, and often found a human target.

So no one would come out and dust for fingerprints, let alone search for strands of hair — not when the explanation was likely the same as before: either a neighbor with extreme PMS or one of Jack's classmates acting out. One of Jason's law enforcement pals had suggested of the letter that it was probably one of Trevor's autistic pals. "They don't understand what's funny and what isn't."

Perhaps Alex could "make a few calls" and have a crime lab assigned to investigate, and while for the sake of Jack and Trevor I would call in that favor, I was the target here, and this didn't seem like the time to involve Alex in anything having to do with Jason and me.

Jack and Ashleigh were playing Scrabble at her house. It was his third lesson and she said he was doing well. He only tried to play Scrabble once before, at a birthday party when he was nine. It was Scrabble Jr. and he just wanted to line up the tiles. He thought he was doing a good job because he was lining them up in order, the As and the Bs (there were 10 "A"s but only three "B"s which was very upsetting) but after a while the birthday kid's mom said he didn't have to play anymore, and 16 minutes later his mom showed up to take him home.

Ashleigh was laughing. "'O-I-O' is not a word."

"Check the dictionary."

She had her MacBook on the floor next to them, and she hit a few keys. "It's *not* a word, Jack."

"Doesn't it — doesn't it spell 'Ohio'?"

She slapped his hand lightly. "That has an 'H' in it, silly. Besides, we can't use proper nouns, remember?"

"Oh, right."

He wanted to make the Crime Conqueror words "Zomb," and he waited ten turns to get the "Z." Then Ashleigh figured out what he was doing and told him that that wasn't a good strategy.

Strategy was hard.

Jack studied the board. Reading words had been easy for him as far back as he could remember, but understanding them was a different matter.

"I can make the word 'I'!" he declared. "I can just put the 'I' over here."

He lay the tile down on one of the corners, where it says TRIPLE WORD SCORE. "That's three points!"

"You are so funny!" Ashleigh said that to him on the day they met, and she said it more than ever these days. When she laughed she put her head back and he could see the skin of her throat. There was an upside down rocket-shape that was paler than the rest. "No, you *can't* do that."

At their first lesson she explained how the special colored squares like DOUBLE LETTER SCORE only worked the first time you use them. He said that made the game less fun and she said that they could play it so that they did count twice. "Why shouldn't we make our own rules?" she had asked and he had said, "Yeah, why shouldn't we?"

When the door opened fourteen minutes later Ashleigh let out a little yelp. The door was behind him and he could only see Ashleigh's face, which was not-smiling.

"Hello, Mother," she said.

"Hello!"

When Jack heard the voice he turned around. It was a woman. He knew it was Ashleigh's mother because she'd just said "Mother."

"This must be Jack!" the woman said.

She was carrying two big shopping bags. Both of them said NEIMAN-MARCUS.

"Yes, this is Jack," Ashleigh said.

Jack wanted to say the right thing so badly that it made all his English disappear. Then he remembered one of the phrases he memorized as a child. "Nice to meet you."

"Nice to meet you, too!" The woman was coming at him very fast with one hand sticking toward him. It was like being in a tunnel but with the tunnel rushing toward you instead of the other way around. The shopping bags rapped against her legs.

He couldn't say anything about her face, but her voice sounded friendly. She grabbed his hand, which he discovered that he had stuck out, too, and she squeezed it.

"Why are you home so early?" Ashleigh asked.

"I decided to treat myself this afternoon. I went shopping!" Ashleigh's mother put her bags down and gathered up her hair in one hand. She let it fall down chunk by chunk. "What are you young folks up to?"

"Planning a hostile takeover of Paramount Studios."

"They made the SpongeBob movie!" Jack said. He wanted to add to the conversation.

"What does it look like we're doing?"

"Sweetie, I'm just asking."

Ashleigh didn't answer.

"Well, I'm going to take a shower." Ashleigh's mother picked up her bags again. "Jack, it really was very nice to meet you. I've heard a lot of lovely things about you from Ashleigh."

"I think I have a word," Ashleigh said. She was looking slyly at Jack — at least, that's what he thought her expression was. "I already have a 'C.' "

"I'm going out tonight," Ashleigh's mother said.

"I'll alert the media." Ashleigh rearranged her tiles. "I also need a 'U.' "

Jack tried to find where 'C' and 'U' could make a word. Yes! There was a 'T'! She could make "cut." It wasn't very many points, though.

"I might be home late." Ashleigh's mother's voice went up and down, like she was singing.

"Like I give a shit what she does," Ashleigh whispered to Jack.

As Ashleigh's mother was walking away Jack thought of a really good thing to say.

"Have fun tonight!"

CHAPTER 18

The first time Marissa snuck into Daddy's office she felt bad about it, but the second time was easy. She got the newspapers out again and she didn't even think about getting caught.

Then she brought the articles to school to show Emma, who reads not as good as Marissa, but who knows more about grownup things. Emma could get snotty about that, but Marissa needed help too much to care.

"Rumors are mean things you say about other people," Emma explained to Marissa during morning recess. "Abound … that's when a ball comes back to you."

Marissa could tell that Emma was faking that one but when Emma also pointed out that if Marissa's parents were divorced in February like the article said, then Marissa must have been born when her parents were already divorced, she knew she was right.

Marissa wasn't ashamed of her parents being divorced, because at least half the kids had divorced parents and a lot of them had step-sisters and step-brothers. Though Kaitlyn's parents weren't divorced and Kaitlyn acted snotty about that sometimes.

At lunchtime Emma had a new idea. "Maybe you're adopted."

"Adopted?" Marissa had never thought of that.

Adopted kids weren't wanted by their own mommies, because adopted kids didn't have real daddies. The adopt*ing* parents went to a big hospital where they picked out babies from about a hundred cribs.

When Marissa was born Mommy wasn't living with Daddy, so there was no way she could have been pregnant.

"You shouldn't feel bad," Emma said. "They pick out the best ones when they adopt."

Marissa's cheeks got hot. She remembered then that Emma was the one who, long, long ago, when Marissa was still living with Mommy, asked her why Jack was so weird.

So Emma must know that they picked Marissa because Marissa wasn't weird.

"Can they send you back?" she asked Emma. *If you turn into weird later?*

Emma thought for a minute. "I think they can."

"No they can't!" Marissa shouted. "You think you know everything, but you don't know anything!"

"You're not my friend anymore!" Emma shouted back, and they didn't speak the whole afternoon, not even when they got put in a group together for chemistry class.

Jack was so excited that afternoon that he wasn't counting his steps as he walked. He was walking faster than usual, too, even though his backpack was extra heavy. Ms. Gonzales was always lecturing him about stopping at his locker before he went home, but he did stop at his locker. The real reason was that he didn't feel right unless he had all his books with him.

His backpack was extra heavy today because he bought a chess set at the variety store. A few days ago he asked Ashleigh if she could teach him to play chess. She said she only knew how the pieces moved, but she could show him that. "You could probably beat me," she laughed, but he thought, if they played he would let her win. Nowadays girls were supposed to win.

He broke his stride to shift the backpack to one side, not that it helped.

"Jack!"

He turned. Cars had been passing him all along the way like they always did but now one had stopped in the street alongside him.

"That looks heavy!" The driver was a woman and the car was white.

"Jack!" He didn't wonder how she knew his name because it happened so often that people knew him but he couldn't recognize them. "Come talk to me!"

He didn't like her voice. It was like she was trying to be nice, but it was pretend nice.

He came up to the open window.

"Your mother sent me to give you a ride!"

Her voice was too loud.

"Whaa-at?"

"Your mother sent me to give you a ride!" She patted the seat next to her. "Get in!"

She was even louder now. The loudness made a pounding in his forehead, so that though he did hear her words, he had extra trouble translating them. She did that gesture, pounding the empty seat, again, and that was what told him that she wanted him to get in the car.

"Your mother's name is Anna, right?"

She was softer and a little bit of un-pretend nice, too. She obviously did know his mother or she wouldn't know her name. "She didn't want you to walk home with that heavy backpack, so she sent me to get you."

That made sense. How else would the Woman know about the backpack that Ms. Gonzales and his mom were always nagging him about? He leaned in the passenger window. The car was so clean it looked like no one had ever used it before and it smelled like mango, which he smelled a lot because Marissa liked it and his mom always bought stuff that smelled like that for her.

"Come on," the Woman said and the color of her voice had become cotton candy: sweet soft pink that dissolved into sticky sugar. He started to pull the handle of the door.

But Mom had told him, *never get in a car with a stranger.* He stepped away.

"Jack, I didn't want to tell you this and make you scared. But your mom is in the hospital. I have to take you to her."

The hospital! He remembered her going to the hospital almost six years ago. She came back with the baby that turned out to be Marissa. Could it be — ?

"Jack, we have to hurry!"

"How do I know — how do I know — "

The Woman laughed, but it wasn't a real laugh. His muscles tensed. He wanted to flee. The only thing that stopped him was that he knew how rude that would be if he was wrong and he might even get a lecture about it. He hated those lectures. He did a pretty damn good job of pretending that he didn't care but he did, oh, he did.

The Woman patted the seat again, but now hard and fast. "Look. Your sister's name is Marissa. How would I know that if I didn't know your mom? Whose name is Anna?"

Something told him that the last thing she said was a joke but he replayed it in his mind and couldn't see what could possibly be funny about her repeating his mother's name.

"She's sick and she needs you," the Woman said.

Mom was sick and she needed *him!* Not Dad or Jason or —

He got in.

"Fasten your seat belt!" the Woman said cheerfully, which reassured Jack that he was doing the right thing.

The car accelerated suddenly, before he'd had time to snap the belt in place.

"We're going for a ride!" the Woman cried as she made the car bolt ahead. It felt the way those huge rollercoasters that hang you upside down must feel.

She didn't stop at the corner. You're supposed to stop at the corner, or at least slow down. He learned that on his lesson with Mr. Hu.

Suddenly the Woman took a sharp turn, such a sharp turn that her wheels shrieked.

"Is this the way to the hospital?" he asked. Something was wrong. He made a mistake getting in. Why did he do such stupid things?

The Woman turned on the radio to a station that was playing rap music, turned it way up loud so that it hurt his ears. "No!" she shouted over the sound. "We're going to the beach instead!"

"But you said — you said — " He wanted to say, *You said she was in the hospital,* but the words wouldn't come.

"Don't you want to go to the beach?" she shouted even louder.

The beach? What did the beach have to do with anything? Jack liked the beach, except for the sand, but you didn't go to the beach in January, everyone knew that.

"I don't want to go to the beach!" he shouted back, even more loudly. "Take me home!"

But now he knew that she wouldn't take him home.

He had to jump out of the car. He'd seen people jump out of cars in the movies lots of times.

But he was scared. His heart was throbbing louder than the music.

The Woman kept singing along to that music, but it was just more noise. It made it so very hard for him to think. *Jump, jump.* In the movies they said to roll. That meant to make yourself into a ball. *Just jump. It won't hurt too bad.*

They were passing nice houses, houses that had a little bit of lawn, and if he jumped and he rolled at just the right moment he might land on the grass there … no, there … she was driving so fast! Why don't they get a speeding ticket? If a cop stopped them he could make some sign that he was in trouble. Maybe Jason would stop them and then he'd be safe.

But they kept driving.

Now … now.… He closed his eyes and pulled on the door handle. Nothing.

"Don't worry, Jack!" the Woman shouted. The radio was louder than he would have thought possible. She must have turned it up. "I have the child lock on! Isn't that great? You're totally safe!"

THEY DROVE on and on and it felt like the thumping noise from the radio and the screechy noise from the Woman singing were coming from inside his head.

Just when he thought he couldn't stand it anymore and that he was going to start screaming in a way that he hadn't in a long time, the car stopped. He opened his eyes. He didn't even know they were closed. But he opened his eyes and he saw the ocean down below him.

"Come on," said the Woman, hopping out of the car.

As she opened her door he grabbed his handle. He was going to run for it.

Still locked.

Then the Woman was filling the window, leering over him, opening the door from her side, grabbing his wrist before he could get his feet on the ground. "We're meeting your mom here. Her name is Anna, right?"

She made that sound that wasn't a real laugh again.

"And your sister's name is Marissa."

She dragged him down the steps that led down to the sand. He knew he should scream for help but his throat had closed up. It was a cold, overcast day, and there weren't many people around.

"Don't you want to see the beach?"

He heard himself whimper. Like a baby. Why was everyone so far away? But not everyone was. Why didn't someone see that The Woman was dragging him where he didn't want to go? Why didn't someone help him?

She was pulling him through the sand. He tried to make it hard for her by making his shoes dig deep into the sand but his wrist was hurting so badly that he had to move with her a little.

Then they were on the smooth part of the sand, the dark part where the water used to be. There were the waves that scared him so badly when he was two. He was a baby, just like the other kids used to call him, and he was a baby still, so he deserved whatever happened.

"We're going for a swim," the Woman said. She sounded crazier every time she talked. Because that's what the laugh sound was. Crazy.

"I need my swimsuit," he said.

"We don't need swimsuits," she said happily. He could see all of her teeth. "People float in saltwater."

They did? Maybe, but — but he remembered that you couldn't swim in Ocean Beach. The water was dangerous. There was something that dragged you down, and he thought of all the times he pretended that he lived in the ocean with SpongeBob with shame, because he knew that real people couldn't live in the ocean, even if Sandy the Texan Squirrel could live there with a fish bowl on her head.

People drowned.

"Don't you want to go swimming, Jack?" She walked towards the water, so close that it lapped up against her own shoes. And then again, *"Don't you want to go swimming, Jack?"*

His wrist hurt so very badly that he was almost ready to follow her. *But if my hand hurts then maybe her hand hurts, too.*

He yanked hard, hard, hard. He was free.

He ran. Five steps and he was off the hard part of the sand and onto the soft yellow part, the part you couldn't run on because the sand would keep pulling you down. The crazy Woman was after him, but she couldn't run, either. He kept stepping, but he wasn't moving. But she didn't catch him, either. He heard her heavy breathing, getting heavier and heavier. She panted, "Stop ... stop...."

It was like those dreams where you were running from something, but you couldn't get away. Maybe it *was* a dream.

Then he reached down. He grabbed a fistful of sand and though most of it fell out between his fingers, when he threw it at her enough got in her eyes that she cursed him, but stopped chasing.

After school Marissa went straight to her room. As always, Leonora had cleaned it up so that the only sign that Marissa had ever even been here before was HannahSophia, lying with her pink head on the pillow.

Marissa lay down and put HannahSophia on her chest.

Now Marissa had a name for how she'd felt since she came to live with Daddy. Adopted.

So it was good that that afternoon Daddy was coming home early — really early, four o'clock — to take her to spend the weekend with Mommy, and for the whole weekend, not just one night. He was going to take an airplane to a contention center and he said he'd come get her Sunday night, which meant that he'd send Leonora to do it....

Leonora is driving fast and they go through a stop sign without stopping and Marissa hears the siren of the police car.....

Marissa startled as the siren became the sound of the approaching vacuum. She must have fallen asleep.

"Vacio un otro lugar!" she called out. *Vacuum somewhere else.*

Daddy told her not to be rude to Leonora, but Marissa was kind of the boss of her. Besides, she didn't have to listen to Daddy, since he wasn't her real Daddy.

"*Si tu no tomas alimentos por toda la casa la alfombra no sería sucia.*"

That wasn't Leonora's voice. It was Dania.

"*No vengas en mi habitación!*" Marissa shouted back.

Marissa heard Dania rolling the now-silent vacuum away. "*Vuelvo enseguida!*" Dania promised.

How long was she asleep? Marissa wondered. She looked at her watch. Daddy picked it out. It didn't have any numbers on it but he taught her how to tell Big Girl time. She was still so sleepy that it was hard to see the little lines and even to remember which line was which number. The big hand was on the 6 and the little hand was on the 4. So that must mean that it was 6:20! How could Daddy be so late?

Daddy forgot her.

He just went to the airport and left her here.

She could call Mommy herself. Mommy would come pick her up.

Some of Marissa's friends had cell phones, and Daddy said that as soon as she got a report card with all As she could have one, too. But for now it didn't matter, because she'd broken the don't-go-into-Daddy's-study rule so many times that it felt easy to go in there now. And she'd been using the phone on her own for practically forever.

Daddy's phone had a lot of buttons and symbols on it that other phones didn't have, but he taught her how to use it for emergencies. She even knew how to use the speaker phone part and she pushed that now and filled the room with the honking sound of a dial tone.

Tap-tap-tap-tap-tap-tap-tap.

Then she heard, "Yeah?"

It's a man's voice. It must be Trevor or Jason.

"Is my mommy there?"

"Who's this?"

"It's — it's Marissa."

"You've got the wrong number." *Click.*

She tapped the seven numbers again and again the man told her she got the wrong number.

She balanced on one foot by putting the other foot on her knee, like a flamingo. When Daddy was with her it was easy, and he let her call his friend Paul by herself.

So she tried again.

"Stop calling here, brat! What part of 'you've got the wrong number' don't you understand?"

Bang. The man slammed the phone down hard.

The receiver was shaking in Marissa's hand. She had to try three times before she could get it back in its cradle. She couldn't call again. The man would call the police on her.

What did she do wrong? She knew her number! Mommy made her memorize it when she was in pre-school.

She said it out loud. It ended zero, six, seven, four.

Or was it....

Seven, six, zero, four...?

All the numbers were whirling around in her head. Even Daddy's books were a blur, as if she were spinning to make herself dizzy and fall down.

Her neck was all hot and damp. Now she had no way of getting to Mommy.

Leonora must have left for the day if Dania was here, and Dania couldn't drive. And Dania must be about to leave anyway, because Marissa was supposed to be gone by now.

So Marissa would be all alone in this big, dark house. Burglars could come in any window and she wouldn't know it. They could come in and hide in one of the zillion closets until it was totally dark and then jump out and get her. Or what if the house got on fire? She knew how to dial 911, but even firemen wouldn't be able to find her before —

Just when her heart was beating so fast that she could hardly breathe, she knew what to do.

She could get back to Mommy herself. She knew the way. Easy-peasy!

She couldn't let Dania know. So she tiptoed down the big stairs in front, and then she hid in the little inside garden next to the kitchen until she saw Leonora go down the basement stairs where the laundry machines were. Then she went to the refrigerator to see what to pack.

She wasn't scared of finding her way home. She'd been back and forth between Mommy's and Daddy's houses a *gajillion* times, so she knew exactly what to look for: first, there was the gas station with the big orange 76 sign, then there was the hospital, then there was a whole lot of plain little houses that Daddy said were for People who Dropped Out of School.

To get to the gas station she had to go five blocks, then turn left, then go three blocks. Easy-peasy....

What should she take?

Water. Snacks. She slipped a bottle of Crystal Geyser into her school back pack, which she'd just emptied onto her bed. She got two Z Bars from the cabinet. Fruit. Fruit was always good. She didn't see any fruit that was easy to pack so she decided to take some of Daddy's chocolates from the white box instead.

That was all she needed because she'd be home with Mommy in half an hour.

After he threw sand at the Woman, Jack started running again. His backpack kept banging against him and that slowed him down. The sand was worse, the way it pulled him down, but finally he got off the sand and onto the sidewalk by the ocean.

By then he had a stitch, so he couldn't run anymore. He clutched his side and looked all over for the Woman. The sun was lowering itself into the ocean, cautiously, the way he dipped his toe into a cold swimming pool before he got all the way in. But he couldn't see the Woman anywhere, so he limped across the road.

He was only across the street from the ocean. He could hear it whoosh-whooshing. He never noticed how loud it was.

Now he'd been walking for a while. He was thinking how he could never tell anyone about the Woman because they'd know how stupid he was to believe her story. Unless — ? He really knew that the Woman was lying, but he'd feel better when he saw his mom, so he had to get home.

Jack knew how to take the bus. He could get downtown by bus and he could get home from school by bus when it was raining and even get to his Dad's house. But there weren't any buses that went to the ocean.

He was supposed to carry his Fast Pass and emergency money in his backpack all the time but he forgot them today. He remembered his cell phone, but the battery was dead. He was supposed to charge it at night, but he forgot to do that, too.

He was getting a little tired, but if he walked a while he'd probably see his house. It still hurt when he took a deep breath, so he walked slowly. A flock of birds flew overhead, but they went too fast for him to count. The blue of the sky was draining away.

Then he saw that the park was only a block away. He lived near the park. But nothing on his side looked like it was near his house.

So his house must have been on the other side of the park. And he could take a short cut through the park. The park was just a big rectangle, so if he went straight across it'd be a short cut and he'd be on the right side.

Marissa didn't know where she went wrong. She had it all written down in her head. Daddy said she could keep things in her head because she was so smart. He never said that that was why he picked her out at the adoption place, but now she knew.

The pavement was so hard and her shoes had gotten thinner just since she'd been walking, so that she could feel it through the soles. She didn't know how long it had been because she left her watch at home. She didn't want to take anything that Daddy gave her.

And now it was getting dark. The sun disappeared behind the buildings a little while ago. She never realized how fast it got dark. And how the wind was blowing! It wasn't like this when she started out.

So she kept trudging down the strange street, holding her thin jacket closely around her, wrapping her arms so tight that her hands almost touched in back.

Suddenly she stopped walking. Now she remembered! It was way back there, when she was so tired, and she sat down at a bus stop and ate all the chocolate because it was starting to melt. When she got up from the seat she mixed up the right-left-count-the-blocks pattern that she had memorized. That was Daddy's fault, too, for telling her she didn't need to write things down. She had to go back to the house and start over.

But when she returned to the corner, though she looked first one way and then the other, she couldn't see the bus stop, and she couldn't remember which direction it was in. She walked up a block and turned and she was more lost than ever, and now it was all the way dark.

She felt like she was going to cry, and it wouldn't matter if she did, because no one could see her, but then she looked up and saw bright lights straight ahead. Lights meant a busy street, a street with people, so a safer street.

When she got to that corner there were no more houses, just stores and restaurants. And she'd been on this street! She was pretty sure there was a Jack in the Box somewhere, because Daddy'd taken her there. He said that there were dangerous men inside sometimes so he locked her in the car and let her hold his cell phone and told her to honk if she didn't feel safe and said he'd come right out, and when he did....

Her stomach groaned at the thought of the hamburger and milkshake and curly fries he always brought her. She'd only taken three pieces of chocolate and she was really hungry, and hungry for something real, not junk food.

She couldn't see the Jack in the Box anyway. Maybe it wasn't even on this street.

Suddenly a whole bunch of loud, smelly men tumbled out of one of the stores. They were laughing like Jack laughed, but in a scary movie way. One of them stumbled almost to the curb and Marissa was so afraid that he was going to knock her down that she turned around and ran. Her backpack was pounding against her back, *thump thump,* and she kept running and then she heard a loud steady honk and a *screeeeeech* and there was a car stopped right next to her! She was crossing the street against a red light!

She jumped up on the curb again. Crossing the street on a red light was against the law. She could get in trouble with the police.

Police. Jason was a policeman. He wouldn't let her get in trouble. But she didn't know how to find him. And if a different policeman saw her, he might not know Jason. And she made that man on the phone so mad, he probably called the police on her already.

And running away must be against the law too!

So whatever happened, she had to hide from the police.

She walked regular now, because that would help her not get noticed. She looked down at the sidewalk and carefully avoided stepping on the cracks.

There was another bus stop up ahead. She could sit down and have that other Z bar. There were a couple of grownups, but they were women and they didn't look too dangerous. Marissa pulled down the remaining fold-up seat. And the bus stop was sheltered from the wind a little, so....

That was when she remembered.

HannahSophia.

She forgot HannahSophia. She left her on the bed at Daddy's house, under the pile of stuff she emptied from her backpack, the workbooks and the Thermos and....

HannahSophia would be so scared! She'd be all alone and so scared!

"You okay, little girl?" one of the women asked. She had a gray scarf around her neck that almost touched the ground.

Maybe they would help her. But she couldn't know that for sure. And what about all the times that Mommy and Daddy and every teacher she ever had had told her not to talk to strangers? Even if they didn't kidnap her they might think that she was running away and call the police. And then even if she told the police about knowing Jason they could still put her in jail. Jason told a funny story at dinner once about how he gave a speeding ticket to a man he knew from high school, except that it didn't seem funny now.

"Hey, kid," the other woman addressed her, and this one didn't sound as nice. She had a big instrument case on her back, maybe for a guitar. "We're talking to you."

"I'm okay," Marissa said.

"Do you know where you're going?" the one with the scarf asked.

Marissa looked away from them. There was a bus coming! This could be the bus that went to Mommy's house!

"Yes," Marissa said, trying to talk like Daddy: in a loud, deep voice.

The one with the scarf shrugged and they went back to talking to each other.

The bus gets closer and closer. But it didn't slow down. And it didn't stop.

The two women said bad words.

Marissa put her jacket over her head so that they wouldn't see her cry.

I pounded unceremoniously on Alex's door, screaming his name, and his nannies' names, in between and simultaneously.

I was one pissed-off lady.

Alex was supposed to have brought Marissa home to me by 5:30, as I was right on his way to the airport. He was late more often than not, so I didn't get nervous until 6:00, and I wouldn't have gotten nervous then if I hadn't known he had a plane to catch. Maybe he switched to a later flight. Maybe he'd delegated Marissa's delivery to Leonora. But by the time 6:30 came around and I hadn't heard anything I called his cell phone (straight to voice mail) and then his house.

After the time that the language barrier had forced me to bribe Rose Gonzales, I complained about the problem to Alex. His response was, first, that I was pretty insensitive to want him to replace two women who needed jobs and second, had I considered taking Spanish classes?

That night, no one answered the phone and so I had plenty of time, listening to the hollow sound of its ring, to recall that conversation and begin working up a head of steam.

During the drive to his house, I failed at calming myself down.

Finally a woman answered the door. I had never seen her before, but I could see that she'd been crying. And when she let forth an agitated stream of Spanish I deduced that she was either Leonora or Dania.

"My sister is upset."

A young man had come up behind her. The family resemblance was striking in prominent cheek bones, a high forehead and an aquiline nose. "And you are — ?"

"Roberto. Mrs. Kagen?"

"Where is my daughter?"

"Mar-ees-sa! *Hija!*" Roberto's sister poured forth more Spanish, ending in a sob.

"Yes, my daughter Marissa!" I screamed.

Roberto was calm. "Please come in."

If I hadn't been nearly hysterical I might have appreciated the irony of being invited by a complete stranger into the home I had lived in for ten years.

"Alex? Mr. Kagen? Is he home?"

When the woman who was either Leonora or Dania said, "No home," I thought Roberto was going to have to pull me off her.

"Calm down," he said. "Mr. Alex probably took her to the airport with him."

"That doesn't make any sense. He's going to Las Vegas. How would she get home from the airport?"

Roberto grinned. His teeth were stained yellow. "What happens in Vegas — "

That was as far as I let him get. "WHERE THE FUCK IS SHE?"

"We were just about to call the police," Roberto offered and though I was itching to put my hands around his neck, I grabbed my own cell to call Jason. Everything else was wasted time.

Only minutes later I had the dubious pleasure of riding shotgun while Jason was at the wheel of his cruiser. He had friends, on-duty and off, also looking. We were not pulling any strings; she was a missing child and that first hour ... that first hour....

I chewed ferociously on my left thumb. Since I'd given up acrylic manicures all my fingernails were a mess, but I was breaking new ground on my cuticles as we drove, mostly silent except for Jason's platitudinous reassurances, and the reports that interrupted the static on the radio.

ROBBERY ON 2100 BLOCK OF CHESTNUT, SUSPECT FLEEING ON FOOT....

Crackle ... crackle....

DOMESTIC DISTURBANCE 55 VINTON....

Crackle ... crackle....

NO SIGHTINGS OF UNACCOMPANIED MINOR ON CALIFORNIA STREET BETWEEN 25TH AND 15TH AVENUES....

"We'll find her," Jason said. He was not speeding, nor did he have his siren or roof lights on. We had to move slowly. But once we moved downtown, into more heavy traffic, the lights and the siren came on and no man nor woman would stop Jason Armstrong.

Jack went straight across the park so why wasn't he on the other side yet? He'd been walking for 48 minutes. It seemed like he should be there by now.

The road he was on started to curve so in order to keep going straight he had to walk on the grass. Now he was in a part where there were lots of trees that all looked exactly the same.

A flock of birds flew overhead, but they went too fast for him to count. In fact, he could just barely see them: The sky was the color of one of Ashleigh's sweaters. It was a pretty color, but it was making it harder to see.

Then he saw the green beer can. He'd seen it before: lying at the bottom of one of the trees.

He'd been going in circles.

When he first heard that expression, it was when one of his teachers said to another student, "You're going in circles." But the student was just sitting there. Later he learned that it meant that you were repeating yourself. But he also knew that when people got lost they went in circles. And this for sure was the same beer can he saw before. There had been other cans, soda and beer, and there had been lots of other litter which was disgusting because people shouldn't litter, but right now he was only thinking about how he'd been going in circles.

He recited a *Crime Conqueror* script for a while, staring at the can, until he thought of something.

His shoulders hurt when he shrugged off his backpack. He didn't realize how much it was hurting until it fell on the ground.

He pulled out the chess game. By itself it was light. When he looked at the picture of the board with the pieces scattered around, he thought of how he was going to spend the afternoon playing the game with Ashleigh but instead he did something so stupid. He hoped she wasn't worried about him, but he kind of hoped that she was now.

He could use the chess pieces to mark where he'd been. That way if he saw them he'd know that he was going in circles and that he needed to go a different way from the way he did when he put the piece down.

He dumped the whole box on the ground. Jack knew a lot about chess pieces because his dad played chess a lot and now he played with Marissa. Jack knew about pawns because when he was little he used to carry one in his pocket. There were sixteen pawns, but they all looked alike so that wouldn't help him, except he could use one black pawn and one white pawn.

After he put the first chess piece next to the can he had to put his backpack on again. It was so much heavier now that he'd had it off. After a few steps he tried carrying it by one of the straps but that was even harder.

So to cheer himself up he thought about Ashleigh, and not about how he didn't get to see her today, but about the times he'd see her later.

He was so excited about his driver's license. He pictured himself in a car, one hand on the steering wheel and one arm around her shoulder, just like the kids on TV.

Drake didn't get his driver's license on the first try, but Josh did, and later Drake did get his, so sometimes you had to keep trying, just like everyone said.

Then he thought about Ashleigh's birthday. It wasn't 'til June 3rd, but Jack loved birthdays, and he had to plan what to do for hers. A big party. Not a DJ, but a real band. And where could they have it? His house was too small. Could they use the school cafeteria? Or his Dad's house?

It didn't take long before he ran out of chess pieces and then he had to start using things from his back pack. Precious things, and it was hard to let go: the packet of ketchup from Burger King, the Ziploc bag of grapes from the week before, and the green beer can he'd just picked up.

Every time he put something down, he went right. Then if he saw it again he went left.

When he got onto a paved road he knew he was going to be all right. A road could go in a circle but not forever because then there'd be no way to get on or off. Now that he was learning to drive he could figure these things out.

So he followed the road and after a while his surroundings looked familiar. There was a big building that he was sure he'd been to. And now there were cars parked along the side of the road.

His house was still far away, but he knew he could get home.

He was stupid to get in the car with the Woman, but he got away from her. And now he'd found his way home.

He wasn't stupid. He just had to do things his own way.

Marissa stopped crying after only a couple of minutes, because she saw the lights of another bus coming in their direction.

This bus stopped right in front of Marissa, grunting and wheezing like Daddy after he climbed the stairs too fast. The doors opened and she saw two giant steps.

Marissa raised her knee as high as it would go and pulled herself up. She could only remember being on Muni once, though supposedly Jack's old babysitter Mairead took her on Muni sometimes when she was a baby. The time that she remembered was when her class was going on a field trip and something went wrong with the chartered bus and they had to take the regular bus.

So Marissa knew that she didn't have to pay because she was still only five, so she started walking down the aisle, but then the bus moved really suddenly and she almost fell down, but she grabbed the back of one of the seats just in time.

"Watch it, kid," said the person in the seat. People on the bus were mean. But everyone was being mean today.

She sat down at the first empty seat. Even through her leggings she could feel that it was really sticky. She slid over to the window so she could look out and maybe see her house. Now she was glad that HannahSophia wasn't with her, because HannahSophia would be even more scared. As soon as Marissa got home, Mommy would get HannahSophia back for her.

Then an old lady yelled at her that she wasn't allowed to take up two seats.

Marissa had left her backpack next to her. She silently pulled it on her lap and the old lady sat down. She had a lot of wrinkles around her thin mouth where her red lipstick was leaking. She was making a *tsiu-tsiu* sound like she was sucking on candy.

After a while the old lady asked, "Where are your parents?" She had a square purse on her lap and she was gripping it tightly, like Marissa might try to steal it. Her nose was narrow and pointy and she sounded like she knew that Marissa was doing something wrong.

"They're at home."

"Do they know where you are?" She leaned in toward Marissa and her breath was all old lady smells, that mint-and-mouse-cage smell.

Mommy always smelled fresh, the way it smelled just after the rain stopped.

"Yes." Marissa looked over her shoulder and saw that there were other empty seats so why did the old lady sit next to her? Was she spying on her? Marissa crunched herself up to the window as tightly as she could.

A mechanical voice had been calling out words as they went and Marissa thought that it was just a foreign language, but then she heard the word "vanness," and she knew that that was the name of a street, because it was the street that Daddy drove down with her all the time. She sat up straighter. If they were calling out street names, then all she had to do was to wait until the voice called out the name of her street, Highland, and then she'd get off the bus and she'd be home.

But the streets were getting darker. Outside the window there weren't as many lights or people anymore. One of the last big signs she saw was the drawing of a naked woman in lights.

The old lady was gone. Marissa didn't notice when she got up to leave. Maybe she was a witch and she got out by magic.

The bus pulled over. It was lighter at that corner and Marissa drew a deep breath, thinking how she was being silly about magic, but then there was noise and bad words, lots of bad words, and a whole bunch of teenage boys got on. She could tell they were teenage boys because they looked like the boys that went to Jack's school. They were swearing and saying the F word more times than she'd ever heard it, and they were punching each other, though they were laughing, but laughing in the same way that the other men were before, the men who almost knocked her over.

Marissa stiffened. What if one of them sat next to her?

They didn't; they passed by her going to the rear of the bus where there were the most empty seats. She tried to make herself really small again, and wished the old lady hadn't disappeared after all.

Then she heard one say, "I'm going to kill that mother-fucker."

Marissa didn't wait for the voice to call out another name. She clung to the standing-up bars and when the bus stopped again she took the two steps down.

BUT SHE ended up on this really *really* dark street. Was she still in San Francisco or had she ended up in a bad Magic Land?

She passed a long, high chain link fence. On other side was a huge, deep hole that made her think of a grave for a giant. There was a tall machiney-like tower looming over it.

Someone called out, "Hey, there little lady!"

But it couldn't be a person. She didn't see anyone, just a long skinny shadow cast against a brick wall.

Ghosts.

Ghosts weren't real! Daddy told her that. But Daddy … Daddy didn't know everything.

Maybe the ghost escaped from the big hole that was a grave because they forgot to bury him.

Then she saw other must-be-ghosts. They were far away and dressed in dark clothes and some were pushing carts.

She didn't know where to go.

Was this her punishment for wanting magic to be real?

Was this her punishment for being mean to Trevor, and especially to Jack? She wasn't mean to them when she visited during vacation, though, was she? She used to be mean. She was mean when Trevor started coming over all the time. She wasn't real mean to him out loud, because Mommy wouldn't let her, but she was really mean to him in her head.

Maybe she'd be stuck here forever.

Daddy had told her about how little girls disappear forever. He wouldn't tell her how, just that talking to strangers was one way and getting in a car with a stranger was a for sure way.

No one tried to get her into a car, though. Cars had been passing her all this time, but no one has stopped. At first she wanted one to stop but now she didn't.

"Hello, little girl!"

It was one of the women ghosts. She was covered in black and Marissa couldn't see her face, but then the headlights of one of the passing cars lit it up and *it's the wicked queen after she turned into a witch!*

Marissa ran.

She ran in the street and heard horns honking and tires screeching and people shouting, but she kept running.

Suddenly she was in an alley. It looked like a regular street when she ran in, but now she saw that there was no way out.

JACK SAW the Princess Tiana doll in the window from really far away. He could tell it was Princess Tiana from the shape.

Suddenly he could feel how tired he was: He felt like he could fall right through the sidewalk.

The last few houses were the worst. It had gotten cold and his feet were so heavy he could hardly lift them.

But then — home! There was Princess Tiana, up close and beautiful. There was every light on in the house. What a beautiful house he had. What a wonderful family.

The next thing he knew he was pounding on the door because he couldn't find his key but finally Trevor opened it.

"You're really late," Trevor snorted. "Really late. Where have you been?"

"I — I don't know."

He couldn't think of anything else to say; he was too tired. He went to his room — he couldn't wait until Trevor had his own room — and lay down.

After a while he could think. It was weird that Mom and Jason were out, but lucky. They wouldn't know that he was really late.

He didn't want to tell them what happened, because they'd be mad at him for falling for the Woman's lie.

But a few minutes later Trevor came in. "Let's play Guitar Hero."

"I'm too tired."

"Where have you been? Where have you *been*?"

"Nowhere."

"You can't be nowhere," Trevor snorted again. "How can you be nowhere?"

Jack really wanted to tell someone what happened. "It's a secret."

"I can keep a secret!"

"I got kidnapped." Now that he was safe, now that it was over, the word had a thrilling sound. And he escaped!

"No, you didn't."

Jack sat up and it made him feel dizzy. "I did!"

He told Trevor the story. It took a long time because he needed so many words, and when he was finished he felt like he hadn't told it good enough. But Trevor, although he interrupted many times to say he didn't believe him, was really excited.

"You can't tell anyone."

"I won't!"

"Promise?"

"Promise." Trevor put his hand up in the high-five position.

Crackle ... crackle....

SUSPECTED DRUG DEALER IN DOLORES PARK....

"Cross Market," I said.

"Okay." Jason punched one of the many mysterious buttons on the dash.

"I took her to a birthday party at the Zeum once — not that long ago."

"The Zeum...."

BURGLARY IN PROGRESS AT JEWELRY STORE, 649 WEST PORTAL....

"You must have taken Trevor there...." *but maybe....* "It's an interactive — oh fuck, it's at Yerba Buena. Moscone. Just head down 3rd."

Crackle ... crackle....

MUNI DRIVER SAYS HE SAW FEMALE ANSWERING TO CHILD'S DESCRIPTION....

"Why...."

"She might recognize the streets, okay? Just *go.*"

Crackle ... crackle....

MUNI DRIVER SAYS GIRL DISEMBARKED AT KEARNEY....

"*Go!*"

"There! There! Stop!"

I almost fell out of the car.

We'd been crawling along at no more than five miles an hour, covering streets South of Market, starting with the Muni line, the 14, where she was last reported seen.

It had been the longest hour of my whole life.

She was sitting next to a dumpster in an alley between a shuttered video store and a closed bakery.

"Marissa! Baby!"

For a second I was afraid that it wasn't her or that it was her, propped up but already ... or....

"Mommy!"

She raised her arms to me.

Her face was smeared with dirt, the tracks of tears making muddy rivers down her cheeks.

EVEN WITH Jason in charge it was hard to get Marissa into the car. He finally did it by holding her tightly against his chest, and easing himself in backwards. I came in from the other side and he eased her onto my lap, then buckled the seat belt over both of us.

Her face was pressed so hard against my chest that I was afraid she'd suffocate. I kept trying to shift her head, and she kept resisting, so her occasional soft moans were perversely reassuring.

It was very creepy, sitting in the back seat of a patrol car, with that thick metal fence between me and Jason. Through the windows, the city had never looked so dangerous. In the dark streets South of Market there were dirty needles and dirtier men. Loose sewer grates. Drunk drivers.

Alex was a failure. His job, his promise, his sworn oath, his *raison d'etre,* was to make the city safe. But his own little girl had been out here, and if it hadn't been for Jason with his police radio and a lot of luck and maybe, just maybe, the grace of God, Marissa might be....

I remembered a Jewish proverb: *If you save one life you save the whole world.*

I kissed the top of Marissa's black hair.

"Are you cold, baby?"

No answer.

"You must be hungry."

No answer.

"Let's just get her home as fast as we can." Jason's voice through the barrier was slightly muffled.

I nodded.

"You know I can't see you if you nod?"

"Then how did you know?"

"I knew."

I sighed. "It's such a relief, you know? It puts other things in perspective."

"Keep that thought."

Another police car had pulled up alongside us at the light. Jason gave the policewoman in the passenger seat the thumbs up and she returned it. Thanks again to the radio, every law enforcement officer in the city and county would know that Marissa had been found.

"What do you mean?" I resettled myself, still trying to give Marissa access to more air. "'Keep that thought'?"

"I'm just coming out with it."

"Good."

"Fascist!" a passing driver shouted. "You're all fascists!"

"So come out with it."

"Now listen, Annie — this is hard…. Denise. I found Denise today. I was going to tell you when I got home, but then you called about Marissa…."

If Jason could be believed — and up until now he could be — Denise actually *was* a little…. He'd said that she was bi-polar.

"She wants to see Trevor."

"Oh! Well, she should. I hadn't wanted to say anything, but I know he thinks about her a lot."

"Why didn't you want to say anything?" Jason sounded suspicious.

I hesitated. "Because I thought it would make you unhappy, when there was nothing we could do about it."

He was quiet in a way that made me nervous. I wished I could see *his* face. Then I had a thought. "How did you find her?" *And for how long have you been looking?*

"Your tires. Remember how I said it looked like someone had used a nail gun? Denise used a nail gun on one of our neighbor's cars once. She told the police it was because she had PMS."

He told me the rest as we bolted up Pine Street. After he'd seen my flattened tires, he'd tracked down the lawyer whom she'd initially left Jason for before disappearing. Lawyer Kenneth was now divorced as well, was working at a distinctly unprestigious non-profit, and yes, he had heard from Denise recently. "So yes," Jason concluded, "she wrote that horrible letter, too. Do you want to hear something funny?"

"Is it really funny?"

"She copied it off the Internet. Some woman in Canada left it in another mother's mailbox."

CHAPTER 19

Jason had been right. I should never, never have let Marissa go back to Alex's house.

Sunday night I went into her room, three, four times. More, but I lost count after that. I stroked hair off her face, but made every effort not to wake her up.

I'd already decided to keep her home from school the next day. It wasn't exactly a tough call.

I was an idiot, an incompetent mother — but there was one person more at fault than I, and he came to my door Monday morning.

"Thanks for knocking," I said nastily. "Do you know what — oh fuck it, just give me back my goddam house keys."

Alex was actually hanging his head.

"This must be your version of looking contrite." I breathed slowly through my nose to keep myself from screaming, though only because Marissa was still asleep. "Oh, and aren't you supposed to be in Las Vegas?"

"I turned around at McCarren and came — "

Suddenly sarcasm wasn't enough. "You stupid, stupid asshole. Do you know what could have happened?"

Alex raised his head, and did something he rarely did with me: He made eye contact. "How is she?"

"Still asleep."

"I could put a gun to my head and pull the trigger," he said.

"Prove it, big talker," I sneered. "I have one of Jason's guns in my room, and yes, it's loaded."

My first indication that I was making an impact with Alex was that he did not respond with an impassioned reminder that keeping a loaded weapon in a house with children, let alone autistic teens, was pretty stupid. I had just been trying to get to him: We had only the one unloaded weapon, and that was locked up.

"I *should* do it. Only … well, I brought this."

He dragged a large wheelie across the threshold. It was fiberglass, with a pink leopard pattern. I took the handle and propped it upright on my side of the door. "There's a lot more," he said. "I'll send it over." He shuffled his oxfords on the welcome mat.

I would never, ever forgive him, but for my own amusement I wanted to hear what lame, self-justifying excuse he came up with. "How did this happen?"

"You met Roberto."

"I had the pleasure, yes."

"Well, he went outside to smoke a cigarette."

"Start from the beginning." I held out my hand. "But give me my keys back first."

Alex dropped a small key ring into my palm. The fob was from a souvenir shop on the Wharf and had a picture of a cable car on it.

I closed my fingers around it. "You were supposed to bring her here on the way to the airport."

"I ran out of time."

"So...."

"I called home to say that Leonora should take Marissa here."

That's what I would have thought; similar situations had arisen, but there hadn't been a problem. I guessed what the problem had been this time. "You gave the message to Dania, and she never gave it to Leonora."

His mouth opened. He closed it.

"You know I do as many background checks as I can without being labeled paranoid."

"You might want a second opinion on that."

"Maybe if I *weren't* so meticulous...."

"Don't even go there."

I might have imagined that his lower lip trembled slightly.

"I trusted them."

"I trusted you!"

"Dania — "

"Are you sure you know which one Dania is?"

"I suppose I deserve that."

"I suppose you do."

"Dania has — had been having an affair with a married man. He broke it off, but she kept hounding him, and when she showed up at his house ... that night, he had her arrested."

"San Francisco's finest on the job."

"Well, yes, and ... Leonora went to bail her out. She did not leave Marissa alone. It's very important that you know that. She wanted to help Dania. She's a woman who respects family."

"Roberto is her brother."

"Yes, and I know him — *I* would have left Marissa with him. He's documented and he works at City Hall."

"I hear he smokes."

"He swears he wasn't outside the house for more than ten minutes, and not even outside the house, just on the deck."

"This is just as lame as I expected," I said. "But I suppose I have to give you credit for at least coming over to 'explain.' "

I could see from the way Alex was shifting his weight that he was tired of standing, but I was not ready — might never be ready — to have him inside my house. Which was awkward, since in one sense it was his house: He'd bought it for us as part of our divorce agreement, and he made the mortgage payments.

Alex was looking up at the sky. "You were right. I couldn't take care of her. Every night I promised that I'd do better the next day, but the next day … something would come up or I'd just be so tired."

I didn't forgive him, but I pitied him. And I suddenly understood, really understood, his obsession with making Marissa into a Girl Genius. She was his legacy. He was simultaneously an atheist and an old father: 53 when she was born. When I'd met him he thought he was going to be governor one day, at the very least, but he'd sat out the last Attorney General's race — in part, I was pretty sure, so that he could micromanage her formative years.

"Heh-heh." It was a sad attempt at his knowing chuckle. "I never did appreciate how much work it must be for you, with the two of them."

I was about to ask sardonically how he came to this realization, when he'd spent the past three months continuing to do none of it, but fortunately, he kept speaking. "You need much more child support than I've been giving you."

My mouth opened. I closed it.

"Would you accept more? It isn't a peace offering. I just never realized how much it cost."

No, it wasn't a peace offering: It was penance and protection. If he gave me more money for the kids I'd never be able to reproach him for his negligence again.

Jason was the kind of man who wanted to support his family, but I would explain how that was the pre-feminist paradigm. He could let me take the money — which would help us all indirectly — or be a sexist.

"Thank you," I said. And it wasn't because of the money, really, that I took the cable car key ring out of my pocket. "You keep these," I said. "But remember, they're for emergencies."

It was Jason who had taught me to believe that, after all, there were good men in the world.

And Jason was one of those good men in the world. But he'd married very young.

So had I, and I had used it as an explanation (read: excuse) for the disaster that my marriage had turned out to be. I couldn't blame him for his wife: In fact, he'd stood by her longer and better than most men would.

He'd wasted no time in arranging for Trevor to see her, and to see her alone, although he would be (very) nearby. That was where he had been, conveniently enough, when Alex had appeared with Marissa's pink leopard suitcase.

They came home in the early afternoon. Jason took Trevor down to the basement to admire the progress of his room. I was a little disappointed that he hadn't come in to say "hi" to me. But: *you're too old for high school games,* I told myself. *You've got work to do.*

I made an extra strong pot of coffee and, exploiting its brief buzz, I forced myself to start cleaning out my closet to make more space for Jason.

A quick assessment told me that it would be easy. To collect data for my psychologist bosses and their various studies I often visited people in their homes. Some of these studies were so frivolous ("Does the stress of sleep-deprivation affect workplace performance?") that I wondered why they'd been funded, or, to put it bluntly, who was blowing whom. But mine was not to question why: mine was to wear suits (not pantsuits, suits with *skirts*), heels, and some high-quality fashion jewelry ("fashion" being a euphemism for "costume"). Sometimes I laid on the jewelry a little heavily.

Or rather, I had. As I surveyed the row of suits, dresses, and trousers hanging upside down, I saw clothes I hadn't worn in months. I hadn't noticed exactly when I'd downscaled my look, but these days I sometimes even wore — the horror! — jeans to work.

An hour later I had three bags of clothes to give away, plus a fourth bag made up entirely of stilettos.

When Jason came in I pointed to it proudly. "Look, I — "

"We have to talk," he interrupted.

"Those are the four most dreaded words in the English language," I said lightly. "Don't tell me I shouldn't have had your birthday present engraved." I didn't dare look in his direction.

I had hoped my teasing would prompt him to reassure me that he merely wanted to talk about postponing the painting of the kitchen cabinets, but when he sat down on the bed, his body made such a heavy *ka-thunk* that my hopes collapsed with him.

"How did it go with Denise?" I asked. Had she demanded joint custody of Trevor? Had she seduced Jason? Why hadn't I remembered to worry more about this meeting and thus repel the evil eye? "Where is she living?"

"At a hotel in the Tenderloin."

The Tenderloin was near City Hall, a neighborhood of recent Southeast Asian immigrants, drug dealers and prostitutes. "But she's looking for an apartment."

"Too bad she's not in the housing market. Maybe Ashleigh's mother could help."

I still hadn't dared to look at him. I busied myself with the clothes in the bags. I had a vermilion suit that was a real beauty — maybe I shouldn't give it away just yet.

"Trevor told me something this morning."

I put the suit on the floor. That would be the "reconsider" pile.

Then Jason blurted, "Denise took Jack for a ride."

"Took him for a ride," I repeated. "You mean, she scammed him out of money? I don't know how. He doesn't have any money."

"Annie." He took me by the shoulders and turned me around. "Look at me."

I was facing him but my gaze was on the far wall.

"Trevor told me while we were on our way to see Denise … Jack was very late last night and he told Trevor that someone tried to kidnap him. He didn't know it was Denise, but I put it together."

I laughed — not a little hysterically. "Trevor must have gotten it wrong. No offense, but he couldn't get a job as a fact-checker. Or — " I didn't want to put the blame solely on Trevor — "maybe Jack made it up!"

"She didn't deny — well, she denied trying to *kidnap* him. She said she wanted to spend some time with him to get to know him better."

I turned back to my bags.

"She's had a tough road, Annie."

I covered my face with my hands. Four hours earlier there had been good men in the world, and he was the best one in mine.

"I'm not defending her," he said.

"I hope to God you're not."

"She says that she's on a new regimen of meds, they're brand new on the market, and … well, you've always said yourself.… What is it you say about hope? I mean, word for word."

"I don't remember." But then I patted his thigh. "This isn't your fault."

He squeezed my hand. "I do feel bad, but I can't rake myself over the coals too much. I haven't even known where she was for eight years."

"Timing is everything in life."

We were silent for a bit.

I rose, and looked longingly at the bag of stilettos. I should go through them again before I gave anything away. "You know, I kept telling myself that this was too good to be true."

He sighed deeply. "It sucks. But look at it this way — " his expression was suddenly playful — "we probably don't have to invite her to the wedding."

I had just picked up my bag of shoes, and now I let them drop. "The wedding?"

"In fact, let's make wine out of these sour grapes. Even if you don't drink wine. Let's make this our reason to finally set the date. We are not leaving this room until we set the date. You have a calendar around here somewhere, don't you?" He went to my desk. "Don't panic, I won't look at your laptop.…"

"Jason." I said his name slowly. "I — we.…"

I'd done it again: I ignored all the signs. He'd told me right at the beginning — well, almost at the beginning, that his ex-wife was … yes, crazy, though he never used that word, but had I paid attention?

Jason's new expression told me that he knew what I was trying to say. "No no no no no." He spoke rapidly while shaking his head. "Don't do this. No. C'mon. Now that we know — this won't happen again. Trevor made it sound scary, but we haven't even talked to Jack yet! Annie, don't do this."

But I had to.

Jack was waiting for Ashleigh at her locker.

They'd met here every school day since school started in August. That was 102 days. Both of them had perfect attendance records. Jack didn't like to miss school.

He slid down against the wall of lockers until his butt was on the ground even though it hurt his back. He was worried about her. He was not going to leave until she got here.

Jack was pretty mad at Trevor for telling Jason and his mom what happened. His mom asked him over and over why he didn't tell her. When he told her that he had learned his lesson, she hugged him and said that she was really grateful that he was safe, but she kept asking him to tell her the story over and over.

The second bell rang. The halls had emptied out.

She was late. Maybe she was sick. Wouldn't she have texted him?

His phone was 52% charged, but there were neither texts nor voice mails.

Then a boy he didn't think he knew was standing over him. "Dude, aren't you supposed to be in class?"

"Yeah."

"Well, get going then."

"I can't. I'm waiting for Ashleigh."

"I don't give a fuck who you're waiting for. Get your ass to class or I'm giving you a detention slip."

Jack looked down at the floor between his legs.

"All right, Dude," the boy said. There was a tearing sound that hurt Jack's ears and then a yellow slip of paper. "The office gets the other copy of this so you'd better show."

Jack put the yellow slip in the pocket of his jeans and didn't think about it anymore.

Jack's fists pumped up and down, telling me that he was too excited to speak. I went on unloading the dishwasher.

"What's wrong, Boychik?"

"She *didn't* come to school *today.*"

I didn't have to ask who "she" was.

"Hasn't she ever missed a day of school?" I asked. I was wiping the water that collected in the ridges on the underside of the plates. What was the goddam point of a dishwasher when the goddam dishes came out wet?

"No!"

"She's like you, then," I said wistfully. "Very healthy and takes school seriously."

I knew how important Ashleigh was to Jack. You knew by the time you were 40, that to a teenager (and on or off the spectrum was irrelevant) love is always true, eternal and irreplaceable. Weren't Romeo and Juliet in their early teens?

And you knew that because *you* were a teenager. Once upon a time.

And you wish very hard that someone could have helped you back then, when you were grieving so hard for the One You Couldn't Have: could have given you the perspective you have now, twenty-plus years later.

And you know that no one could have, and you know you can't now.

I tried to put my own sadness away along with the dried plate. I not only couldn't give Jack the perspective of being 40, I couldn't even get him to help me with the dishwasher.

Jason had left with Trevor five minutes after I had broken our engagement and we hadn't spoken since. The Armstrong men had never officially moved in: All that there was at my house were the extra clothes in addition to Jason's uniforms, his medals, and Trevor's best video games.

Everything they'd both left behind would fit in one large box. Jack, Marissa, and I would return to being the mere outline of a family, like a page in a coloring book left blank.

I'd thought about nothing else since Saturday afternoon. I didn't count how many times I'd picked up the phone to beg him to forgive me. It would have to have been an equal amount of times that I had thought, *no, it's just too dangerous. Who knows what she's capable of? I don't care if she sends me hate mail. But she might hurt one of the kids. What if next time, instead of driving nails into the tires, she cuts the brakes?*

I'd also harassed poor Jack for the story of his encounter with his almost-stepmother enough times that I had absorbed the full impact of the danger he'd been in.

"I haven't seen her since Friday!"

"Hon, lower your voice." I made a downward motion with my flattened palm.

"I haven't seen her since Friday!" he repeated, more loudly.

Marissa might be happy when she found out that she wasn't about to have a new stepdad and stepbrother, but Jack was going to be crushed. I was surprised he hadn't asked about Trevor or Jason; the day before was the first Sunday we hadn't spent with them since early September. I was almost glad that he was worried about Ashleigh, since it meant that I didn't have to tell him yet.

"Had you made plans for the weekend?" I pulled out the last item from the dishwasher: It was the large crimson Starbucks mug, the San

Francisco-themed one with the Golden Gate Bridge, that Jason had adopted as his favorite, though he didn't swill the java the way I did.

"We've got to make sure she's all right!"

"Hon, I'm sure she's — "

"Now!"

I imagined that when Kimberly put me on her mailing list she hadn't considered how that would put me in possession of her work phone.

Troublesome things, those extensions. Caller I.D. doesn't always show up.

"Kimberly Allen."

Such a sweet, well-modulated voice. No trace of a British accent today.

"Hi, Kimberly." I wanted to be as ingratiating as possible. "Ashleigh didn't come to school today."

"I know," she trilled. "I bet that sharp boy of yours noticed."

I cleared my throat. "Well, Jack is worried about her. What's up?"

"If you must know," she said, irritation now audible, "Ashleigh went to visit her aunt in Portland."

"Why?"

"*Why?* Her aunt took ill suddenly and you may or may not have noticed — I know you have your hands full with Jack – that Ashleigh is a very giving person."

I had no reason to disbelieve Kimberly — yet I did.

"And a caring person," my new best friend continued. "And a *polite* person, if you catch my meaning."

"She's not answering her cell phone," I said. "Jack — "

"Perhaps she doesn't want to talk to Jack right now!"

Perhaps she didn't.

Still, I asked, "I suppose you've let the school know about her absence. How long do you expect her to be gone?"

"Of *course* I've notified the school. Now why don't you mind your own business?"

It was time — past time — to let the matter drop.

"Maybe she *is* in Portland, Boychik." Why not, after all?

"No," Jack insisted. "She's not."

MOMMY LEFT the light on the first night that Marissa was back in her real room.

Before Mommy left, Marissa told her how Emma said she was adopted. Mommy said, "Oh, honey, no, you're not," and then Mommy explained how it took nine months for a baby to be born, and how a mommy and daddy didn't need to live together the whole time if they were together at the beginning of the nine months, and Marissa only said, "Oh," but her chest felt normal again.

That first night Marissa had had really bad dreams about the dark street and the scary cars and the really scary people who might have been ghosts. She woke up in the middle of the night a bunch of times.

The second night Marissa thought maybe she would sleep with the light off, but then she decided that HannahSophia might be scared.

So even though she was in bed and supposed to go to sleep she could see everything: all the Barbies, and the white chest of drawers that Daddy bought her a long time ago, and DVDs that Jack wasn't supposed to touch but sometimes did.

It wasn't as big as the room at Daddy's house. There was even some dust. But Marissa didn't care about dust. She wiggled down deeply into the sheets. She could feel a few crumbs from the last night she spent here when she snuck a cookie in. She liked feeling the crumbs and she spent a couple of minutes trying to find them with her toes.

Jack was right: crumbs weren't bad.

Maybe Mommy should change the sheets tomorrow, though.

The next day Marissa went to school. She told everyone how she ran away and had a big adventure and how she rode home in Jason's police car. Emma thought she was making it up, but Marissa said, "I am not!" and everyone believed her instead of Emma. She and Emma were sort of friends again and sort of not.

Now it was the third night. She still had the light on, but she only liked it on because it made it easier to think. She hugged HannahSophia and wondered if Daddy was lonely in that big house without her. Maybe he was scared.

Once a really long time ago Mommy said, "your father can take care of himself," but Marissa wasn't so sure.

My job was more "job" than "career," but it was usually a decent escape from real life. I spent that morning interviewing Alzheimer's caregivers for Dr. Someone's article, and came away feeling depressed but also well aware that others had it much worse than I.

I wore the vermilion suit.

Marissa was not only back in school for the second day, she had a playdate with Emma afterwards. So I picked her up, and dropped her off. *Pick 'em up, drop 'em off.* Sing it to the theme song from the TV show *Rawhide* and make it the soundtrack for the rest of my life.

Then it was time for my regular afternoon Starbucks stop.

I had planned to order my standard venti-raspberry-whole-milk-mocha and head out again, but when I walked in the door I saw, in my peripheral vision, the navy uniform of the SFPD. In the space of a second I had time to wince, to recognize Jason, and to consider fleeing in my 4" heels.

But even as I was identifying the exit, my heels moved on their own toward him. He was so handsome, and I missed him so much. I ached to feel the cotton of his uniform sleeves sliding against my skin.

"Coincidence?" I sat down across from him. "You be the judge."

"I'll tell you this. If I have one more caramel coki-shmiatto I'm going to start gnawing on this table like a beaver."

"Knock yourself out. There's no wood in this furniture." I rapped my bracelet against the table. "Not a coincidence, then?" I asked hesitantly.

"No. I've been here over an hour." He half-grinned. "Jack could tell us exactly how long. Anyway, you're later than usual."

I took this in. After a moment I asked, "Have you been able to cite a lot of the customers for bad haircuts? Or is this just a power lunch break?"

"I'm not on duty." He touched the brim of his cap. "I thought you'd be swayed by the uniform. And right now my presence here makes this the safest Starbucks in the city and county."

I turned my head. The place was so packed that customers sipped their beverages while leaning against windows. The tables immediately behind and in front of us, however, were empty. Perhaps I wasn't the only one with an instinctive fear of the police.

"We might be safe from crime, but I wouldn't be surprised if there were a fire code violation," I said. "Besides, there are *dogs* in here. Dogs aren't supposed to be here, are they? Except service dogs?"

"Gotta check the manual."

We went back and forth for a few more minutes, making nervous observations on increasingly irrelevant subjects until we both fell silent.

Finally, "You know I love you," I said hoarsely. "But — you told me she tried to commit suicide once. So I keep picturing her going back to the beach and this time he doesn't get away and she doesn't care if *she* — "

"I truly believe that nothing like this will happen again."

"Still, we can't — *I* can't trust her."

"You don't have to trust her," he replied. "You have to trust me."

"I did trust you."

"I may be the best-looking and smartest man you'll ever meet, but even I can't see the future. Didn't I come to tell you right away?"

"That doesn't change — "

"Is it possible that you don't want to trust me?"

I shifted. The chair squeaked and my pantyhose stuck to my skirt. "I'll be the one with the psychological insights, thank you."

"Let's talk more about safety." He leaned on his forearms. "Let's talk about the risk of our children growing up — or finishing growing up, or trying to grow up...."

"Yes."

"Growing up without both of us."

The lonely days — the lonely years — before Jason's and even Trevor's arrival came back to me in a fast-running film. Freeze-frame: Jack staring out the window, talking to himself while Marissa begged him to play with her.

"I had a surprise wedding gift for you," Jason resumed, "but I think I need to give it to you now."

He must be about to offer to finish the basement bedroom. Last I'd heard it only required another two weekends before painting.

"With a little help from a plumber friend I can build not just an extra room in the basement, but a third bathroom."

"What? Really?"

"Big enough for the boys to share."

"Are you sure there's room?" I pictured my van and the nearly-finished bedroom and tried to see where this phantom toilet and presumably shower stall would fit.

"You'll have to clean out a few boxes. But then you can have your own bathroom or share with Marissa, or Marissa can have her own bathroom."

A third bathroom.

A third bathroom!

Marissa would never have to deal with Jack and Trevor's manly habits. *And I would have my own bathroom.* I could never have imagined, when I teenager myself, that the possibility of an extra bedroom and bath could feel so life-changing. *Welcome to your 40s, Anna Kagen!*

"I need my espresso if we're going to continue this."

"Allow me."

I made an insincere gesture of protest, then watched all the MacBookers watch him in what suddenly became a very short line.

"A 'venti-Annie.' " He set it down in front of me, and I took three gulps. *Aaahh.*

"Besides, Trevor's got other shit to deal with," Jason said. "You've heard that Coach Takanawa is leaving the school?"

"No! When?" I managed between further, not-so-attractive-sounding gulps.

"I think really soon."

"Does Trevor know yet?"

Jason nodded. "He's taking it pretty hard. But no tantrums."

"Good for him."

"He doesn't know about us. I told him we were back in our apartment because 'your' house was being painted."

"Jesus, you learned about guilt trips pretty fast."

"I've learned at the feet of the master."

"You mean 'mistress.' "

Jason leaned forward and I heard the bump of his nightstick against the table leg. "I don't want you to be my mistress. I want you to be my wife."

His hand was resting on mine and for another few moments I let it stay there, contemplating the restoration of my future.

Then I withdrew mine. "My sister, you know, she always put her love life — even just her sex life — before her kids. They've been living with their dad for about four years now." *She* was still engaged — to Sean.

"Meaning…?"

"What if I'm like her? What if I'm blinded by what we have and Denise comes after — "

"She won't."

I chewed on my thumbnail.

"Let me talk to her in person."

"And if you're satisfied — ?"

After Jason had left on Saturday, I'd taken off my engagement ring and put it in a small zippered pocket inside the tote bag I carried. I'd been carrying it with me since. Freud would have something to say about that.

Now I unzipped the pocket and slipped the ring back on. "If I'm satisfied, I'll have this sutured to my finger."

CHAPTER 20

Jack memorized Ashleigh's locker combination the second day of school, just by watching her twirl the dial. He had so much trouble learning how to use the combination on his own locker: the idea of spinning the dial that extra time confused him so badly. But finally he got it, and once he got it, he never had trouble again.

He was at school early when there would be hardly any people around. He twirled to the right: 64. Then to the left, careful to pass the zero, but only once, to stop at 16. Then to the right again, going to 38.

Cah-lick.

He'd seen the inside of her locker many times: the poster on the door that proclaimed, "THERE IS ENOUGH IF YOU SHARE. FEED THE HUNGRY NOW." against the backdrop of a wheat field, and the different-colored binders lined up next to the textbooks that belong to the class. That was how she explained it to him, anyway, when she was trying to organize his locker the same way. Finally she said that he didn't have to.

He yanked out a binder from the middle, which made the books and binders on the side fall in to the center with a thud. He couldn't help but let out a loud, delighted laugh at the noise and harmless disaster. But it was short-lived.

He squatted to look through the first binder. It had one of those notebooks with the whirly wires hooked inside. He opened it. Her handwriting was so neat! It looked like printing in a book. But it was all about some kind of science. Or maybe it was social studies. It wasn't what he was looking for, he knew that, so he let it stay open on the floor while he yanked out another one. A couple of books fell out, too — *splat* on the floor.

One by one he went through them all. There were a lot so he had to be patient, and it was hard for him to be patient.

Now there was only one binder left. It was blue. Or maybe purple. Everything else in her locker was just books, and they were all piled in the center now in a big mish-mash, what was left of them, anyway, because most of them were on the floor.

He was still holding the blue-purple binder in his hand when he saw a different kind of book. He could tell it wasn't a textbook because there was no writing on the front, just some kind of design, and there was a red ribbon sticking out, too.

He knew right away that this was what he was looking for.

Jack remembered everything Ashleigh had ever said to him. So he remembered that she told him that she kept her journal in her locker so her mother wouldn't see it. He didn't know what a journal was, but another time she explained how it was everything she was thinking that was private. He had wished she would tell him what was private but he didn't say so.

His legs hurt too much to squat anymore so he just sat.

On the first page was the date of the first day of school. When he saw the date, Jack's heart leapt. They met that day! He remembered how her hair almost touched the floor when she bent over his spilled papers.

Below the date he read:

My goals this semester:

1. Pay it forward once every day. Remember that no good deed is too small.

2. Get as good grades as possible. My goal is 3.8. NO! 4.0=GO FOR IT!

3. Raise a minimum of $5,000 or more for charity TBD

4. Face my fear and go to the dentist.

5. Clean out my closet and donate all extra clothes to Goodwill.

He flipped to the next page, hoping to see that she wrote about meeting him. No: There was stuff about her classes that he didn't understand but he didn't see his name.

Three pages later there was a mention:

Jack walked home with me again today. I like him, but something's wrong with him and I can't tell what.

He had to stop reading for minute after that.

She wrote a lot about AIDS in Africa, and water there, too, and he saw the words Peace Corps. He knew all the words individually but often he couldn't string them together to understand what they meant.

He was a slow reader, especially of cursive, and there weren't even any lines on the pages.

He looked at his watch. Five minutes until the first bell rang. He had to be alone to study this.

He stuffed all her binders and textbooks back into her locker. He couldn't get it to look the same way it did before, but he didn't have time to fix it.

Then he put the journal under his jacket and hurried out the side door of the school. A long way past the main building were the T-buildings.

He went behind the farthest one and sat on the rough ground that hurt his butt.

She'd written dates between the entries, writing them all out, like September 4, 2009. There was a lot about the One World Club and how she liked Mr. Takanawa for helping them.

Once in a while he saw his name:

I think that the kids are getting used to Jack now. I hope I've helped.

The first bell rang.

Then there were a lot of pages that were harder to read than the ones before, because the words were blurry, but he recognized the name Dylan after a while because she kept writing it and he knew a lot of kids named Dylan.

The second bell rang.

He could go late to class. No one would care.

There were lists, and he figured out that they were part of her making plans for the big field trip they took over winter break. On the second day of the field trip she printed in all caps: I WANT TO WORK WITH AUTISTIC KIDS — but that was all.

Then there were some days missing.

After that the journal got even harder to read. Her writing was smaller and not as neat, and he had to read most of the sentences two or three times. But finally he figured out that the week after the field trip she started going to Mr. Takanawa's condo (a condo was like an apartment) which was one of "those ugly ones across from Ocean Beach." There was a lot of description of what she wore each time she visited. Mr. Takanawa had a cat named Sojourner Truth and he wouldn't let Ashleigh have any wine.

He told me that his parents were so right-wing they were practically fascists, and he grew up believing what they believed, but then he came to Boulder to teach and he saw how wrong they were and he was a socialist for a while. Now he believes in regulated capitalism. I kept nodding while he talked. Who can I get to help me understand this so I don't have to appear so ignorant?

He let the journal fall from his hands. He had to take it to someone and have them read it and tell him what it said, the way his mother did with his homework. He couldn't take it to his mom, because she was at work, but when she came home....

But no. He couldn't wait that long. And he couldn't show his mom.

When he lifted the journal up from the ground it was gritty and that hurt his fingers so bad that he almost dropped it again. But he held on to it, and he kept reading.

Mr. Takanawa gave her books to read and they talked about them. When he saw, "David says we're like Pygmalion and Galatea" he had no idea what that meant and there was nowhere to look it up, and he didn't even know who "David" was at first, but then he remembered that David was Mr. Takanawa's first name.

Two big 1ˢᵗs today! First, he showed me some of his poetry for the first time.

But before that he got out a bottle of wine. He said he needed it for courage. He said I shouldn't have any, but I said it wasn't fair if he did and I didn't so he said OK!!

His poetry is so beautiful. I want to get some copies.

Then I asked him why he didn't send it out, and it turns out that he has! And he's published some of it! He showed me the magazines where they were published.

He didn't want the people at the school, the kids or the admin to know about it b/c it was personal and besides, he didn't want to share that part of himself.

A history teacher who wrote poetry and then kept it secret sounded pretty stupid to Jack.

It happened. I can't believe it happened, but it happened.

I'm supposed to feel like a WOMAN now. I feel different but not in that way.

I don't know what I expected. That's really, really funny, because I've thought about it so much for so long, but I really didn't know what I expected. The other girls have teased me about it for so long. I stayed strong because I knew it was good to wait, but I never told them that. I felt sorry for them, making this beautiful gift to womankind into something like ping-pong, but worse. And now I can't even tell them!!

I can say that I expected it today. We just had one of our usual visits, and I had just one glass of wine, which he still says is my limit!

Then he said, "you know, you're a very beautiful woman."

I didn't know what to say. I hung onto the mug like it could transport me to another universe.

He got up very, very slowly. I knew he was going to kiss me. And then he did. He's kissed me before, but it's been like friends kissing.

I've always wondered how it is in the movies when men and women kiss, how it is that they know they're in love. It never made sense to me, because love is about what's inside. But what can I say, the movies *are right. The moment I felt his lips on mine it was like electricity. He didn't even have to put his tongue on my mouth. But then, when he <u>did</u>, I thought I was going to die. I thought I could die. And I even thought, maybe this is what it feels like to die.*

It's hard to write about the rest, but I want to so that I'll always be able to remember it, even when I'm old and have Alzheimer's.

He didn't take his lips off mine when he started pulling my shirt off. But of course he couldn't take my shirt off without taking his lips off so we both laughed about that. I think I shocked him then, because I just started peeling off clothes. I didn't want him to think I was easy, but I'd been waiting for this for so long. I ~~think~~ <u>know</u> he was surprised.

We went into his bedroom. He led me by the hand. His bedroom is really beautiful and he has a king size bed with sheep and clouds on the comforter so he can count them when he can't sleep.

It was soft as a cloud and he took a long time, but then, yes, it started to hurt. My girlfriends warned me about that. I was always asking them, then why did they want to do it so much? And they said because after a few times I'd start to you-know and that was worth <u>everything</u>. I knew what they were talking about. But you don't need a man for that so I still didn't get it back then. I wanted to be held by someone. <u>That's</u> what you can't do by yourself.

Anyway, I didn't want <u>him</u> to know that it hurt, so I bit down on my lip really, really hard but when he got in deeper I couldn't help making some noise. Fortunately, he thought it was because I was enjoying it. I'm so glad I didn't have to hurt his feelings.

Then afterwards there was blood on one of the clouds. He put his finger in it and some of it came off. He said like he was really surprised, "I'm your first."

I said, "I was waiting for you."

I know I wasn't <u>his</u> first. He's way too old for that. But he'll always remember that he was <u>my</u> first, and that makes me special to him right there.

I hate to say that my mother was right about anything, but she was right about waiting for the right person.

What kills me is that I can't tell anyone!! After all this time they've been teasing me about being a virgin I have to pretend that I still am!! The one I <u>really</u> wish I could tell is Parker. I try <u>really</u> hard not to have evil thoughts about her, but I just have to keep praying on that, too.

I really wish I could tell Jack, too, but I'd better not. No, I mean I can't, obviously. I feel so guilty about him!

Jack had never understood what people meant when they said they felt guilty, but he had the same sensation that he did when there'd finally been a sunny day and he saw the fog creeping back in.

We spent a lot of time talking tonight and we have plans now. We're going to Africa, but we're going on our own. He wants me to graduate first. I'm going to talk him into running away at the end of the school year. I can get my GED online. What's the point of taking fucking <u>physics</u> when I can get started? 2 yrs is too long to wait when the crisis is so great.

We can start our own organization. It turns out that he knows a lot about organizing. He started an underground campus newspaper when he was at Boulder. They found out about it and put a stop to it. He did a bunch of other stuff that's hard for me to remember right now, but I'll write it down when I do.

So we don't have to deal with all the bureaucratic gov't b.s. He knows about starting a non-profit and we can run it and make sure that the $ goes where it's supposed to.

Now all I have to do is to prove to him that we should go now and not wait!! Two years might not seem long to him, but it does to me!!

We spent a lot of time tonight talking. I wish I could remember it all and write all of it down so that I could re-read it whenever I want. I have a good memory, but it's not like Jack's. It's funny that I wish I were more like <u>him</u> that way!

Jack re-read the last paragraph a few times.

One thing I really do remember is that he teased me about being an actress. I reminded him and <u>he</u> didn't remember. He said something back then about an old time actress. Then he remembered what he said that night and he said he wasn't teasing! He said I was so gorgeous that it wouldn't even matter if I couldn't act. He said I could have Hollywood eating out of my hand in two weeks. I could rock their world!

After that we made love. It really is "making love" and not "~~fucking~~." I crossed that out because I don't want to use the "F" word anymore.

The wind blew through Jack as if he wasn't even there.

The last date he saw was the date from three days ago. That was the last date he saw her. When he flipped the page and it was blank he got scared. He'd been sure that he'd be able to figure out what happened from the journal even if he didn't understand all of it.

He turned the very last page so that there was only the inside of the back cover. But there on the back of that last page she'd written a bunch of letters and numbers in black. Everything else in the journal was written in blue.

There were numbers and letters. Like: SW LAX BUR $109 1914 709 3:05pm.

In less than a minute he'd memorized them all.

More gradually he saw a pattern: The letters "SW" over and over. The letters SFO over and over. LAX, BUR, SNA and ONT. The numbers didn't make any sense to him, but....

Then he understood.

His dad had taken him to Disneyland for the last five summers. Jack always stood in front of the arrival-departure screens and memorized the flights.

They always flew Southwest. Dad said they had the most flights in and out of the San Francisco airport, and he didn't want to drive to Oakland. On the screens it didn't say Southwest, it said "WN" which bothered him, but his dad said, "Try not to worry about it."

These were flight times, flight numbers and airport codes.

Jack had never cut school before. He'd missed a few days over the years: He stayed home on Yom Kippur and twice, once in third grade and once in eighth grade, he was too sick to go. But he'd never *cut*.

Today he'd have to.

Denise called out, "It's open!"

Inside, I was surprised to see not only a smile on a welcoming face, but arms spread out to embrace me. I approached with caution, imagining a pen knife tucked somewhere in the folds of her shalwar kameez, a traditional Indian garment that Marissa's erstwhile teacher had often worn.

Denise hugged me tightly. My back tingled and I let my arms drape loosely over her shoulder. From that position I could see that the room was so cluttered that the bed — assuming there was one — was completely hidden.

The only window had a torn shade. Between that shade and the glass, a trapped fly buzzed.

Finally Denise loosened her grip. She looked me up and down much as a grandmother might. I half-expected her to say, "Look how you've grown!"

Instead: "You are gorgeous! I'd fall in love with you myself if that was my style. Do you cover the gray? And you certainly are — " she feigned a cough — "well-endowed, shall we say?"

I had pictured *her* as stout, with eczema and at least one missing tooth, preferably in front, but she was taller than I, and willowy in the silk outfit.

This would have been the standard Second Wife meets First Wife ritual if I were not truly, in spite of my sardonic inward remarks, afraid. When I asked Jason if I could speak to Denise on my own, he had said it was a good idea: that after talking to her I would see how quickly she was stabilizing on her new meds and that we need not fear her.

I had planned to come here and to be direct. To insist that she take responsibility — not for harassing me, which was unimportant now, but for her attempt to kidnap Jack.

I was strong.

I was invincible.

I was Anna Kagen.

But the night before I had had a nightmare about Maleficent appearing in flames. *Sleeping Beauty* had scared the shit out of me when I first saw the video as a child.

And now I was very afraid. Jason thought it was safe, yes, but the most level-headed of us see people the way we want to see them. And no matter how the new Miracle Meds might eventually help, they hadn't stopped her from taking Jack for a ride just a few days before.

I thought of calling Jason to see if he could wait outside the building while Denise and I talked … or screamed … or when she put a gun to my head … but I was ashamed. For all the years of our marriage, Alex had accused me of being "hysterical and overreacting." I wasn't going to start my second marriage by proving him right.

I had tried, but failed, to score a Valium from Darya.

"I'm so glad you wanted to get together. Jason told me what I did. I mean, I guess I must have done it, unless — and we *cannot* rule this out — I have been cloned by the government?"

"I guess we can't rule anything out."

"But I can explain it." She'd been speaking quickly, and with humor — I was *pretty* sure that the cloning had been a joke — but now she continued in a calm and authoritative manner. "When I have a manic episode I'm not responsible for what I do. I don't even remember that day."

Be direct. Be direct. That was what I had planned to do but I no longer could remember what I was going to say that was so direct.

"Didn't Jason tell you? I came back to California a few months ago. I was going to surprise Jason and Trevor and tell them I was ready to be a family again. The very *moment* I pulled up I saw him driving away and I followed him to your house. They went inside and they didn't come out until the next morning." She wagged a finger at me. "You are a naughty girl! When you're traveling a lot, how can you keep up with one regimen? This doctor, that doctor, this town, that town ... why don't we have single payer health care? I went off the meds because Sri Bannerjee said they were poisoning my body."

"Who is — "

"So I'd been off the meds for a long time, and doing so well. It's not about illness. Big Pharma wants you to think it's about illness but — "

"But you're taking medication now?"

"Yes! Now I have the good stuff. It's new stuff. I'm feeling better than I ever have. I miss Sri Bannerjee but he said I had to make peace with my family and then when I got here — I know what I did and I am so sorry, but I don't remember that day. I'm so glad you came! Sit down. We crazy ladies love company. At least I don't have a cat yet. I'm thinking about it but they're hard to travel with. And of course if I get one cat, I have to get a dozen. You can't be a crazy cat lady unless you have at least a dozen." She laughed, a little loudly. "What you need to know is that I'm *not* crazy. I found a doctor, he's fallen in love with me, and we've started something entirely new, it's still experimental, actually, and he officially pronounced me stable! I said to sit down. Make yourself at home."

There was no place to sit. I still couldn't see a bed. It might have been behind one of the many piles of various objects, shaped like haystacks and almost as tall as I. The dominant theme was dirty laundry, although I was no one to pass judgment on that. There was a strong, nauseating smell from incense, burning unseen, and I remembered Jason's story of a fire started somewhere under her watch, but the details had escaped me.

"Sit there! It's comfy."

Denise indicated a shorter pile, this one composed primarily of stuffed animals. I didn't like to sit on them: their button eyes looked out at me like trapped souls. But my knees were literally shaking, so I plunked down — cautiously, lest I hurt the stuffies more than necessary.

"My daughter used to love stuffed animals," I said. "She's kind of narrowed her focus to one special one now. She talks about her like she's real, I mean, like the stuffed animal — " Another case of nervous=babbling, but Denise interrupted.

"Do you need some water? I have some bottled at the Ganges."

"It's a pink leopard — not for drinking?"

"It has healing powers!" She produced a green bottle from behind one of her piles. The water inside was murky. "You do have to drink it, though." She extended it toward me.

Though my body was frozen in place, my mind was formulating a plan to scoop up both Jack and Marissa and head to the airport. They were both at school, and their schools weren't close to each other, but —

"Your face!" Denise laughed. "You should see your face!" Denise was still laughing when she hid the bottle again. "It's Diet Sprite. I took the label off."

"But — "

"Oh, that. I added a handful of dirt. Your face!" She laughed again. "You don't mind a little practical joke, do you? I wouldn't have played it on you, but like I said, I don't get many visitors."

"Denise — "

"Call me Mrs. Armstrong," she cut me off.

"Oh-kay."

"Don't look so scared! I was just *kidding*. Pretty soon I'll be calling *you* Mrs. Armstrong."

"I'm going to keep my name," I said, before I could consider what reaction that might trigger.

"Like the man said, 'What's in a name?' I prefer to be addressed as Coyote Weeping Tree, anyway."

"Maybe 'Tree' for short?" I suggested.

"Yes, I like that. But you're wondering how I got that name in the first place, am I right?"

"Yes," I lied.

"I'm going to share my journey with you. Then you'll understand."

She attacked one of the piles of dirty laundry, throwing one piece at a time — blouses, long skirts, scarves, and jeans — over her shoulder. She stopped more than once to display some of the hand-crafted items she uncovered: sock puppets and knit hats that she'd made herself. As more and more laundry went from the pile, though, creating a new pile of nearly equal height behind her, the tension in her voice rose proportionately. "They're here, I know there here!"

"What exactly are you looking for?" Though if it were a firearm, would she tell me? Why hadn't I demanded that Jason give me a weapon?

"They're here! I know they're here!" was Denise's only answer, which, especially as it was in the plural, had me trying to measure the distance between myself and the door. The door — where was the door?

I got up to look. There was no door! I was about to question my own sanity when I realized that that entire wall was covered with a bead curtain. I'd been too nervous to register the multi-colored strings when I came in. Now all that I could see — when I finally saw it — was the plain hardware store doorknob that protruded between two of the strings.

"Here they are!"

I looked back from the door to see her holding a canvas bag upside down. Small black hard cover books were raining onto the floor.

"I knew I had them! I wouldn't leave my journals behind." She whispered, "Sri Bannerjee says they're not wordly goods. Sit down," she commanded again.

"I'm all right." I preferred to stand close to the door.

"*I said to sit down.*"

I did.

Jack had trouble getting to the airport.

He got on a bus that was called an "Airporter" but it took him to the San Jose airport. His mom taught him how to ask for help in an emergency, though: Say, "Excuse me sir or ma'am sir for a man and ma'am for a woman my name is Jack and I need help but not money," unless it *was* money and she hoped-to-God-it-never-was, that was why he should keep the $20 in his shoe and not spend it on Doritos again.

After asking a lot of people who just ignored him, he found a nice man who sat down with him and drew a map of how to get to a special bus that would take him to SFO, and wrote down "Monterey Airbus," which is what it would say on the front, even though it wasn't going to Monterey.

He told Jack how to take another shuttle that went around the San Francisco airport and to get off where he saw the sign for Southwest.

When Jack got to the airport he couldn't find the shuttle. But he decided that he would just walk until he saw a Southwest sign.

He didn't think it would take him long because of all the times he'd been to the airport, but it turned out that the airport was much bigger than he'd ever realized. He remembered being lost just a few days before. In the airport it was light and not so scary in that way, but he didn't have much time. He didn't know what flight she'd chosen, but he'd narrowed it down to either the one that left at 3:05 to LAX or the one that left at 3:40 to BUR.

He asked some people, "Where do people go to get on Southwest planes?" A couple of them asked, "What's in the backpack?" and when he said, "my books for school," they made a *grrrr* sound and then moved away.

The same announcements kept playing over and over. *Do not leave bags unattended. Smoking is prohibited at all times. Report suspicious activity.* And people said that *he* repeated himself.

He passed by a restaurant. Through the window he could see the front part of a really big plane and the tube that people used to get on them. He had to find *that* place....

But he got distracted by watching a man at the counter eating a hamburger. Jack was really, really hungry. He was going to buy lunch at school, but he spent that money and some other money he had and the $20 in his shoe just getting to the airport.

"You okay?"

It was a woman and he could tell from how she was dressed that she was a waitress. Her voice was gravelly, like Ms. Gonzales's, but her face was the usual blank of strangers.

"Yes."

"You been standing here a real long time."

Had he? He was so hungry that he forgot to keep track of how long he'd been there.

"People say you staring at them is making them jumpy." She looked inside the restaurant. "Yeah, like you really look like one a them terrorists. Are you with your parents?"

He didn't like to lie, but.... "Yeah."

She folded her arms across her chest. That pushed out her name tag. It said VERNELLE. "You want to tell me what's going on?"

"I need — I need to find the Southwest planes." He wondered if the plane he saw through the window was the plane he needed.

"Bernard!" Vernelle shouted to the inside of the restaurant. "I'm taking my break now. Oh, yes, I am," she added after a pause. "He's gotten on my last nerve," she said, but not to anyone. Then to Jack, "you come with me."

Jack was scared at first because of what happened with the Woman in the car. He'd been scared thinking about her since then. But she didn't pretend that his mom was in the hospital and she told him her name was Vernelle, even though he already read it on her front.

They walked a little ways and there was a store that sold tons of candy and she bought him a Hershey bar. He'd never tasted such a good Hershey bar.

"Now, why don't you tell me what's *really* going on?"

He wanted to tell her the whole story: how he met Ashleigh on the first day, how they started walking home from school … everything. But there wasn't time. He said just enough to make her understand that he needed to get to Ashleigh.

Vernelle sighed a lot. It reminded him of his mom.

"I'm gonna take you over to the next terminal," she said. "Just … just be careful."

"Terminal" is where planes leave from, but "terminal" also means that someone's going to die. That was another stupid English word.

While they were walking Vernelle started telling him about her son. He was 27. He was smart. She kept repeating that, that he was smart. He shouldn't have been fired from the job he had with stocks because they didn't give him the right instructions. The stocks were too heavy for him anyway. And it was hard to get a job when you couldn't drive, she said. He got a license but they took it away. Probably for the best. He was for sure gonna kill someone some time.

"I'm going to get a driver's license," Jack said.

But as soon as he heard himself say it, he knew it wasn't true.

Two hours had gone by and I was still sitting, now with a pain in my back and two legs not asleep but comatose. I had crushed the poor stuffed animals nearly flat.

The immediate threat to me was boredom. But how long would she stay on these pills? What else was she capable of doing that she would claim not to remember later? She was a grenade with the pin pulled, no matter how many pairs of earrings she fashioned from pebbles and wire. (That's right, she was a jewelry-maker now.)

Denise hadn't started the journals until Sri Bannerjee told her that it was the next step in her path, so her tale was non-chronological. What I sorted out: After Kenneth-the-lawyer went back to his wife, Denise had followed another man to Taos, where she fell in with an artists' collective and "discovered myself as a creative spirit." She shaped pottery and mastered decoupage. She also discovered herself sexually, with a number of partners, in a number of combinations.

There was one particular man, though, not the one who had taken her to Taos, but the one who bestowed upon her her Native American name, who departed the collective without warning, tipping her into a depressive episode. The other members secured enough money to give her "the only truly priceless gift there is, the gift of a new life, a gift beyond compare:" that was, money to travel somewhere else, and she chose Mumbai.

For the past three years she'd been living there as one of the followers of Sri Bannerjee, her guru and the man she was in love with now, "the man who taught me what true love was about."

There were three volumes left unread when she sighed, "the rest is too personal." That felt as good as any Valium could have.

"I don't want to hurt your feelings," she said, "but I have to go back. I see that now."

"Back...?" I was terrified that she meant back to reading.

"Back to Mumbai."

Relief wasn't the word. Gratitude. That was it. Gratitude so profound that I whispered, "thank you, God."

Denise began repacking the journals. She moved slowly, never lifting her head, and radiating sadness.

"Trevor loved seeing you." I hoped that would cheer her up.

"H'm." Silence for a bit while she methodically replaced the books. "I see he's still a picky eater."

"Not as much." During our first outings, Jason had brought Trevor's food and it was always (and only) peanut butter sandwiches and a Diet Dr. Pepper.

Denise held the final black notebook in both hands. She stared at it long enough that I thought that she'd forgotten I was there. When she did speak, she was addressing the notebook. "Maybe what Sri Bannerjee really meant when he sent me back here is that I should bring Trevor back to India with me."

What? What? What? I don't think so!

"He doesn't have a passport," I said.

With great effort, Denise shrugged. "You can get them really fast on the Internet. Just because I have a past doesn't mean I'm stupid, you know."

"No, of course not — "

Denise was staring in the direction of the window, where the fly still buzzed. She was unaware of me again, so I mentally floundered, like one of Trevor's fish fallen from its tank. She couldn't take Trevor away. We needed him: Jason, Jack and even Marissa. He'd entered our lives as one more set of grating habits: talking endlessly about the same subjects, missing the toilet when he urinated, forgetting to pay for a candy bar and being accused of shoplifting....

But looking at this pitiable woman, my strong and even more surprising thought was *you can't have him.* He was truly Jack's brother now. I couldn't sever him from Jason any more than I could cut off Jason's arm. And when I pictured the house *sans* Trevor it felt empty. We were crowded, we were loud, and we quarreled — but we quarreled over silly things, the silly things that meant all the more that we belonged together.

My initial physical revulsion toward Trevor had evaporated. Now he was almost as much the same extension of my body as Jack. I had not thought myself capable of loving another woman's child. But he was Jason's son, and as I had fallen more in love with Jason, my affection had slowly spread to Trevor.

Denise finally spoke. "That fly is driving me crazy."

The fly's erratic buzzing had bothered me, too; it was the one sound that could have, and did, make Denise's sonorous reading more irritating.

"I. Am. Going. To. Kill. It." Denise spoke each word with a chilling calm. Then, startling me nearly out of my skin, she leapt toward the window and attacked the shade, banging hard with her fists at random places.

"Whoa!" I shouted but then, "Whoa...." this time soothingly, as I tried to pull her away. "I'll get it."

"I'm going to kill it!"

After a split second's hesitation, I put my arms around her from behind and squeezed — firmly, as firmly as I could, but while whispering, "I'll take care of it, I'll take care of it," and other vague but reassuring promises. Gradually her rage flowed into me where I let my own body absorb and digest it.

When I began to feel her relax I let go, and she slumped to the floor. "I surrender, Mr. Fly. Or should I say 'Ms.' Fly. You win."

"Not yet." I tried to open the window. It wouldn't budge. *Oh, yes, you will.* I shoved the frame. It was painted shut. We were doomed.

I tried once more and it opened — not very far, but enough. In contrast to the behavior of flies throughout time, this insect buzzed to freedom. We were too crazy for him. Or her.

I slammed the window closed.

Denise was sitting cross-legged on the floor. "Trevor likes his coach."

"He's told me," I said.

She frowned, sending a deep crease up the middle of her forehead. "He talked about school, but you know, he repeats himself *so much*."

I didn't argue. The fear came back to me but it brought hope on its back.

Denise wasn't talking to me when she continued to complain about how difficult it was to have a normal conversation with him.

"You have to enter their worlds." I was thinking of both boys. "Crime Conquerors and tropical fish are their *lingua franca*."

"You know what I really learned from Sri Bannerjee?" Denise asked rhetorically. "Some women are just not meant to be mothers."

When I walked out of the decrepit building, I saw a police car double-parked on the other side of the street. I had trouble, at first, seeing through the driver's side window, but yes, it was Jason behind the wheel.

When he and Vernelle got to the security line for Southwest Jack knew where he was. This was the place you had to go through to get on a plane. You had to take your shoes off which he hated because of the way the floor felt.

Vernelle said she had to go back to work and she was sorry she couldn't stay with him.

There was a line in front of the security place, and it folded back in on itself just like the lines to the rides at Disneyland. One, two, three … there were six folds. Everyone was standing close together, so there was a lot of bumping of suitcases and backpacks and wheelies, and the line moved slowly, but it kept moving, so it looked like the people were all waving in the wind. He stood on tiptoe, and waved his own body back and forth, so he could see between the people when they moved.

Where the folds ended there was a woman in a uniform like Jason's who was stopping people. Then the line stretched out from her, so long he couldn't see the end.

He went along that line, looking for Ashleigh as he went. He saw coffee cups and cell phones and lots of people with their arms around other people.

Twice he saw someone with long red hair and he said, "Excuse me," and the girl turned around and it wasn't her and he wondered how he made the mistake. Then he said excuse me to someone he really hoped might be her but it turned out that it was a man. Jack could tell by the red beard. "You got a problem, man?" the man said and Jack said, "no," but then he tried saying, "Have you seen," but he couldn't get past the word "seen." The man with the red beard faced someone else and made that hand sign with the finger doing a circle around the ear. Jack had seen that sign many times and he knew what it meant.

By the time he got to the end of the line there were signs for a different airline, US Air.

His shoulders sank. She wasn't there. She must be gone already. He thought about going home, because after what happened over the weekend his mom would kill him if he didn't come home when he was supposed to, and he was already cutting school.

But he always gave up on things, like soccer in fifth grade after just one game. He gave up on science projects and his dad got him out of having to take a foreign language at school. He wouldn't give up now. He knew she needed help.

He went all the way back to where the line folded. His back pack was getting awfully heavy, and even though he couldn't tell by anyone's face he felt like people were suspicious of him.

He lay down on the floor. It was a good way to calm down. He recited the script of the Crime Conquerors episode because that would help him think of what to do next.

Then all of a sudden he was in the air.

There were two Uniforms, one on each side of him, holding him up.

"What is the matter with you?" one of them said. "We've been talking to you for forever."

"I've only been here thirteen minutes!" he protested.

They let him down so that he was standing but they each held on to one of his arms. They were both talking fast. He heard the words "looks weird" and "people complaining."

Then he heard, "It's here, I know it's here."

It was Ashleigh's voice!

He tried to run to her but the two Uniforms didn't let him go.

So he did something he hadn't done since he was a really little kid: He went completely limp.

"C'mon kid," one of them growled. "Get up!"

They both pulled, but they couldn't get him to move.

Then they loosened their hold just for a second. But in that second, with all the strength he had, with strength he never knew he had, because he wasn't strong, not like Trevor, Jack wrenched his arms away from the man holding him and ran to Ashleigh. "I found you! I found you!"

"What are you doing here?" Ashleigh didn't sound happy to see him. And she didn't look right, either: there were black smears under her eyes, and her hair was sticking out.

"I need your government-issued i.d.," the Lady Uniform said, holding out her hand to Ashleigh, who was waving a piece of paper in *her* hand.

With her other hand Ashleigh was digging around in her WORLD IN PIECES tote bag. "I know, I know! I have it!" Her wheelie had fallen to the floor.

"C'mon, kid." The two men were tugging at him again.

"It's okay, I know him," Ashleigh said to the men, but as if she wasn't even happy about knowing him.

"Are *you* all right, Ma'am?" one of them asked.

"I'm not a 'ma'am.' "

There was a roar like the ocean behind Jack, a roar like people were mad and impatient.

"You'd both better step out of line," Lady Uniform said.

"But I've got to get on a plane."

"She can't!" Jack insisted.

"All right, all right." Ashleigh stuffed the paper back in her tote bag. Jack wanted to pick up her wheelie but when he tried it fell down again.

"C'mon, Jack," Ashleigh said and she tugged on him once before she grabbed her wheelie, but he was glad it was her and not those other men, and he followed her.

From behind the roar-like-the-ocean got louder, and it sounded like the ocean was really angry.

There were some empty chairs next to a big window. Cars and buses were on the other side.

They huddled close together because Ashleigh didn't want anyone to hear. That's what she said, anyway. He liked huddling close together. He could feel her breath on his face. Her breath wasn't as nice as it always had been, but for once, for the first time maybe, he thought, *I haven't brushed my teeth since yesterday and my breath must be gross.* He wished he'd brought a toothbrush with him, but what would he have done for toothpaste?

"Why do you want to go to Disneyland?"

"I'm not going to Disneyland, Jack. I'm going to Hollywood."

"Hollywood!" That was where they made a lot of the TV shows, but not Nickelodeon, because they were in Florida. Then he asked a question he almost never asked, "Why?"

"That's where — that's where someone told me I should go. A girl like me. To — to rock the world." She said more softly, "To be a Hollywood Whore, more like it."

"What's a Hollywood Whore?"

"A beautiful girl who fucks her way to the top."

"To the top of what?"

"I was going to show *him,*" Ashleigh said.

He knew she meant the "him" of her journal.

"That's all he thought I was good for," Ashleigh said, in that voice people used when they didn't care if you really listened.

Except. "You said — you said I was a good listener." She said that one time when he walked her home from school.

"I did, didn't I?" She put her hand on her head and pushed her hair back. "Oh, God, Jack, now that you're here — I've got to tell someone."

He listened as carefully as he could.

It was dark when she left the house, and so cold. Why didn't she grab her sweater, her coat? They were in her room. Ashleigh wanted to keep them hanging on a hook by the door, but no, that was too "working class" for Kimberly. So there she was out in her pajamas.

The lights from the street lamps ran down like paint that wasn't dry. It was the tears in her eyes making them drip. Or was it raining? Maybe it was both.

Wasn't it funny how your mind wandered when you were so very hurt you didn't understand how it was that you kept breathing, why your heart hadn't simply stopped beating? Your mind wandered to try to trick you into forgetting what happened. You saw everything around you as if you'd never seen it before, as if it was on another planet, as if *you* were from another planet. You weren't going to be part of this world again. No, you *wished* you weren't going to be part of that world again. But you would. That's what sucked. Right now was when you could go to that doughnut shop on Irving that was open all night. You could eat doughnuts all you wanted because it didn't matter right now. But tomorrow would come.

Tomorrow would come. She could put off going to bed (she had no home now to sleep in anyway), but the dawn would break. The only way to keep back the morning would be to travel west, to outrun the sun, but the Pacific Ocean was just ahead....

Why was she always surprised when she walked a few blocks and began to hear the ocean? She'd walked more than a few blocks, though. She'd walked a long time.

She still couldn't *see* the ocean; you could only see the ocean from there on a very clear day, and then it was a little cup of slate blue at the bottom of the sky. But if she kept walking long enough she'd get to it: the mighty Pacific, the largest ocean in the world, which covered 46% of the surface of the earth.

San Francisco was so small. There was nowhere to hide. You were surrounded on three sides by water. You might just as well have been an island. Alcatraz had been such a perfect place to house criminals. How weird it must have been to have the most dangerous men in the world on an island in the Bay. What did people do, just go sailing right around it on weekends? Did they think of the men inside?

But how much worse for the men on Alcatraz, to look out the filthy windows of the dining hall to see the lights of the world's most beautiful city.

And then it hit her again.

She realized that she'd been hearing the ocean for a while now, the susurration that was the heartbeat of the sea. Because now she was standing in front of it, and she didn't know how she got there. It stretched out, invisible, all the way to the other side of the world. All that proved its existence were the cuticles of white that trimmed the waves as they spent themselves on the sand. All other light was far behind her, or to the north or south.

The sky was black and wholly without stars. She left them all behind in Marin, at the hostel where it all began.

The water would be cold. So cold. That was how they kept people locked up on Alcatraz: If you went into the water you would drown from hypothermia. How sad. Did anyone ever do anything to deserve to be on an island where they could see San Francisco while they were being sodomized? *Of course they did.* The world was full of such unfathomable evil. The Armenian genocide. Then the Holocaust. Now prisoners waterboarded — by the Americans. The good guys.

But all over the world people were torturing other people. In so many different ways.

Why, though? Were bad people solely victims of their environment? They discussed this in social studies last year. Nature vs. nurture. No answer.

She knew one thing: the evil was in people.

The other thing she knew was that there was no God. She was an idiot to think there was.

She couldn't live another 60 years knowing all this. The years of her long, long life stretched out as a punishment, as if she had to spend them on Alcatraz herself.

Shussssh, went the waves. Why was she drawn to the sea now? It must be what her science teacher said back in 7th grade: that we came out of the sea millions of years ago. The sea was our home, to the sea we returned, not to be part of something greater, only to disappear. People died from hypothermia before they got far enough out to be sucked in by the undertow. Ocean Beach was spotted with signs warning against swimming, but still someone drowned here last year.

How long would it take? How awful would it be? Choking … burning lungs … no, she couldn't bear it. She'd always thought that she wasn't afraid to die. She'd sometimes imagined the doctor telling her that she had six months to live. She would face it with Hemingway's grace under pressure. She would quietly give away her few things. She had almost nothing of monetary value, only a copy of *Tuesdays with Morrie* inscribed by Mitch Albom that Freddie found in the symphony thrift shop.

The beach itself was deserted. Behind her were the cookie-cutter condos along Great Highway. They looked so innocent if you didn't know what was inside.

Sometime back in the 50s or 60s there was an amusement park where the condos were. An amusement park, a family amusement park, becoming condos … *the center will not hold....* She couldn't remember where she heard that, but it was clear to her now that the universe wasn't expanding, it was shrinking, and it would keep shrinking until it became a flat disc: On one side would be the Mall of America and on the other a refugee camp, the haves and have-nots joined together for eternity.

She wanted out.

She walked across the sand. It was high tide and a short walk to where the incoming water flattened out and then retreated. She walked a foot or two into the shallow waves so that her feet sank into the sand and the water lapped at her ankles. It rolled in, just an inch or two high at the edge here, and when it retreated she had the sensation of rushing backwards, even though she knew that she was standing still. It was a game she learned from her mother when she was a little girl, and they came to the beach and held hands.

She took two big steps deeper into the ocean. Now the water coursed above her ankles on its way out. How many more steps? She took two, three. It was gathering around her shins. Another two, three, four steps and it would take her down.

See? It was so cold at first but now she was used to it.

Jack wished so hard that he understood what Ashleigh has been saying, but he didn't. Why was she so unhappy?

"I can't say anymore. Shit, what do I look like? I haven't showered...."

She unzipped her suitcase. She had such strange things in there. Things he remembered from her bathroom, like bottles and brushes and funny bars of soap. She took out a brush and ran it through her hair. "Want to borrow this? You could use it, too."

For the first time in his life he brushed his own hair.

"You're handsome with your hair combed," she said. "I suppose if I'm going to tell anyone...."

She got home really late, and she was relieved not to see her mother's Mercedes in front of the house; she did *not* want to deal with Kimberly that night. The lights were on as usual, but Kimberly always left them that way, so that burglars would think they were home. Ashleigh thought that if anyone were able to carry out Kimberly's Stairmaster or 60" plasma TV they should be rewarded for their enterprise.

She let herself in, punched the code on the burglar alarm and tiptoed upstairs straight to her bedroom.

Even if the house were empty, Ashleigh was glad to get to her bedroom. She'd learned from David about the "Free-gan" movement and it was like a whole new world. Better than garage sales: no money changed hands at all! Just a few days ago she'd picked up a rusty garden chair that was left out on the sidewalk. She had to spray it with Lysol real heavy before she touched it, but it was in her room now. She could have brought home a whole roomful of furniture if she'd had a van and someone to help her.

She'd spent the past three hours at a St. Elizabeth's junior board meeting. A board meeting on a Friday night was a real commitment. David had told her how important it was to keep to her commitments, so she did, and she felt bad that she didn't feel the excitement that she had when she first signed up. Meetings went on like forever.

She put on her red plaid pajamas — her mother bought them for her for Christmas, and she hated them, but she wore them so her mother wouldn't ask her why she *wasn't* wearing them — and she lay down, ready to go to sleep.

Then there were footsteps in the hall, two pairs of them, and a muffled giggling that she knew was her mother even though her mother never giggled like that.

Her mother had a guest. The footsteps were heavy enough that Ashleigh thought it was a male guest — but Kimberly never had male guests.

Maybe it wasn't her mother at all. Maybe they were intruders. Ashleigh regretted her glib thought of moments before: Ever since that terrible night with Dylan she hadn't really even felt safe in her own bed. She hoped they'd take her mother's jewelry and....

Then she heard her mother's distinctive *shush!* and a low voice.

So it *was* her mother — and a man.

And then ... the shower running?

At least they weren't burglars. But Ashleigh still wanted to keep her mom out. The metal chair was fate: She got up as quietly as she could and pushed it against the door, even lifting the chair as she moved it so the legs wouldn't squeak against the floorboards. There was still no doorknob from when her mom had taken it out but at least it got the door firmly closed.

The shower stopped.

Ashleigh got into bed and hoped she didn't have to get up to use the bathroom.

There was a knock.

"What is it, Mother?"

"We just want to talk to you."

Kimberly's voice sounded weird.

Ashleigh got out of bed grudgingly, thinking that she should be grateful that Kimberly didn't just shove the door open and slam the chair into the wall.

Standing next to her mother was David. He wasn't wearing anything except a towel around his waist, one of her mother's prized plush teal towels, with monograms on them.

But it couldn't be him. It had to be someone who looked like him.

"Darling," her mother said. She took one of Ashleigh's hands in both of hers. "May we come in?"

Kimberly was in her bathrobe, but the bathrobe was falling open at the top so that Ashleigh could see between her flat breasts, almost all the way to her navel. "Honey, it's time I told you everything."

Ashleigh knees buckled. She was standing close enough to the bed that she ended up sitting on the edge instead of crumpled in a heap on the floor.

"When I was in high school I fell in love," Kimberly said. "I mean, I thought it was love."

What was her mother saying? Kimberly kept talking but Ashleigh didn't hear anything for a while because she was thinking how maybe David had an identical twin that he'd never told her about or that someone on the junior St. Elizabeth's board put a hallucinogen in the decaf.

"I only let Brandon take my virginity because we were engaged...."

Ashleigh saw a teeny-tiny bug on the floor. She started to step on it but the bug was running so fast for a bug that she imagined it was thinking, "Please, please, I want to live!" — and it knew that it could never outrun her, but it kept trying.

"I wanted to have an abortion and I could have had one — Mama said she'd drive me to Indianapolis and Daddy didn't need to know — but she didn't want me to have an abortion. She said it was just like murder. Then Brandon convinced me that he wanted to get married, that he was going into his dad's business ... Yada, yada, yada, am I right?"

Kimberly had always told her the opposite: that her parents were going to force her to have an abortion and they could have because she was a minor.

"I didn't want to throw my whole life away with a baby. But there was so much pressure. And then before I knew it, it was too late."

The bug had disappeared under her bed. Kimberly kept randomly talking: about what a small town was like and how her father was really a prick, which was all the more reason not to trust men, but Brandon even had her father fooled, too, which proved that he could fool anyone. Oh, and she lied about something else: She was 19 when she had Ashleigh, not 17. So she was 36, not 34. David said that she had to be honest about everything from now on.

"And then Brandon disappeared! Totally disappeared. His family said they didn't know where he was, but they were lying. So the day after you were born I came out here and reinvented myself. All for you! I never told you about your father because he didn't want you and I knew how that would hurt you. And I know you think I only care about money and success and being in the *Nob Hill Gazette* but I've only done all that because I want you to be proud of me."

Ashleigh was looking at her hands, wedged between the legs of her plaid flannel pajamas. They didn't seem part of her body: They were more like anvils that someone had sewed to the end of her arms. They were so heavy that she couldn't lift them even to brush her hair out of her eyes. And her head was heavy, too. She couldn't raise it to see if it really was David there after all. He hadn't said anything, and David was such a common name. She kept staring at the floor and wishing the bug would come back so that she would know that it was okay.

"We both knew right away that we were soulmates. Now I have to thank Brandon because if he hadn't run out on me I never would have come to California, and I don't think you would ever have come to New Palestine, Indiana, would you, David?

"David made me see my *potential*. How I've been holding myself back. I don't have to be 'realtor to the stars.' I can be the star. With so many houses under water I'm going to stop making money for that silly Dummy and Whitebread and make it for us. All I need is a few hundred thousand and when the market comes back — " Kimberly snapped her fingers — "hand over fist. I'm a little bit psychic, you know. The market is going to come back in two years and we'll all be sitting pretty."

Kimberly took Ashleigh's hand back. Ashleigh couldn't figure out how she had the strength to lift it. Ashleigh's eyes were just high enough that she could see Kimberly take one of David's hands at the same time. His towel was loose.

"And if it hadn't been for that stupid camping trip I never would have met David. I went to tell him he had to stop it, but he told me why it was a good idea. So you have a real family now. We'll be a threesome."

Then David took Ashleigh's other hand and Ashleigh finally raised her head. They made a circle, holding hands like this, like they were going to have a séance or sing "We Shall Overcome."

Kimberly said, "It'll be beautiful." She was beaming like the Madonnas in Renaissance paintings in Ashleigh's European history textbook from last year.

"A threesome would be beautiful," David said, and now she knew that for sure it was him.

Ashleigh was chewing on a clump of her hair.

When Jack read her journal, he got that she was in love with someone else. Now he knew that it was Coach Takanawa.

"He made me believe in myself — fuck! He pulled the same shit on my mother that he pulled on me. Made me see my 'potential,' " she said in a funny voice.

Do not leave bags unattended.

"But he was going to mentor me! It wasn't just about sex."

They had sex together, Ashleigh and Coach Takanawa.

"Then he turned out to be like all the men my mother was trying to warn me about — but she made the same mistake." Ashleigh spat the hair out of her mouth. "She made it twice! *Brandon.* It's so pathetic."

"But where have you been for three whole days?" Jack needed to know. "I was worried about you!"

"I stayed with my friend Sue — she's not really a friend anymore, but she let me crash in her basement while I got my shit together. I had to go to the bank and get all my money out. And I had to sneak home to get some clothes." She was quiet a moment and then she said, "She said some really mean things. But I need all the friends I can get."

Smoking is prohibited at all times.

"I'm your friend." He said "friend" on purpose instead of the title he could brag about for such a short, precious time: *boyfriend.*

"I know. And I'm sorry about — about pretending to be more."

"That's okay." He'd looked into her eyes before but never like this, never for more than half a second, but now it was as if he had all the seconds he wanted. He knew her eyes were green but they had gold flecks in them, too. And she had freckles. He could see every single one. There were so many. They reminded him of the stars on the night of the field trip, the night she kissed him.

"How can it be okay? I used you."

"Because ... because...."

It took him a really long time, but she waited for him to find the words just like she always had.

"Because I *did* have a girlfriend. Now we're breaking up, but on TV boyfriends and girlfriends break up all the time and they stay friends." He felt himself smile even though a big part of him was sad. "Why do you have to go away?"

She dropped her head between her knees and moaned. "Everyone's going to know what happened. I can't live with that."

"You told me — you told me not to care about what people think."

"That's right. That's what makes me a hypocrite. Jack, I had such big plans!" She tilted her head all the way back; her hair fell past her waist and she talked to the ceiling. "I was going to be this big heroine but it turns out that I'm just as spoiled and selfish as my mom. As soon as things got hard I just became a — but I thought that at least I could help *you*...."

"But you did help me," he said.

"*How?*"

How? So many ways he couldn't put into words no matter how patient she was.

Just talking to him. No matter how often people said he was smart, they didn't think he was smart at all. Everyone talked about everything in front of him as if he was not only stupid, but completely deaf.

Just hanging out with him.

Not treating him like a charity case.

If only he had the words in English! If only he had the words in any language — in freaking sign language because then the hearing-impaired kid in Mr. Weesley's class could translate for him! But there were only the words in his private language, the language he heard in his head but couldn't speak.

Report suspicious activity.

When neither of them had talked for six minutes, Ashleigh moaned again. "I wanted to save the whole world."

Which made Jack remember something he heard the cantor say when he was getting ready for his Bar Mitzvah the last year.

"If you save one person, you save the whole world."

"Huh." She chewed on her hair again. "I don't see how."

"It's something like ... something like...." The words were dangling up high in his brain. He had to strain for them like in the grocery store when things he wanted were on a shelf he couldn't reach. "One person is like infinity."

That was the best he could do.

If he had more words he could tell her that she gave him confidence. That he knew that she cared about him, even if it wasn't *that way*. She liked him even though it wasn't cool to like an autistic boy.

And that's why he might have another girlfriend, a real girlfriend — she *was* a real girlfriend but someday....

Ashleigh put her hand on his thigh and his skin tingled. "I missed that plane by now."

"Good!"

"There's another one."

His stomach tightened. "The 4:30 to SNA?"

"Yeah."

"You can't go away."

"Why not?"

He did have those words. People said those words on TV all the time. He couldn't speak for a minute because he was afraid, but then he said, "Because — because I love you."

When people said "I love you" on TV, sometimes all their problems went away because that was what the other person had been waiting to hear. Other times it didn't work out.

EPILOGUE

That was the last time I saw Ashleigh in person.

She left me and went through security.

My mom and Jason tried to find out what happened because I asked them to, but they couldn't. Then finally after 23 days I got an email from her. It turns out that she went to Hollywood, but she didn't have any money and one night she slept outside and then the police found her and made her come back home. Because of what happened with Coach she didn't want to live with her mom anymore. But it turned out that she had an aunt that she didn't even know about in Indiana and that's where she is now.

We email a lot. This was one of her first ones:

I DESERVE TO BE IN THIS PLACE B/C I USED YOU SO AWFULLY. I WANTED TO HELP YOU BUT IN THE END I JUST USED YOU.

This was another one:

THIS SCHOOL SUCKS. IT'S ALL WHITE PEOPLE. I DON'T THINK THERE ARE ANY CATHOLICS. THERE ARE HARDLY EVEN ANY BRUNETTES. AUNT DARCY IS KINDA CHILL. HOW WE SPEND MOST OF OUR TIME TOGETHER IS DISSING MY MOM. BUT SHE MAKES ME GO TO A REALLY AWFUL CHURCH. SOMEHOW I HAVE TO LAST 'TIL I'M 18 WITHOUT SHOOTING MYSELF.

I was scared by what she said about shooting herself but she wrote back and said she was kidding and that she was really okay. Then after two more emails she wrote,

I ASKED IN THE PRINCIPAL'S OFFICE ABOUT JOINING THE GAY-STRAIGHT ALLIANCE. THERE IS NO GSA AND THEN SOMEHOW EVERYONE KNEW THAT I ASKED AND NOW THERE'S A GROUP OF KIDS CALLING ME "LESBO." I THOUGHT I KNEW WHAT IT WAS LIKE TO BE GAY WHEN PEOPLE DIDN'T ACCEPT YOU BUT I HAD NO IDEA.

Everyone knows that it's okay to be a lesbian! And every school has a Gay-Straight Alliance, but I was unhappy that she was unhappy.

I HAD NO IDEA WHAT IT WAS LIKE TO BE YOU, JACK.

AUNT DARCY WENT BALLISTIC WHEN I TOLD HER ABOUT THE KIDS CALLING ME LESBO, AND SHE WAS GOING TO GO TO THE PRINCIPAL, BUT I DECIDED THAT I DIDN'T WANT HER TO, BECAUSE I THOUGHT OF YOU. YOU NEVER GIVE UP, NOT WHEN YOU GET BULLIED OR MADE FUN OF, AND I CAN TELL IT'S HARD FOR YOU TO WRITE, TOO. BUT YOU KEEP ON TRYING.

So when I want to shoot myself (JK!) or just feel like giving up, I think of how I want to be like you. Let them call me Lesbo. I'm going to keep on trying and maybe by next year there will be a Gay-Straight Alliance here at Ronald Reagan High. Maybe that's the reason God sent me here!!!

And one from a few days ago:

It's hard making friends here. I feel like I can't trust anyone anymore. Freddie was my BFF and I almost never hear from him!!!

So it turns out that you are the truest friend I ever had. I'll try to be a true friend to you, too, even from far away.

Coach Takanawa never came back after the day I cut school, and Trevor is having a hard time. Jason says it'll take time for Trevor to get over it so we all have to be patient. But that's hard, because it's hard the way that Trevor keeps asking the same question over and over.

I know why Coach left, but I can keep a secret if I have to (not like Trevor), and that day at the airport Ashleigh asked me to keep this secret.

Jason and Mom got married at the beginning of February. Jason had two best men: me and Trevor. Marissa was the flower girl in a white dress with a basket of petals. Dad came and because of Dad the mayor came and he did the wedding.

So we really are like *Drake and Josh* now.

Trevor has a really big aquarium in his room next to where Mom parks her car.

I'm not allowed to use Marissa's bathroom, but if I have to go in the middle of the night I do. I don't see what the big deal is.

Last night we were sitting down to dinner all five of us when Dad came over. Mom said he should have called or knocked, but Dad said he wanted it to be a surprise, he had a present, and he gave me a really big envelope.

"Open it."

It was season tickets to the Giants. "For three," Dad said.

Marissa said, "I don't want to go to a stupid baseball game!"

And Dad said, "Not you, Wissy. We're going to take Trevor!"

The thing about Dad is that he cancels at the last minute a lot. But when he can't take me and Trevor to the games, Jason can take us. Having two dads is really handy.

Dad said that he had a feeling that 2010 would be the Giants year. Maybe it'll be my year, too.

☺

THE END
of
HE COULD BE ANOTHER BILL GATES

ACKNOWLEDGMENTS

I would like to thank a few people who made this book's journey possible:

My agents, Michael Larsen and Elizabeth Pomada, cofounders of the San Francisco Writers Conference, and an inspiration to writers around the country.

The best writing group in the universe: Sheri Cooper, Terry Gamble, Suzanne Lewis, Phyllis Florin, Mary Beth McClure, Alison Sackett, and Linda Schlossberg.

The visionary Steven Drachman, my fellow Chickadee Prince author, and David Groff, editor extraordinaire.

Drew Johnson and Nelson Lum of the San Francisco Police Department.

Camilla Bixler, Dr. Hackie Reitman, Laura Shumaker, and all the members of the Bay Area autism community.

For editorial assistance and encouragement: Donna Gillespie, Douglas Wm. Gordy, Hether Ludwick, Ed Rucker (a fine writer also published by Chickadee Prince), Christine McDonagh, Michael Bernick, and Gary Kurutz of the California State Library.

And of course I thank you, the reader, for picking up this book and making it all the way to the last page. If you enjoyed my story, remember that Chickadee Prince Books, the publisher who brought this to you, is a small independent press devoted only to quality work, and it needs your word of mouth to survive. Please tell a friend and write a review of this book or other CPB books.

Donna Levin
March 2018

OTHER BOOKS FROM CHICKADEE PRINCE
THAT YOU WILL ENJOY

In Love with Alice by Alon Price
The Thirtover Novels - ISBN: 978-0991327454

"A spellbinding love story that is both intimate and universal ... a novel about the missing pieces in our lives — first loves, absent siblings, parents dead or distant — and how we are haunted by them. *In Love with Alice* is a complex tapestry of tortured relationships that will stay with me for a long time. And I'm a little bit in love with Alice myself."
> — Clifford Garstang, author of *What the Zhang Boys Know* and *In an Uncharted Country* (Press 53)

" 'It was great being young and rich' says a main character. But was it? *In Love With Alice* is an unapologetic look at lives most of us can only imagine, lives carefully drawn with shadow ... make us excited to get home at night, after our mundane day has ended, to pick up the book again. Just to see how it all keeps coming together, the latching and unlatching of these mysterious lives."
> — *Nina Gaby,* editor of *Dumped: Stories of Women Unfriending Women* (She Writes Press)

*

Rebecca Zook's Amish Romance by Granville Wyche Burgess
Book 1, ISBN: 9780999756904; Book 2, ISBN: 978-0991327492

"Like a quilt woven with many dexterous hands, Burgess weaves a page-turner tale of intrigue and romance.... A witty novel, full of humor and intelligence, with memorable characters who feel life-like enough to hug."
> — Elizabeth Oberbeck, author of *The Dressmaker* (Henry Holt & Co.)

"A sensitive story about finding oneself in a community."
> — *Kirkus Reviews*

CPSIA information can be obtained
at www.ICGtesting.com
Printed in the USA
LVHW082333151118
597350LV00010B/117/P